Best Practices in Change Management – 2012 Edition

650 participants share lessons and best practices in change management

© 2012 Prosci Inc.

ISBN: 978-1-930885-59-2

Acknowledgements

Editors – Tim Creasey, Jeff Hiatt
Study design – Tim Creasey, Jeff Hiatt
Data collection, graphs and tables – Tim Creasey
Study analysis – Tim Creasey, Mike Davis, Michelle Haggerty, Annie Hiatt, Garrett Knight, Denise Onofrey, Allison Seabeck, Avery West
Reviewer – Judith Larrimore

All rights reserved. No part of this report may be reproduced or transmitted in any form or by any means, electronic or mechanical, including photocopying, recording, or by any information storage or retrieval system, without the prior written permission of Prosci, except for normal reviews and quotation.

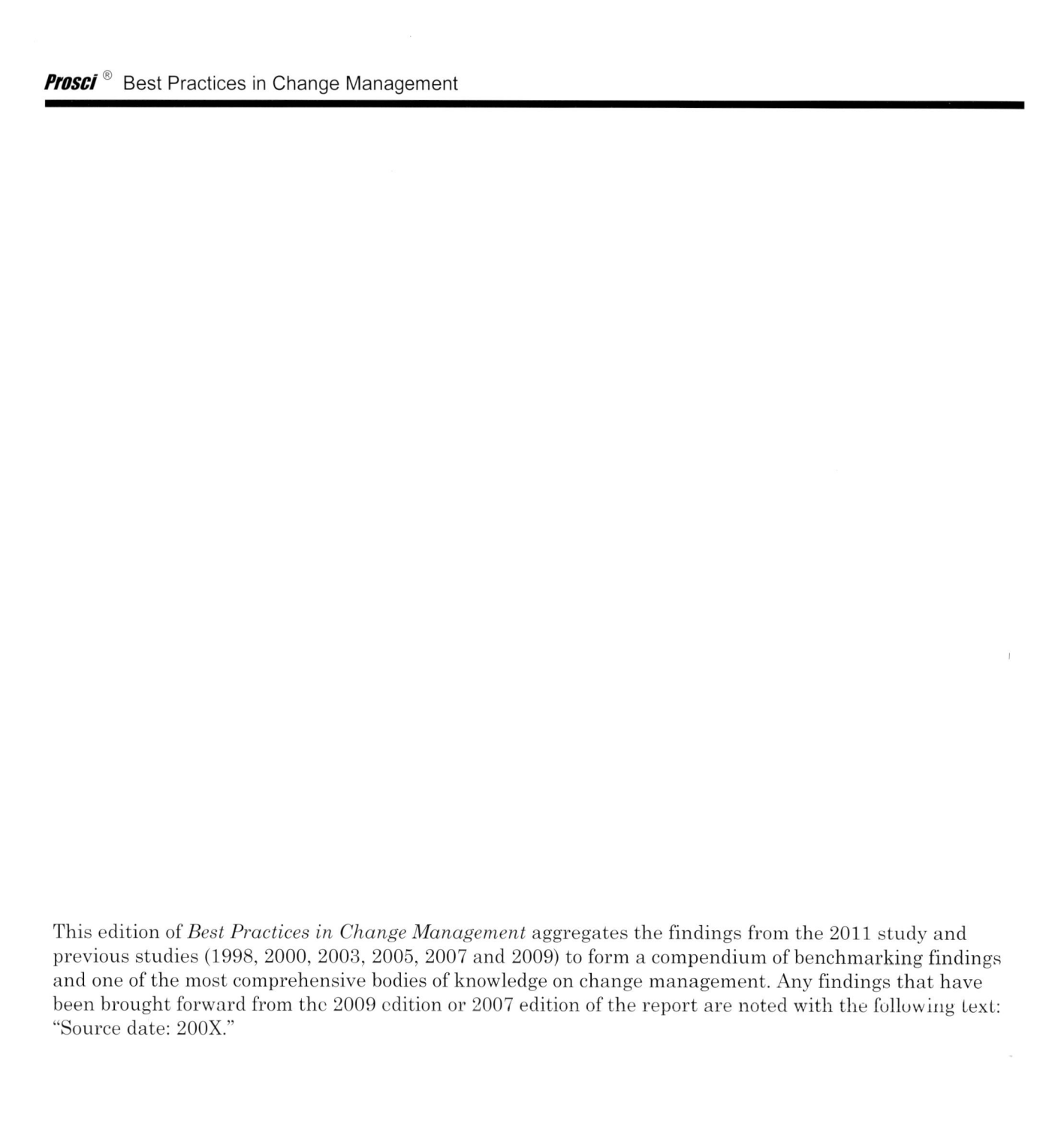

Prosci ® Best Practices in Change Management

This edition of *Best Practices in Change Management* aggregates the findings from the 2011 study and previous studies (1998, 2000, 2003, 2005, 2007 and 2009) to form a compendium of benchmarking findings and one of the most comprehensive bodies of knowledge on change management. Any findings that have been brought forward from the 2009 edition or 2007 edition of the report are noted with the following text: "Source date: 200X."

Table of contents

TABLES AND FIGURES 4

OVERVIEW
- EXECUTIVE OVERVIEW 7
- GREATEST CONTRIBUTORS TO SUCCESS 14
- GREATEST CHANGE MANAGEMENT OBSTACLES... 16
- WHAT TO DO DIFFERENTLY ON THE NEXT PROJECT 18
- CHANGE MANAGEMENT TRENDS 19
- ADVICE FOR PRACTITIONERS 21

STRUCTURE
- MOTIVATION FOR CHANGE MANAGEMENT.. 24
- USE OF METHODOLOGY 26
- CHANGE MANAGEMENT TEAM AND STRUCTURE 33
- RESOURCES AND BUDGET 41
- PROJECT MANAGEMENT AND CHANGE MANAGEMENT INTEGRATION 48
- CHANGE READINESS 52

METHODOLOGY AND PRACTICE AREAS
- CHANGE MANAGEMENT ACTIVITIES.. 54
- SPONSORSHIP 59
- MANAGERS AND SUPERVISORS.. 71
- COMMUNICATIONS... 78
- TRAINING 89
- RESISTANCE 90
- REINFORCEMENT AND FEEDBACK 98
- CONSULTANTS.. 101
- TRAINING ON CHANGE MANAGEMENT 107

ENTERPRISE CHANGE MANAGEMENT
- CHANGE MANAGEMENT CAPABILITY AND COMPETENCY........................... 110
- CHANGE MANAGEMENT EFFECTIVENESS AND MEASUREMENT 125
- JUSTIFYING CHANGE MANAGEMENT 133
- CHANGE SATURATION AND PORTFOLIO MANAGEMENT 135
- UNIQUE CHANGE TYPES 141

APPENDICES
- APPENDIX A – PARTICIPANT DEMOGRAPHICS 145
- APPENDIX B – PROJECT PROFILES... 147
- APPENDIX C – CHANGE MANAGEMENT MATURITY MODEL........................ 150
- APPENDIX D – 2011 STUDY PARTICIPANT LIST 153
- APPENDIX E – 2009 STUDY PARTICIPANT LIST 157
- APPENDIX F – 2007 STUDY PARTICIPANT LIST... 161

Tables and figures

Figure 1 – Geographic distribution of participants 7
Figure 2 – Role of participants 7
Figure 3 – Correlation of change management effectiveness to meeting or exceeding objectives 9
Table 1 – Contributors to success over time 15
Figure 4 – Use of particular methodology 26
Figure 5 – Use of particular methodology by region 26
Figure 6 – Use of particular methodology by industry 26
Figure 7 – Impact of use of particular methodology on overall change management effectiveness 27
Figure 8 – Methodology used 28
Figure 9 – When did change management activities begin? 29
Figure 10 – Organization has a change management permanent position / job role 33
Figure 11 – Team structures used 34
Figure 12 – Level of experience and expertise of change management resources 39
Figure 13 – Project had dedicated change management person or group 41
Figure 14 – Relationship between dedicated resources and overall effectiveness 42
Figure 15 – Average FTE vs. project investment 44
Figure 16 – Average FTE vs. project scope 44
Figure 17 – Average FTE vs. employees impacted 44
Figure 18 – Average FTE vs. duration 44
Figure 19 – Percent of project FTE dedicated to change management vs. project investment 45
Figure 20 – Percent of project FTE dedicated to change management vs. project scope 45
Figure 21 – Percent of project FTE dedicated to change management vs. employees impacted 45
Figure 22 – Percent of project FTE dedicated to change management vs. duration 45
Figure 23 – Average budget vs. project investment 46
Figure 24 – Average budget vs. project scope 46
Figure 25 – Average budget vs. employees impacted 46
Figure 26 – Average budget vs. duration 46
Figure 27 – Percent of project budget vs. project investment 47
Figure 28 – Percent of project budget vs. project scope 47
Figure 29 – Percent of project budget vs. employees impacted 47
Figure 30 – Percent of project budget vs. duration 47
Figure 31 – Project teams' view of the role of change management 48
Figure 32 – Did the project you reported on for this study apply project management? 49
Figure 33 – Integrated change management activities into the project activities? 49
Figure 34 – Percent of project team with change management training 51
Figure 35 – Took steps to evaluate change readiness 53
Figure 36 – Change Management Activity Model 54
Table 2 – Change management start-up activities 55
Table 3 – Change management design activities 56
Table 4 – Change management implementation activities 57
Figure 37 – Sponsors' understanding of roles and responsibilities 61
Figure 38 – Ineffective or extremely ineffective sponsor role fulfillment 61
Figure 39 – Correlation of sponsor effectiveness to meeting objectives 61
Figure 40 – Sponsor symptoms 62
Figure 41 – Sponsor left during the course of the project 63
Figure 42 – Sponsor at right level in the organization 64
Figure 43 – Sponsor characterization at beginning of the project 65
Figure 44 – Access to sponsor 65

Figure 45 – Correlation of sponsor access to meeting objectives 66
Figure 46 – Frequency of meeting with sponsors - actual and desired 66
Figure 47 – Sponsor communication frequency 66
Figure 48 – Sponsor Activities Model 67
Table 5 – Sponsor start-up activities 68
Table 6 – Sponsor design activities 69
Table 7 – Sponsor implementation activities 70
Figure 49 – Adequately prepared managers and supervisors 73
Figure 50 – Effectiveness at coaching employees through personal transitions 73
Figure 51 – Effectiveness at managing resistance 74
Figure 52 – Preferred senders of messages 78
Figure 53 – Use of social media and Web 2.0 85
Figure 54 – Most resistant groups 90
Figure 55 – Percent of employee resistance seen as avoidable 93
Figure 56 – Percent of manager resistance seen as avoidable 95
Figure 57 – Best provider of reinforcement and recognition 98
Figure 58 – Used consultant 101
Figure 59 – Provision of training on change management 107
Table 8 – Average days of change management training 107
Figure 60 – Days of training for change management resources 107
Figure 61 – Days of training for project team members 108
Figure 62 – Days of training for executives and senior leaders 108
Figure 63 – Days of training for managers and supervisors 108
Figure 64 – Days of training for impacted employees 109
Figure 65 – Prosci Change Management Maturity Model 110
Table 9 – Maturity Model results by region 110
Figure 66 – Maturity Model data for the United States 111
Figure 67 – Maturity Model data for Australia and New Zealand 111
Figure 68 – Maturity Model data for Canada 111
Figure 69 – Maturity Model data for Europe 111
Figure 70 – Maturity Model data for Africa 111
Figure 71 – Maturity Model data for Asia and Pacific Islands 111
Figure 72 – Maturity Model data for Latin America 111
Figure 73 – Maturity Model data for Middle East 111
Table 10 – Maturity Model results by industry 112
Figure 74 – Actively working to deploy change management 112
Table 11 – Maturity Model ranking for those actively working to deploy 113
Figure 75 – Participants actively working to deploy by region 113
Figure 76 – Participants actively working to deploy by industry 113
Figure 77 – Participants actively working to deploy by organization size 113
Figure 78 – How long has deployment been underway? 114
Figure 79 – Originator of the effort 114
Figure 80 – Have Change Management Office or functional group 117
Figure 81 – Location of Change Management Office or functional group 118
Figure 82 – Number of employees in the functional group 118
Figure 83 – Success of deployment effort 120
Figure 84 – Single, common, shared definition 122
Figure 85 – Project leader and project manager recognition 122
Figure 86 – Executive and senior leader recognition 123
Figure 87 – Middle manager recognition 123

Figure 88 – Front-line manager and supervisor recognition *123*
Figure 89 – Solution developer and designer recognition *123*
Table 12 – Percent of projects applying change management *123*
Figure 90 – Percent of projects applying change management *124*
Figure 91 – Correlation with meeting objectives *125*
Figure 92 – Correlation with staying on or ahead of schedule *125*
Figure 93 – Correlation with staying on or under budget *125*
Table 13 – Change management effectiveness factors *126*
Figure 94 – Overall effectiveness of change management program *127*
Figure 95 – Measured change management effectiveness *127*
Figure 96 – Measured whether change was occurring at individual level *129*
Figure 97 – How well were project goals and objectives defined? *129*
Figure 98 – Speed of adoption *130*
Figure 99 – Ultimate utilization *130*
Figure 100 – Proficiency *130*
Figure 101 – In line or better than expected speed of adoption vs. change management effectiveness *131*
Figure 102 – In line or better than expected ultimate utilization vs. change management effectiveness *131*
Figure 103 – In line or better than expected proficiency vs. change management effectiveness *131*
Figure 104 – Participants who had to justify change management to leadership team *133*
Figure 105 – Level of change saturation *135*
Table 14 – Change saturation by region *135*
Table 15 – Change saturation by industry *135*
Figure 106 – Amount of change expected in the next two years *136*
Figure 107 – Kept an inventory of all changes underway *138*
Figure 108 – Have a structured process for managing the portfolio of change *138*
Figure 109 – Unique change types *141*
Figure 110 – Geographic representation of participants *145*
Figure 111 – Geographic presence *145*
Figure 112 – Industry segment *145*
Figure 113 – Size of organization (annual revenue) *146*
Figure 114 – Project stage *147*
Figure 115 – Project type *147*
Table 16 – Combinations of project types *147*
Figure 116 – Scope of the change *148*
Figure 117 – Project investment *148*
Figure 118 – Employees impacted *148*
Figure 119 – Duration of the change effort *148*
Figure 120 – Meeting objectives *149*
Figure 121 – Projects on schedule *149*
Figure 122 – Projects on budget *149*

Executive overview

Participant profile

Six hundred and fifty participants from 62 countries took part in Prosci's 2011 Best Practices in Change Management benchmarking study. This report combines the findings and data from the 2011 study with Prosci's previous six studies to form one of the largest bodies of knowledge on change management and managing the people side of change.

2011 study – 650 participants
2009 study – 575 participants
2007 study – 426 participants
2005 study – 411 participants
2003 study – 288 participants
2000 study – 152 participants
1998 study – 102 participants

Figure 1 shows the geographic distribution of participants in the 2011 study. Participation increased from Australia and New Zealand, Canada, Europe and Latin America. Participation decreased from the United States, Africa, and Asia and the Pacific Islands.

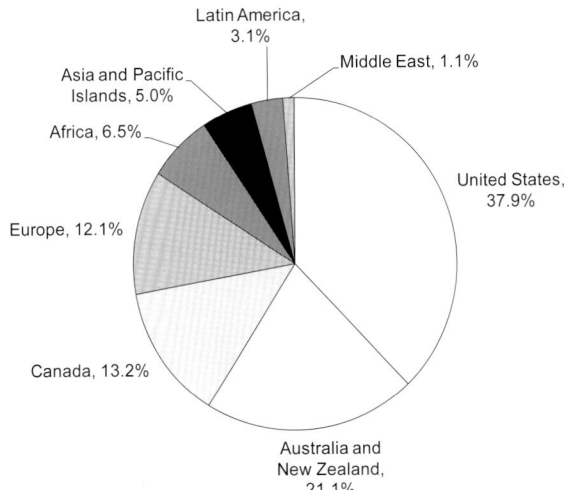

Figure 1 – Geographic distribution of participants

Study participants represented a variety of job titles within their organizations. Figure 2 shows the role of study participants over the last four benchmarking studies. The top three job roles of participants were:

- Change management team leader
- External consultant
- Project team leader

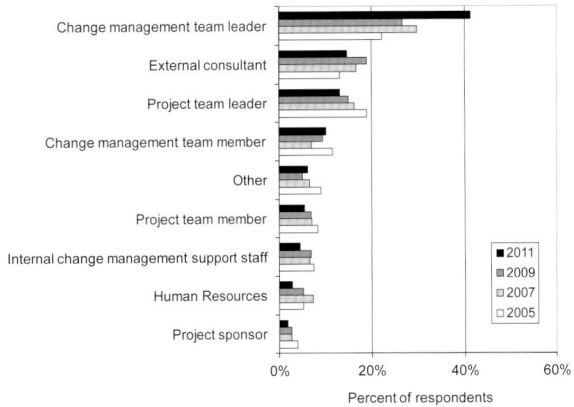

Figure 2 – Role of participants

Study objective

The objective of this study is to uncover lessons learned from practitioners and consultants so current change management teams can benefit from these experiences. Specific attention is paid to what is working and what is not working in all areas of change management.

This report also presents emerging trends in change management, looking to identify the changes that have occurred and the future direction of this discipline.

Because change management is a holistic system that requires involvement by change management practitioners, project teams, executives, managers, supervisors and front-line employees, this report details how each of these different groups is engaged in managing change.

New sections in the report

New questions were added to the 2011 study to expand the scope and depth of the research. These new areas of focus include:

- Motivating factors and reasons for applying change management
- Advice for new practitioners
- Change management performance measures and evaluation
- Team member attributes
- Specific change management activities at project initiation when there is incomplete information on the solution
- Advantages of having a dedicated change management resource
- Consequences of not having a dedicated change management resource
- Change management-specific training
- Change management budget components
- Advanced analysis of change management resourcing, including full time equivalents (FTE) and budget
- Tactics for creating active and visible sponsorship
- Consequences of losing a sponsor
- Tactics for dealing with a sponsor who is at the wrong level
- Biggest skill, competency or tool gap for managers and supervisors
- Preparation of managers and supervisors
- Use of social media and Web 2.0 applications
- Approaches for determining whether employees are engaging in the change
- Change management deployment efforts
- Change management job role

Study highlights

Greatest contributors to success

For the seventh consecutive study, active and visible executive sponsorship was identified as the greatest contributor to success. The second through fifth contributors to success paralleled the findings from the 2009 benchmarking study:

1. Active and visible executive sponsorship
2. Frequent and open communication about the change
3. Structured change management approach
4. Dedicated change management resources and funding
5. Employee engagement and participation
6. Engagement with and support from middle management

Engagement of middle management was a new entry on the list of greatest contributors to success in this study.

Greatest obstacles to success

The top five obstacles to success identified by 2011 benchmarking study participants matched those in the 2009 benchmarking study. Ineffective sponsorship topped the list of greatest obstacles for the third consecutive study.

Insufficient change management resourcing moved up one spot to the second most mentioned obstacle, switching places with employee resistance.

What to do differently on the next project

By a two-to-one margin, the top suggestion by participants for what they would do differently on their next project was to secure sponsorship and ensure sponsor alignment throughout the organization. The next most common response for what to do differently on the next project was to start change management earlier in the project life cycle.

Top trends in change management

For the third consecutive study, the top trend identified by participants was a greater awareness of the need for and value of change management. One negative trend identified by participants that made the list of top trends was underestimating the work involved in managing change and under-resourcing the change management effort.

Change management effectiveness

Projects with effective change management programs were more likely to meet objectives, stay on schedule and stay on budget than those without effective change management. This direct correlation mirrors the findings from the 2007 and 2009 studies. Projects with excellent change management programs were nearly six times more likely to meet or exceed their objectives than those with poor change management programs.

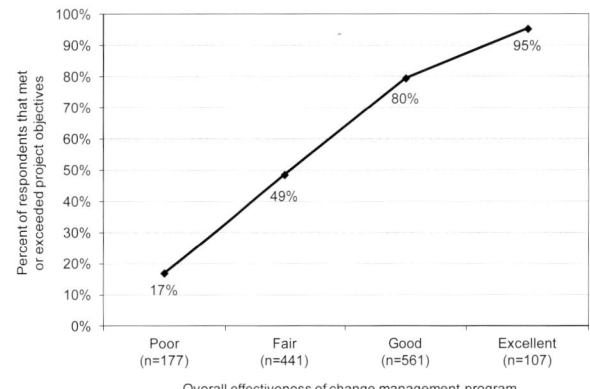

Figure 3 – Correlation of change management effectiveness to meeting or exceeding objectives

Practitioner advice

Experienced practitioners shared advice on how to apply change management. Practitioners identified the three most important activities at the beginning of an engagement, with effective communications being the top recommendation. Participants identified four challenges or hurdles, the top one being ineffective sponsorship. Communication, timing, integration with project management, building buy-in for change management and sponsorship were the five topics of advice for new practitioners.

Motivation for change management

Participants identified two primary motivations for applying change management. The top response was as a necessity stemming from the nature of the change, including the complexity, number of people affected and breadth of impact. The second primary motivator was to contribute to overall project success, as change management was viewed as a key success factor and driver of buy-in and adoption.

Use of a methodology

The percentage of participants that reported using a particular methodology increased to 72% from 60% in 2009, 58% in 2007, 55% in 2005 and 34% in 2003. Ease of use and scalability were the top factors used in choosing a methodology. Participants who reported using a particular methodology reported higher levels of overall change management effectiveness than those who did not.

Change management activities at initiation with incomplete information

Previous studies indicated a bias toward starting change management at project initiation. However, change management practitioners sometimes face a situation of managing a change that has not been completely designed or developed. Participants in the 2011 benchmarking study identified seven specific activities for change management when there is incomplete information about the project or change. The top recommendation was to create a communications plan to describe the desired results and need for change, followed by an assessment of the organizational climate and identification of common risks and resistance.

Attributes of a great team member

Communication skills and change management competencies were the top attributes of a great change management team member, followed by flexibility and interpersonal skills.

Impacts of having a dedicated change management resource

Over three-quarters of participants reported on projects with a dedicated change management resource. The greatest advantages of having a dedicated change management resource were improved focus on change management and a single point of contact with clear responsibility and accountability. The greatest consequence of not having a dedicated resource was neglected change management activities. Use of a dedicated change management resource correlated to more effective change management programs.

Cost components of change management

Participants identified the cost components included in their change management budget. Three costs were identified most often: change management resources, training and communications.

Integration of project management and change management

Participants reported that creating a collaborative working environment was the most effective step for engagement with the project team. Collaboration was bi-directional. Creating a compelling case for the value of and need for change management also contributed to effective integration of change management and project management.

Sponsorship

Participants identified active and visible participation in the project as the most important activity for sponsors in support of change, followed by direct communication to employees, and building and maintaining a healthy coalition of support. Providing behind-the-scenes assistance to the sponsor on his or her role was identified as the most effective tactic by change management practitioners for creating active and visible sponsorship. Failing to remain visible and engaged and failing to demonstrate support were the two biggest sponsor mistakes identified.

Managers and supervisors

Participants identified the most important activities for managers and supervisors during change as communicating the change to their direct reports and advocating for the change. Lack of visible support and involvement was the biggest mistake made by managers and supervisors. Communication skills, change management knowledge and coaching skills were the three biggest gaps for managers and supervisors, as identified by study participants.

Preferred senders of change messages

As in previous studies, an employee's supervisor was identified as the preferred sender of personal messages while senior leaders were identified as the preferred senders of business-level or organizational-level messages about why the change was needed and how the change aligned with the organization's direction.

Communication messages

The business reasons for the change were identified as the most important messages for employees and the second most important for managers and senior leaders, behind only expectations and their role in the change. The 2011 benchmarking study generated extensive lists of the most important messages to communicate to three groups during change: employees, managers and supervisors, and senior managers and executives.

Use of social media

Just under one in five participants used social networking or Web 2.0 applications as part of change management communications. Participants shared which tools they used, the benefits of using these communication vehicles and recommendations. The top recommendations for those considering using social media were "if it works for you, use it" and consider alignment with the culture of the organization.

Communication vehicles

Participants shared the different communication vehicles they used on their projects. The compiled list now includes 107 different communication vehicles, up from 74 in the previous report.

Training

Participants reported on the role of change management in creating project-related training, including the creation and planning of training, and supporting or overseeing training.

Resistance

Participants shared six techniques for identifying resistance to change, with a lack of visible commitment or adoption being the most commonly cited. Mid-level managers were identified as the group exhibiting the most resistance to change. As in the 2009 study, participants felt that a majority of the resistance they experienced could have been avoided with effective change management and proactive engagement activities.

Reinforcement and feedback

The use of surveys and feedback systems for measuring engagement was the most common approach used for determining whether employees were engaging in the change. Participants shared the most effective approaches for reinforcing change at the individual and group level. Communicating successes and sharing results were the top tactics used in both instances. Participants identified the best provider of reinforcement and recognition for individual employees as the direct supervisors, while mid-level managers and the primary sponsor were preferred for group-level reinforcement and recognition.

Consultants

A lack of internal competency or resources was the top reason participants cited for using an external consultant to support change management work. The top reason for not using a consultant was having sufficient internal capabilities. Overall, there was an even split between those who did use a consultant and those who did not.

Training on change management

Participants reported on change management-specific training for change management resources, project teams, impacted executives and senior leaders, impacted managers and supervisors and impacted employees. Participants shared the actual number of training days and the recommended number of training days for each group. Generally, participants recommended about one additional day of training than they actually provided for each group.

Change management capability and competency building

Slightly less than half of the study participants (46%) were working actively to deploy change management throughout their organizations and shared their experience and advice. Leadership commitment to change management was an important factor for building change management capabilities and competencies, and was identified as both the activity with the biggest impact and the most important activity at the launch of the effort. However, securing sponsorship was only the fifth on the list of actual steps taken.

Common and shared definition of change management

Nearly three quarters of study participants either disagreed or strongly disagreed with the statement: "Throughout my organization, there is a single, common and shared definition of change management."

Change Management Office or functional group

Just over one third of participants (36%) had established a Change Management Office or functional group. The most common locations for the group were Human Resources (HR) or Organization Development (OD) and Information Technology (IT). Most functional groups were comprised of five or less employees.

Permanent position or job role

43% of participants reported having a permanent position or job role for change management in their organization. Participants identified 20 responsibilities of these permanent roles, led by applying the methodology and supporting the organization's development of change management capabilities and competencies.

Change management measurement

For the first time, participants shared suggestions for measuring change management effectiveness. Responses for measurement included tips and suggestions for methods, criteria, data sources and timing. Participants also identified five tactics for evaluating whether individual transitions were taking place. Just over one-half of study participants reported measuring change management effectiveness.

People-side ROI factors

Participants reported on the speed of adoption, ultimate utilization and proficiency factors for their projects. Generally, around 10% of participants reported exceeding expectations and around 50% reported results in line with expectations. There was a direct correlation between change management effectiveness and performance of speed of adoption, ultimate utilization and proficiency.

Justifying change management

The most common approach for justifying change management was the use of past failures and the illustration of the negative consequences of poorly managing the people side of change. Past successes with change management and senior-level buy-in were the top conditions that resulted in a team not having to justify change management.

Change saturation

The percentage of participants who reported being near or past the point of change saturation increased from 59% in 2007 to 66% in 2009 to 73% in 2011. When asked what was being done to address saturation and collision, the top response by participants was "nothing" – that the organization was not taking steps to address saturation and collision. Those who were working to address saturation and collision identified the use of portfolio management tools and prioritization as the top two tactics.

Unique change types

Participants provided data on the issues associated with and tactics for managing four unique types of changes: changes with impact across various cultures, changes that occurred over a long time frame, changes that involved layoffs or significant staff reductions, and mergers or acquisitions.

Greatest contributors to success

Study participants identified six factors as the greatest contributors to overall change management success. The top five findings remained consistent with the results of the 2007 and 2009 reports. The sixth contributor, middle-management support, was a new addition to the list and was identified by study participants the same amount of times as employee engagement, the fifth contributor.

1. Active and visible executive sponsorship
2. Frequent and open communication about the change
3. Structured change management approach
4. Dedicated change management resources and funding
5. Employee engagement and participation
6. Engagement with and support from middle management

1. **Active and visible executive sponsorship**
   Study participants reported active and visible executive sponsorship as the number one contributor to success for the seventh consecutive report. Participants cited this factor four times more frequently than any other contributor. Participants reported the need for executives and senior leaders to be involved and visible during all stages of a change, supportive and committed to the change itself, and knowledgeable about the need for change management. Active and visible sponsorship included:

   - Visibility and accessibility throughout the entire project
   - Engagement of leaders and managers early and throughout the duration of a project
   - Alignment of priorities among organization leaders; projects realized better success when objectives were clearly defined and were aligned with the overall strategy and vision of the organization
   - Direct communication with employees and the project team (including change managers) throughout the duration of the project to build and maintain support for the change

2. **Frequent and open communication about the change**
   Study participants reported highly structured and frequent top-down communications as a major contributor to success. Communication messages included a clear and compelling reason for the change, the objectives of the change and the implications of not changing. Participants emphasized that the need for the change was best delivered by the sponsor or leader of the change. Communications needed to be tailored and customized for each impacted group. Study participants also noted the need to communicate with end-users frequently to gauge project success.

3. **Structured change management approach**
   Study respondents cited the use of a structured change management approach as the third greatest contributor to program success. Respondents noted that the use of an established, easy-to-apply methodology helped increase user adoption. Respondents also noted that the earlier change management was applied, the more success the project achieved.

4. **Dedicated change management resources and funding**
   Having dedicated change management staff on the project team during the planning and implementation of the project was the fourth most frequently cited success factor. Having "change agents" across the organization and within organizational hierarchies ensured that change management was being utilized in multiple, if not all, functional groups across the project. According to study respondents, it was also important to provide the appropriate amount of funding and resources required to execute the change management plans that were developed.

5. **Employee engagement and participation**
Employee participation and buy-in to the change were cited as key contributors to change management success. Specifically, study respondents cited the following activities to drive employee engagement:

- Providing two-way communications for employees to solicit feedback

- Creating awareness among the end-users and front-line employees about why the change was occurring and establishing the "what's in it for me" (WIIFM) messages

- Increasing involvement of employees in the decision making process by soliciting and gathering input

6. **Engagement with and support from middle management**
Having the buy-in and engagement of middle management helped to ensure positive and effective communications to front-line employees. Respondents noted that ensuring that managers had adequate change management skills empowered them to be more effective leaders of change and decreased fear of power loss resulting from the change.

Contributors to success over time

The table below shows the ranking of contributors to success over the last seven benchmarking studies. Active and visible executive sponsorship ranked number one in each of the seven studies. The top five factors were identical in the 2009 and 2011 studies. Participants in earlier studies also included comments on the quality of the team and the drivers of change as contributors to success; these factors have moved off the list of top contributors in more recent studies.

Contributors to success	2011 rank	2009 rank	2007 rank	2005 rank	2003 rank	2000 rank	1998 rank
Active and visible executive sponsorship	1	1	1	1	1	1	1
Frequent and open communications around the need for change	2	2	3	3	4	2	-
Structured change management approach	3	3	2	2	5	-	-
Dedicated resources and funding for change management	4	4	4	-	-	-	-
Employee engagement and participation	5	5	5	4	-	2*	2
Engagement with and support from middle management	6	-	-	-	-	-	-

Table 1 – Contributors to success over time

* This item was combined with "Frequent and open communications around the need for change" in the 2000 study.

Greatest change management obstacles

Study participants identified five main obstacles to the overall success of their change management programs. While the top four obstacles matched the results from Prosci's 2009 study, "insufficient change management resources and funding" moved from the number three spot to being the second biggest obstacle on the 2011 list.

The five biggest obstacles identified by study participants were:

1. Ineffective change management sponsorship from senior leaders
2. Insufficient change management resourcing
3. Resistance to change from employees
4. Middle management resistance
5. Poor communication

1. **Ineffective change management sponsorship from senior leaders**
   Participants cited ineffective change sponsorship as their primary obstacle. Common problems included:

   - Inactive or invisible sponsors
   - Poor alignment between organizational direction and the objectives of the change
   - Lack of sponsor commitment to change management
   - Sponsors with competing priorities or changes in sponsorship
   - Sponsors at the wrong level (not high enough in the organization)
   - Little or no access to the primary sponsor
   - Failure to build a coalition of sponsors

2. **Insufficient change management resourcing**
   Participants cited a general lack of resources and funding available to conduct the necessary planning and implementation of change management. Specifically, participants struggled with:

   - Insufficient resources to support change management required for the project
   - Part-time resources; "working in the margin"
   - Inadequate change management skills and knowledge to lead change management activities effectively
   - Adding change management resources to the project team too late in the project life cycle

3. **Resistance to change from employees**
   Employee resistance moved from the number two obstacle in 2009 to the number three obstacle in 2011. Reasons for resistance included:

   - Lack of understanding why the change was needed and the "what's in it for me?" (WIIFM)
   - Employees close to retirement and unwilling to change
   - Employees unwilling to learn new systems or tools (satisfied with the current state)
   - Loss of control or fear of loss of control
   - Change saturation; employees were overwhelmed by the amount of change occurring in the organization
   - Unwillingness to change due to poorly handled changes in the past

4. **Middle-management resistance**
   Middle managers were reluctant to support the change personally or lead the change with their staff. This resistance from middle managers resulted in a lack of consistent and accurate communication about the change to their employees. Participants cited the following reasons for management resistance:

   - Fear of job loss or loss of control
   - Not supportive of the change itself
   - Lack of understanding of the need for change management

- Lack of knowledge or skills to manage change effectively
- Insufficient time to complete change management activities; managers were task focused and unable to commit the necessary time to focus on the people side of the change

5. **Poor communication**
Participants cited a number of reasons that their communications were not effective including:

- Inconsistent messages
- Communications not addressing the need or reason for the change
- Difficulty reaching employees because of geographical separation
- Long gaps of time between communications; poor communication "timeliness"

Additional obstacles cited by participants included:

- **Lack of buy-in for change management**
Study respondents noted challenges getting senior executives and project teams to buy in to the need for change management and realize the financial benefits of change management. Without full support or understanding around the necessity for change management, change management was often either brought on to a project too late, tasked only with communications and training activities, or not utilized on the project at all. Some respondents reported a struggle to get their organizations to realize the benefits of incorporating change management.

- **Disconnect between project management and change management**
Study respondents noted conflicting priorities and misalignment between project management and change management teams as a large obstacle to success. Respondents reported that a lack of consensus on how to integrate the two practices became a large challenge throughout the life of projects and often resulted in change management playing "second fiddle" to project management. Specifically, study participants cited difficulty involving and getting assistance from project managers.

What to do differently on the next project

Participants in the 2011 study were asked to reflect on what they would do differently on their next project. By a two-to-one margin, the top response involved engagement of sponsors. The top five suggestions for what participants would do differently on the next project were:

1. Engage sponsors better
2. Start change management activities sooner
3. Emphasize employee engagement and involvement
4. Secure sufficient resources for change management
5. Improve communications

Below is a full list of the most frequently cited activities participants said they would do differently on their next project.

1. **Engage sponsors better**
   Get the primary sponsor on board and engaged at the start of the project. Ensure sponsor alignment throughout the organization. Engage the various senior leaders that need to be on board supporting the change. Educate and coach sponsors. Increase the active and visible involvement of sponsors. Create a tighter connection and relationship to sponsors.

2. **Start change management activities sooner**
   Begin change management activities earlier in the project life cycle before the implementation phase, preferably at initiation.

3. **Emphasize employee engagement and involvement**
   Increase the focus on employee involvement and engagement, particularly early in the project life cycle. Place an emphasis on stakeholder identification, mapping and involvement.

4. **Secure sufficient resources for change management**
   Ensure that change management has the appropriate level of resources, including time, budget, funding and dedicated personnel.

5. **Improve communications**
   Communicate more. Communicate earlier. Ensure communications are open, honest and precise. Facilitate more face-to-face and two-way communications to increase dialogue.

Additional suggestions from participants were:

- **Structure the change management team**
  Assign a change management lead with necessary experience and expertise. Create a change network. Utilize local change management resources. Improve the visibility and empowerment of the team and create clear expectations of the roles of various groups.

- **Utilize a holistic approach**
  Apply a proven model that ensures rigor. Establish change management milestones and scope. Use concrete deliverables.

- **Engage the project team**
  Create a cooperative and collaborative relationship with the project team. Build the project team's commitment to change management. Integrate change management and project management activities. Educate the project team about change management principles, processes and tools.

- **Ensure clarity around the change**
  Create clarity about the details of the change and why the change is happening. Align individual visions and understanding of the change with a single, clear organizational vision.

- **Enhance planning activities**
  Dedicate more time to planning the change management effort, including readiness assessments, scaling exercises, and impact identification and analysis.

- **Engage managers and supervisors**
  Build necessary skills in coaching and communication. Engage middle managers and supervisors early and build buy-in for the change.

Change management trends

Top trends in change management

Participants in the 2011 benchmarking study identified seven trends in the discipline of change management.

1. **Greater awareness of the need for and value of change management**
   Participants noted an increased level of acceptance of change management as a legitimate field. This increase was derived from greater value placed on change management and its contribution to the success of projects and initiatives. Along with greater acceptance, participants noted more legitimacy in terms of the practice and the competencies associated with change management.

2. **Increased use of methodologies, tools and language**
   Participants observed an increase in the use of established methodologies and structures, including the development of in-house competencies. Along with the use of these established methodologies, participants identified an increase in the use of corresponding tools, technologies and common language.

3. **More engagement and earlier integration with project management**
   Change management activities are being introduced earlier and more often into project management programs. Project managers are asking for change management support and resources throughout the project life cycle.

4. **More resources and positions devoted to change management**
   Organizations are appropriating more resources, funding and time to change management activities, training and tools. Organizations are establishing more internal positions dedicated to change management. Respondents noted that organizations tended to favor experience with change management over training and certification for change management positions.

5. **Greater demand for change management training and certification**
   Participants observed an increase in the demand for change management training and certification in established methodologies. Training for middle and upper management has increased as part of this increased demand. Respondents suggested that the increased acceptance of change management as an established competency contributed to the increase in demand and resources for change management training.

6. **Increased leadership support for change management**
   Leadership (upper and middle management) has increased acceptance and support of change management. Respondents noted that upper management was more apt to accept change management while middle management resisted slightly more. For both upper and middle management, there has been an increase in overall change management competencies.

Some participants did identify one negative trend that they were experiencing.

7. **Underestimation and allocation of change management resources**
   While interest in utilization of change management has increased, some respondents observed underestimation of the work required and subsequent lack of resources and funding necessary for successful management of change. A lack of allocation of resources included funding (due to budgetary constraints), staffing and, most notably, allotted time for planning, integration and execution of change management activities.

Trends from previous studies

The top trends identified by participants in the 2009 study included:

1. Growing recognition of the need for change management
2. Greater demand for change management competency building (training)
3. More dedicated resources for change management
4. Increased use of change management tools
5. Greater application of change management on projects
6. More integration between project management and change management
7. Growing change saturation
8. Increased use of a standard change management approach
9. More frequent establishment of a change management group
10. Increased focus on management of the portfolio of change

The top trends in the 2007 report were:

1. Growing recognition of the need for change management
2. Increased use of more structured and formal processes
3. Better understanding of what change management really is
4. Enhanced integration with project management
5. Greater recognition of change management as a new competency
6. More frequent creation of formal change management job roles and titles
7. Earlier application on projects

Advice for practitioners

Most important activities at beginning of engagement

Experienced practitioners were asked to identify the three most important activities they would recommend a new practitioner complete at the start of an engagement to improve the success of the change management effort. The most commonly cited start-up activities included:

1. **Communication**
   Strategize for effective and efficient early communication. Avoid saturating the audience. Use language that is understood on all levels. Be sure to discuss and agree on roles and expectations. Be explicit about deliverables. Define what involvement looks like. Listen to all levels. Develop a means for accepting input from stakeholders. Develop easy-to-understand plans and be visible and vocal about those plans. Establish a communications plan quickly to develop common language.

2. **Analysis and assessment including stakeholder analysis**
   Identify critical success factors of the project then assess for alignment to these factors. Complete impact and readiness assessments. Gauge and understand the scope of the project. Determine what may interfere with or impact employees' capacity to adopt the change. Spend time and convince others to spend more time during the analysis phase.

3. **Relationship development and coalition building**
   Identify and get commitment from the right sponsor. Establish a relationship with key team members, including business leaders and middle managers. Customize strategy to address leadership resistance. Develop a team of change champions, agents and leaders. Develop team principles and rules. Present benefits and change management methodology to key players. Meet with stakeholders often.

Biggest challenges or hurdles

Experienced practitioners commented on the biggest challenges or hurdles they would recommend that a practitioner be aware of and watch for at the start of a new engagement. The most common challenges or hurdles included:

1. **Poorly selected, waning or disengaged sponsorship**
   Watch for sponsors who lack authority, have insufficient change management knowledge or do not believe in the change. Many participants offered comments similar to *"make sure the sponsor is at the correct level in the organization"* and *"beware of sponsors with no interest, authority or impact on individuals."*

2. **Lack of understanding, buy-in or recognition of the value of change management**
   Challenges include organizations with low change maturity levels, change saturation and lack of strategic prioritization. One participant stated, *"it is too easy for anyone to think they can 'do' change management however it is a specialized skill that requires experts and deserves to be treated properly."*

3. **Lack of resources for the change management team including budget, time allotment and dedicated personnel**
   One participant's comments summarized the general theme identified by participants: *"the challenge is change management resourcing not getting the needed attention, it is too often underestimated and under staffed."*

4. **Lack of project management and change management team integration**
   The biggest integration challenge was a lack of collaboration, including the change management team not being asked to participate in key decisions. Hurdles also included: *"being ignored by project managers"*; *"project managers who don't know what change management is and is not, and who don't understand the change management role"*; *"[being] sidelined by*

project teams who speed through to meet deadlines rather than purposefully plan for change."

5. **Resistance to the change on all levels, including passive resistance**
Participants noted resistance to the specific change in addition to resistance to the change management efforts and activities. Challenges also included verbal support of the change but unwillingness to participate in change activities.

Advice for new practitioners

Experienced practitioners participating in the 2011 benchmarking study provided the two most valuable pieces of advice they would provide to new practitioners. The top responses were:

1. **Communicate early and often**
Agree on who communicates what and when. Engage face-to-face at all levels in the organization. Try to answer the question "what's in it for me?" (WIIFM) on all levels. Identify who can credibly communicate messages about the change. Listen to both formal and informal communication about and within the project.

2. **Get involved early**
Get involved early to participate in or drive vision, outcomes, planning and stakeholder analysis; involvement midway through the project is too late to do this effectively. The change management team needs to be involved at the very onset of the initiative. Establish change management as an integral part of a project from day one. Engage stakeholders, sponsors and employees up front. Involve impacted employees in the change process as early as possible. Engage middle management immediately.

3. **Integrate change management with project management and strategy**
"Don't underestimate the power of project management to override the people-side of projects." Align with the project manager and closely integrate with the project activities. Meet with the project manager frequently (at least twice a week was most commonly recommended). Participants advised that new practitioners view project management and change management as parallel processes. Be clear on the scope and changes regarding the scope of the project.

4. **Establish buy-in**
Ensure the "why" for the change is clear. Educate others on the change management process and the value and rationale for applying change management to the project. Participants advised new practitioners to use a recognized methodology and justify the need for a formal change management program early. Create understanding of the return on investment (ROI) of change management and establish what change management will deliver.

5. **Work with sponsors**
Participants advised new practitioners to be clear about sponsor activities and consider the level of sponsorship. Ensure sponsors understand their role and what is expected of them. Work closely with the sponsors and be confident in the direction you are giving them. Secure sponsorship early and document expectations and specific activities. Ensure the sponsorship is meaningful to all levels of the organization.

Biggest gap new practitioners would like to fill

New change management practitioners identified the biggest gaps they would like to fill. The top gaps identified were:

1. **Change management knowledge, tools and skills**
Participants identified a lack of knowledge and training in key change management skills, tools and methodologies as a gap for new practitioners. They reported needing more expertise in the field of change management.

2. **Selling change management to the organization**
Participants sought out approaches to engage

with project teams, stakeholders and sponsors, and build buy-in for change management with these groups. Participants expressed desire for "*more experience influencing sponsors and leaders*" and sought the ability to position change management as a permanent function by "*clearly articulating benefits of a structured change management approach*."

3. **Sponsorship and leadership engagement**
   Participants identified the ability to engage and coach sponsors as a key gap for new practitioners. Lacking an understanding of how to influence decision makers and build the coalition of support from leadership, participants expressed a desire to learn approaches for creating sustained engagement from sponsors.

4. **Creating effective communications**
   New change management practitioners in this study identified a gap in the deployment of honest and effective communication. They desired improved skills in selecting and implementing the appropriate communication tools and the correct alignment of timing and messages for specific audiences.

5. **Project management integration**
   The ability to effectively and efficiently integrate change management with project management was identified as a gap for new practitioners. Participants described this gap as including competencies both in bridging the differences between the methodologies used in each area and in managing the overlap of the two disciplines.

Motivation for change management

For the first time, participants were asked to identify the motivating factors or reasons change management was applied on the project. The top two reasons, the nature of the change and driving success, were cited twice as often as any other reason.

The top reasons for applying change management cited by participants were:

1. As a necessity stemming from the nature of the change
2. To contribute to overall project success
3. As a result of previous experience
4. As a mandate or directive

1. **As a necessity stemming from the nature of the change**
   - The change had a high degree of complexity. Complexity resulted from a variety of factors, including: magnitude of change from both scope and scale; impact to multiple divisions or parts of the organization; impact that was global or across dispersed geographic areas; or highly political nature of the change.
   - The change had a high degree of "people change," including significant impact on roles, responsibilities and behaviors.
   - The change had many stakeholders, both in terms of sheer number and in terms of varied impact across numerous groups.
   - The change was vital for the organization due to its importance, strategic nature or visibility to the public or customers.
   - The change impacted the culture of the organization.

2. **To contribute to overall project success**

   Change management was viewed as a key success factor that promoted benefits realization, increased the probability of success, ensured achievement of expected return on investment (ROI) and kept the project on track. Specifically, change management helped:
   - To create the necessary buy-in, commitment, understanding and awareness with employees, and prepare them to make the change
   - To increase usage and adoption of the change and to assist employees through the transition so they can absorb and adopt the change
   - To mitigate the people risk associated with the project
   - To minimize the significant risk posed if the change is not implemented effectively
   - To minimize disruption and friction during the change and promote operational continuity and a smooth transition
   - To ensure an effective and efficient implementation
   - To implement a change quickly
   - To ensure the project is implemented within budget and on schedule

3. **As a result of previous experience**
   - The failure on past changes that neglected change management resulted in change management being applied on this project.
   - Prior successes on projects that used a structured approach for change management resulted in change management being applied on this project.

4. **As a mandate or directive**
   - Senior leaders saw the impact of change management and viewed it as a necessity on the project.
   - Direction at the corporate level encouraged change management.

- Change management was mandated or made a requirement for the project.

Additional reasons provided by participants included:

- To ensure more effective communication and sponsorship
- As a result of anticipated resistance
- As a consideration proposed by vendor, consultant or request for proposal (RFP)
- As damage control for projects experiencing problems

Use of methodology

After several years of remaining steady, the percentage of study participants using a particular methodology increased. Starting in 2003, when only 34% of participants cited using a particular methodology, the number has increased. 72% of participants in the 2011 study indicated using a particular change management methodology (Figure 4).

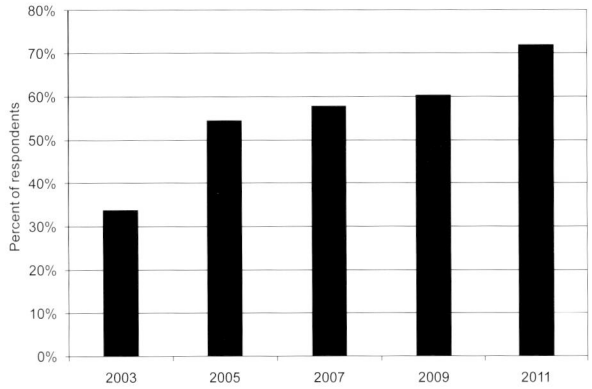

Figure 4 – Use of particular methodology

Figures 5 and 6 below present further segmentation on the use of a particular methodology by industry and region. Results are shown relative to the entire study population average of 72%.

Participants from the United States, Australia and New Zealand, Canada and Africa reported higher rates of using a particular methodology than the entire study population.

Participants in the following industries reported the highest rate of using a particular methodology: Food/Beverage, Government – Defense, Insurance, Health Care, Consumer Goods, Development and Manufacturing, and Government – State or Local.

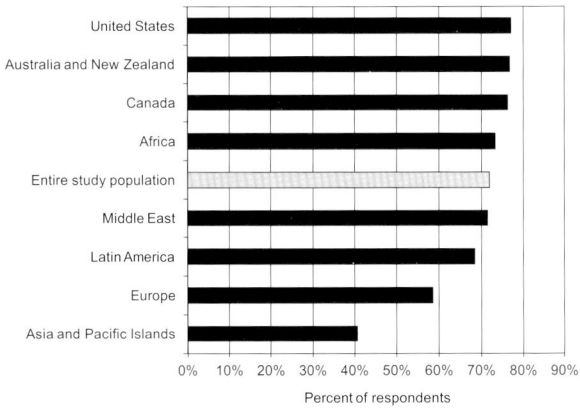

Figure 5 – Use of particular methodology by region

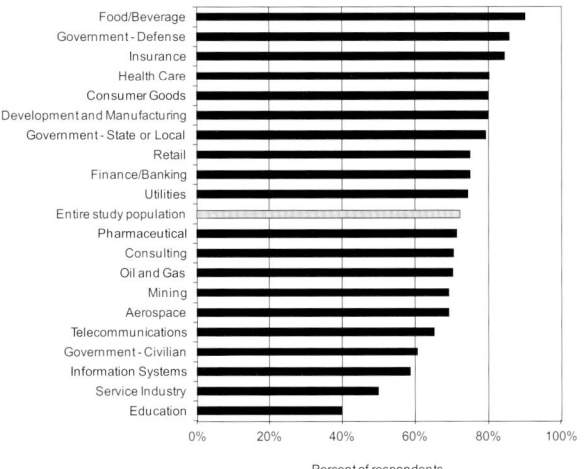

Figure 6 – Use of particular methodology by industry

Participants who used a particular methodology reported higher levels of overall change management effectiveness. 61% of participants who did not use a particular methodology reported "poor" or "fair" overall effectiveness, compared to 42% who did use a particular methodology (Figure 7).

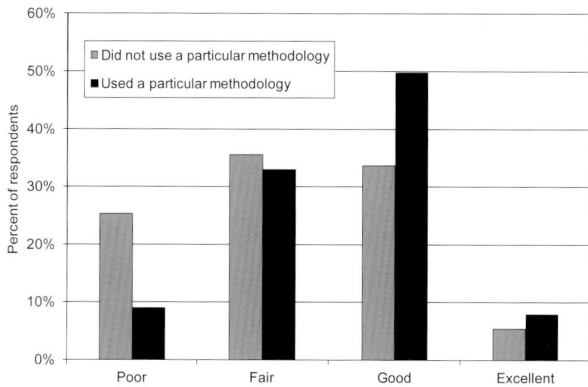

Figure 7 – Impact of use of particular methodology on overall change management effectiveness

Key factors in choosing the methodology

Participants were asked to identify what key factors led them to choose the methodology they ultimately selected.

1. **Ease of use and scalability**
   Participants favored a methodology that was easy to use and could be scaled to meet the specific change that was being managed. Additional characteristics in this category included:
   - Easy to follow
   - Easy to understand
   - Easy to explain to others in the organization
   - Flexible and scalable
   - Quickly adaptable to the change
   - Clear templates, tools, frameworks and structure
   - Accessible and available resources
   - Practical
   - Used business or organizational language as opposed to jargon

2. **Owned internally or able to be licensed by organization**
   A methodology that was either created within the organization, created for the organization specifically or licensed to be used by the organization was preferred. In addition to ownership or right to use, successful results using the methodology reinforced its continued use.

3. **Previously used or experienced**
   The selected methodology had a track record of producing results when used in the organization. In addition to familiarity, this created credibility for continued use on future projects.

4. **Certified or trained in methodology**
   Change management resources already present in the organization were certified in or had been trained in this methodology. The degree of familiarity and amount of previous success with the model by practitioners contributed to confidence expressed toward the methodology.

5. **Compatibility with project, company, culture or industry**
   The methodology offered special compatibility with the type of project, company (e.g. use of language and concepts specific to the organization and its culture), culture (e.g. designed for Latin cultures) or the industry (e.g. designed for IT industry).

6. **Credible, well-known and recognized approach**
   A methodology that was well known, reputable and popular among peer organizations and/or industries was favored over unknown or brand new approaches. Respondents regarded research-based methodologies as more credible and proven.

7. **Comprehensive approach**
   Methodology provided theory and corresponding actionable items throughout the change process. Methodology addressed and related the needs of the organization and the individual in a practical manner.

8. **Recommended by an outside source**
   A trusted source outside of the organization recommended the particular methodology.

Which methodology was used

Participants who used a particular methodology shared which approach they used. Figure 8 shows the results of this analysis.

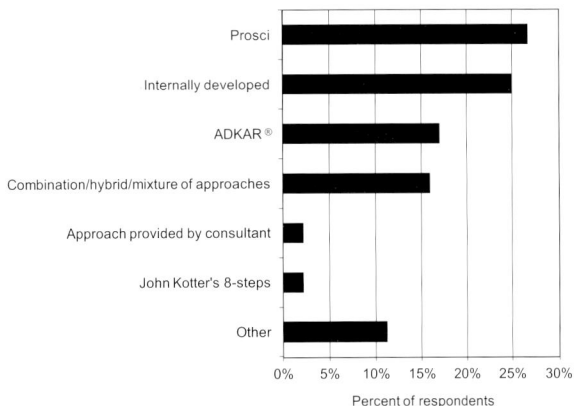

Figure 8 – Methodology used

Editor's note: The change management study invitation was sent to nearly 60,000 members of Prosci's Change Management Learning Center. Because this is not a pure random sample, the rank order of these methodologies may not be representative of a neutral participant group.

The top source material or influencers mentioned by participants with internally developed approaches were: Prosci and ADKAR®, John Kotter, Daryl Conner, Ackerman Anderson and Anderson, Accenture, and Bridges.

The top methodologies or approaches used by participants that indicated a combination, hybrid or mixture of approaches were: Prosci and ADKAR®, John Kotter, internally-developed approaches and consultant-provided approaches.

Benefits of using a structured approach

Participants identified six primary benefits of using a structured approach to change management.

1. **Definition of activities, roles, language, processes, tools and assessments**
   Structured approaches designated and defined key activities and roles, common language, and documentation practices to guide the overall process. Templates, tools and assessments provided by a structured methodology visibly outlined procedures for specific steps. Best practices reports were utilized as a reference for issues unaddressed in the structured approach and toolset.

2. **Systematic structure resulting in a consistent and repeatable approach**
   Structured approaches directed change in a systematic manner. This fostered consistent practices, generating more rapid familiarity with the system and allowing for repetition of activities and results.

3. **Logical, detailed progression of stages**
   Structured approaches presented steps in a logical and consecutive manner. Communicating the motives behind each step gave clarity to the methodology's direction and reasoning, while contributing transparency to the approach itself.

4. **Easier to understand and explain**
   The organized and documented framework of structured approaches made them easier to learn, understand and explain to others. Training further supplemented the ease of understanding and explanation.

5. **Support for value of change management**
   Structured approaches contributed credibility to change management as a practice. Presenting a legitimate, controlled and structured approach helped to dispel the notion that change management is "soft" and vague. This credibility bolstered confidence in the initiative and encouraged buy-in.

6. **Identification of gaps and common mistakes**
   Structured approaches addressed change management thoroughly and comprehensively. A structured approach fostered the anticipation of gaps and resistance. Common mistakes were avoided. This helped to reduce risk and ensure that no components of the process were overlooked.

When to start change management
Source date: 2009

Participants in the 2009 study were asked to indicate when change management activities began on the project they were reporting on and when they would recommend starting change management activities. Figure 9 shows the strong bias participants had toward starting change management activities at the initiation of the project. Over 80% showed a preference to begin change management activities at project initiation, although less than 40% actually started this early.

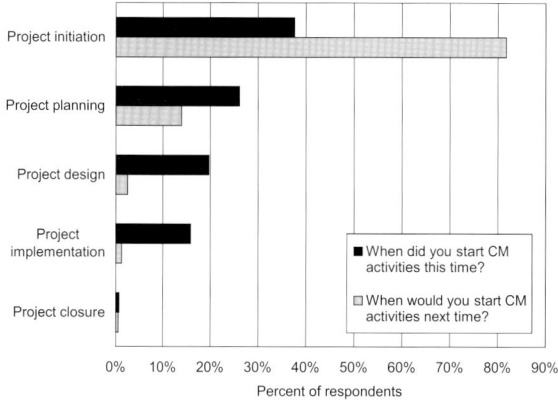

Figure 9 – When did change management activities begin?

What you can do at initiation when there is incomplete information

In the 2009 study over 80% of participants recommended starting change management during project initiation. However, at project initiation there are often many unknowns about the details of the solution.

Participants in the 2011 benchmarking study were asked to provide ideas for specific change management actions that can be taken when change management is started at initiation and there is incomplete information about the project or solution design. The top suggestions from participants included:

1. **Create a communication plan to describe the desired results of the change and the need for change**
   Communicate details of the change openly and often to increase transparency and awareness of the change, including desired results, the need for change and current information gaps. Establish expectations for communications surrounding the change by designating structured channels.

2. **Analyze the organizational climate and its reaction to change and document common risks and areas of resistance**
   Use systematic, measurable assessments to analyze the organizational climate and its reaction to change. Common measures include change impact analyses, change readiness assessments, organizational culture assessments and change saturation assessments. Describe common or historical risks, areas of resistance and pain points for both the organization and this specific project.

3. **Identify stakeholders and involve them in the design of the solution**
   Perform a stakeholder analysis to identify, describe and categorize stakeholders by the extent that the change will affect them. Involve stakeholders and end-users in the design of the solution corresponding with their proximity to the change to encourage engagement.

4. **Develop a flexible, high-level change management plan that includes key deliverables and required resources**
   Create a high-level change management plan that identifies deliverables of the change management function, timing of those deliverables and the required resources. Design this plan flexibly, allowing for adjustment according to future insights and information.

5. **Coordinate change management and project management plans**
   Incorporate change management actions into the project management plans from the initiation of the project to establish change management as a valuable component of the project plan. Express the need for change

management in a business case and document tangible benefits, return on investment (ROI) and statistics on change management success. Logically relate change management activities to the project plan and to deliverables in the project schedule.

6. **Identify and solicit support from sponsors of the change**
   Identify change sponsors at the initiation of the project to proactively identify and remedy resistance within the leadership. Establishing support from change sponsors helps clearly and coherently guide the change in a manner consistent with the project's goals and timeline.

7. **Designate and educate a change management team**
   Designate members of a change management team and educate them fully on the change management methodology chosen for the project. The change management team should build a fundamental understanding of the process to be used across the stakeholder groups by explaining the basic roles and steps of the methodology.

Contributors to starting change management early in the project
Source date: 2009

Those participants in the 2009 study who started change management early in the project life cycle identified the factors that contributed to having change management begin at the onset of their project. The top contributors to having change management begin at the onset of the project were:

1. **Senior leadership directive**
   Senior leaders connected to the project had a high level of experience with or knowledge of change management. They ensured that change management was incorporated into the project by demonstrating support for change management and insisting that it be adequately addressed. In some cases, senior leaders required change management plans for the project.

2. **Acknowledgement by the project manager**
   The project manager or project director recognized the importance of change management and supported its inclusion in the project. Previous experience with change management by the project manager contributed to this acknowledgement.

3. **Previous experience**
   The organization had previous experience with changes where the people side of change was either effectively managed or ineffectively managed. Most responses indicated previous negative experiences where change management was ignored and projects suffered as a result.

4. **Incorporation into project initiation steps**
   Change management activities were incorporated into the launch of the project. Participants stated that risk analysis, assessments and stakeholder identification occurred at the launch of the project. Change management activities were incorporated into the project timeline, budget and charter. Change management plans were identified as key deliverables.

Additional reasons for change management beginning early in the project life cycle included:

- The nature of the project itself – including the complexity, perceived difficulty of the change and importance of employee buy-in

- Resource availability – change management resources were available or assigned to the team from the very beginning

- Integration with project management methodology – the organization had taken steps to integrate the change management methodology into its existing project management methodology

Consequences of starting late
Source date: 2009

Participants in the 2009 study who started change management late in the project life cycle commented on the consequences of this approach. The most common consequences of starting change management late were:

1. **Employees were more resistant and less engaged**
   Because change management was not started early, the project experienced higher levels of resistance from employees. People were not motivated to participate. They were not engaged or committed, and they were slow to get on board with the change. Confusion and misconceptions about the change were exacerbated.

2. **Change management activities were limited and ineffective**
   The role of change management was limited and primarily reactive in nature. Participants felt that change management activities were ad hoc, started too late and often limited to only a single change management activity like training or communications. There was too little time to do change management effectively and the work was often rushed. Change management work was isolated from other project work.

3. **Time was spent playing "catch up"**
   The change management team had an incomplete view of the change effort, including the strategy, direction, expectations, and expected results and benefits. The team expended tremendous energy backtracking and trying to catch up on what had already happened with the project. This effort was viewed as non-value-added work and excessively costly.

4. **Change management was not effectively positioned**
   There was neither support nor resources for change management. Roles were poorly defined, and the change management team had a difficult time building relationships, having influence or getting a "seat at the table."

5. **Project design ignored the people side components**
   In a number of instances, people issues related to the project design were identified late in the project after change management resources were brought on board. The result was rework and having to revisit project decisions.

6. **Project objectives were compromised**
   Benefits were only partially realized or not achieved at all. The project ended up behind schedule or over budget. Results were not sustained.

Action steps if change management started late in the project
Source date: 2009

Participants in the 2009 study provided the specific action steps they had to take as a result of change management being introduced late in the project life cycle.

Overwhelmingly, the most common action steps cited by participants pertained to adjusting the change management approach. These adjustments included:

- Redo, undo and fast-track communication efforts
- Refocus on building awareness and support
- Work to get sponsor engagement and action (escalate critical issues)
- Limit focus to the most critical activities
- Increase resources for change management
- Expedite change management activities
- Provide education about change management
- Control damage – "put out fires"
- Skip steps or cut corners as necessary

The other action steps cited by participants were:

- Backtrack and learn about project developments that have already occurred (become grounded on project work so far)

- Change the project schedule – put project on hold, push out deadlines, slow down efforts, re-plan or, in some cases, re-launch the project
- Expend extra time and energy (overall, the team had to work harder)

Advice to a new team regarding methodology

Participants commented on the advice they would give to a new team regarding change management methodology. The top recommendations included:

1. **Use an established change management methodology and stick with it**
   Respondents noted that the core principles of most change management methodologies are similar. Regardless of which approach was used, respondents stressed the importance of using a structured change management methodology. Use the methodology consistently and utilize its toolset and assessments as intended.

2. **Ensure that the change management approach fits the organization and project**
   Select a flexible and scalable change management methodology that allows for customization based on the organization or project. Understand needs and evaluate multiple methodologies before selecting one to use.

3. **Provide training on the change management methodology that includes practical application**
   Users should be trained in the change management methodology and understand the components. Training should include a focus on practical application, allowing them to modify the approach and adapt it to diverse changes. This could include education on communicating the methodology to others, as well as detailing roles and responsibilities.

4. **Integrate change management activities with the project management plan**
   Change management activities should be integrated with project management plans as early as possible in the process.

5. **Use a practical, comprehensive methodology that is easy to understand and explain**
   When selecting a change management methodology, respondents favored practical, comprehensive approaches designed to ensure no key activities are missed, ease of understanding and an approach that was easy to convey to others.

Change management team and structure

Attributes of a great team member

Study participants identified the most important attributes of a great change management team member. The top four attributes identified were:

1. **Communication skills**
   Able to communicate effectively with all levels of the organization; being an effective communicator including listening to others, accepting feedback, and demonstrating competencies in both written and oral communication

2. **Change management competency**
   Has attended change management training and has experience applying a structured methodology; has experience managing resistance and coaching employees throughout the change

3. **Flexibility**
   Has an open mind and is flexible during times of change; demonstrates resilience throughout the change process and is able to adapt and be creative with what is available

4. **Interpersonal skills**
   Demonstrates strong interpersonal skills with coworkers and has respect from employees within the organization; is people-oriented, trusted and honest in all situations.

Permanent position or job role

Participants in organizations that had created a permanent position or job role for change management (43%, see Figure 10) provided elements of the job description or key responsibilities of these staff positions.

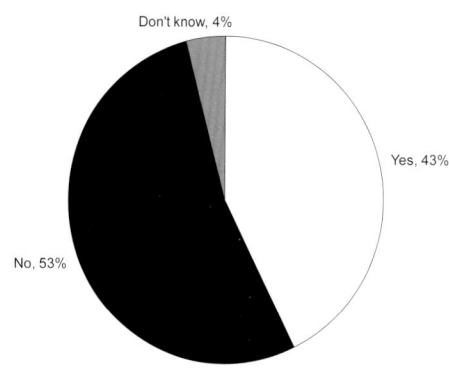

Figure 10 – **Organization has a change management permanent position / job role**

A complete list of the job description elements is provided below, in rank order based on frequency.

- **Apply a structured methodology and lead change management activities** – manage the change management process, and apply change management tools and processes in support of the project or initiative

- **Support change management at the organizational level** – including building change management skills; creating and/or implementing an enterprise framework; supporting other change management practitioners; maintaining a change management network (for example, a Community of Practice or a Center of Excellence); building change management capability; provisioning change management tools; building awareness of the need for change management; and facilitating continuous improvement by capturing lessons learned

- **Support communication efforts** – including the design, development, delivery and management of communications

- **Assess the change impact** – including conducting impact analyses, assessing change readiness and identifying key stakeholders

- **Support training efforts** – including providing input, documenting requirements, supporting the design and delivery, and managing the training program

Additional items included:
- Consult and coach project teams
- Create change management strategy
- Define and measure success metrics and monitor change progress
- Support and engage senior leaders
- Manage stakeholders
- Complete change management assessments
- Coordinate efforts with other specialists (examples included communications specialists, training specialists, and learning and development specialists)
- Identify, analyze and prepare mitigation tactics for risk
- Identify and manage anticipated resistance
- Integrate change management activities into project plan
- Support organizational design and definition of roles and responsibilities
- Evaluate and ensure user readiness
- Manage the portfolio and change load
- Track and report issues
- Coach managers and supervisors

A number of study participants also shared skills or qualifications for the change management position. The top responses included: change management experience and expertise; excellent written and verbal communication skills; existing professional relationships or the ability to build relationships; knowledge of the organization or industry; experience and background in project management; and interpersonal skills including the ability to influence and build support.

Team structure

Source date: 2009

Data was collected on the change management team structure used by study participants in the 2009 study. Participants chose between the two structures shown below or selected "other structure" if their structure did not map to Team Structure A or Team Structure B. In Team Structure A, the change management resources are on the project team. In Team Structure B, the change management resources are external and support the project team.

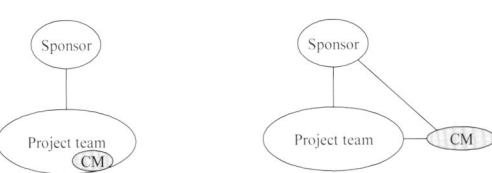

Over 60% of participants used Team Structure A where the change management resources were on the project team (Figure 11).

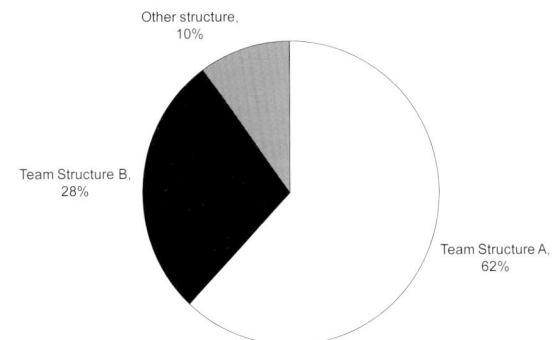

Figure 11 – Team structures used

The most common "other" structure cited was a hybrid of Team Structure A and Team Structure B. Hybrid structures included the following:

- The project team itself was responsible for change management.
- Change management was done by a member of the project team with outside assistance

including facilitation, coaching, support and advising.

- A single change management group from a company-wide Change Management Office supported and participated with projects in all divisions and departments.

Team structure preferences
Source date: 2009

Participants in the 2009 study also expressed which team structure they would prefer and the reasons why.

Advantages of Team Structure A included:

- Increased project knowledge
- Part of the team
- Integrated responsibilities
- Increased credibility
- Ease of communication

Advantages of Team Structure B included:

- Access to leadership
- Objectivity
- Independent from conflicting priorities
- Different scope
- Enterprise approach
- Different skill set
- Elevated status

These advantages are addressed in more detail on the following pages.

Team Structure A advantages
A majority of 2009 study participants reported that a team structure where the change management resources were integrated into the project team was the most effective. The top five reasons to use an integrated structure were:

1. **Increased project knowledge**
   Change resources inside a project team had a better understanding of the business objectives, context and technical details of the project. They gained the benefit of day-to-day knowledge and were able to monitor events as they unfolded.

2. **Part of the team**
   When change resources were integrated into the project team, they had ownership in the project and shared the team's common goals. They personally engaged and made a commitment to project success. There was an opportunity to build trust through collaboration and involvement in decision making.

3. **Integrated responsibilities**
   All team members shared accountability for the success of the project. Change management resources played an integral role in achieving project outcomes, working with the project team from beginning to end. There was also a need for ongoing and active involvement in change activities from other members of the project team.

4. **Increased credibility**
   Change managers within the project team had increased influence. They were seen as a peer with project-specific knowledge, rather than as an outsider. This position provided increased opportunities to raise people issues, coach the project team and influence strategic direction.

5. **Ease of communication**
   Change resources on the project team were privy to the high volume of communications between project team members. There was no need for a third-party relay of information. Change resources could also more directly communicate their change-related information to the project team.

Team Structure B advantages
A smaller but still significant group of participants responded that the most effective team structure utilized change management resources external to the project team. These external resources took various forms, including subject matter experts (SMEs), resources from a Change Management Office, internal Organizational Development (OD) consultants or external consultants. The primary reasons to

employ resources outside of the project team were:

1. **Access to leadership**
   Change management resources were coaches for sponsors. They were in a better position to manage sponsorship activities when they were external to the project team. The flow of communications between sponsor and change manager was direct, not filtered through a project manager.

2. **Objectivity**
   Resources outside of the project team offered neutrality and an independent point of view. They provided objective feedback and more accurately assessed the people impacts of the project.

3. **Independent from conflicting priorities**
   Change management resources outside of the project team had autonomy to maintain the priority of their change work without being "swallowed by project tasks."

4. **Different scope**
   Participants noted that change management required a specific, constant focus on strategies related to the people side of change. It was a forward facing role with an organizational-level viewpoint that often addressed more audiences than the project itself. Change management also coordinated multiple segments of large projects or programs.

5. **Enterprise approach**
   Organizations with an enterprise-focused change management discipline were able to coordinate many projects and ensure stable, consistent implementation. Resources could be allocated to "hot spots" as needed, leveraging skills across the organization and reducing costs.

6. **Different skill set**
   Change management required specialized knowledge and skills such as experience or training in change concepts and tools, as well as strong communication skills. By contrast, project work often involved a very different set of skills in technical processes or systems.

7. **Elevated status**
   Change management gained a greater level of respect when considered separately from the project team. External change managers reported in at the same level as the project team and were seen as a complementary but equal team. They enabled success by coaching both the sponsor and the project team through the change process.

Additional team structure considerations

Source date: 2009

A number of study participants did not indicate a preference between Team Structure A and Team Structure B. Instead, they responded with alternative ideas about the most effective change management team structure.

- The most effective team structure varied from project to project depending on:
    - Nature of the project including size, scope, complexity, impact on people, risk or geographic distribution; responses were equally divided as to which structure was better for which size of change
    - Cultural factors within an organization such as employee response to outside help and fragmentation of groups
    - Resource considerations such as availability of change management skills and experience within the project team and sponsorship coalition

- Hybrid structures. Participants proposed structures that combined resources both internal and external to the project team. These hybrid structures had benefits that included:
    - Balancing project knowledge with outside perspective
    - Having support and expertise from a Center of Excellence as needed, particularly during busy project stages
    - Allowing for business unit representation while building change skills within the organization

- Entirely unique team structures included:
    - Change management owned by all impacted groups, with involvement from all levels – "everyone in the change circle"
    - Sponsor included in the change management team bubble
    - Change management team positioned hierarchically between the project team and the sponsor

Decisions on the number of change management resources

Source date: 2009

Participants identified factors that influenced the number of change management resources on the project as well as those constraining factors that limited the number of resources used.

The top influencing factors were:
- Nature of the change
- Scope of required change management efforts
- Number of impacted groups
- Organizational capacity for change
- Benchmarking
- Geographical distribution
- Phase of project
- Established organizational guidelines
- Strategic importance of the project
- Project team's change management experience

The top constraining factors were:
- Budget
- Availability
- Skill set
- Organizational maturity in change management
- Confidentiality

Influencing factors:

1. **Nature of the change**
   Participants reported that the change itself was a major factor in determining the change management resource requirements. The change characteristics most frequently cited were the type of change (process, systems, reorganization, etc.), the complexity of the project, the number of people impacted and the pace of implementation.

2. **Scope of required change management efforts**
   Resourcing decisions were determined by the amount of change management work to be completed. The scale of the communications plan, training requirements, coaching needs and assessment work were key factors in calculating resource needs. Participants asked themselves, "Do we have enough people to do all the work?"

3. **Number of impacted groups**
   The number of business units, work streams or levels involved in the change affected the number of change management resources required. Study responses underscored the importance of involving key representatives from each impacted group to answer questions and allow for cross-organizational input.

4. **Organizational capacity for change**
   An organization's cultural acceptance of change and change capacity impacted change management resourcing decisions. Factors such as higher volumes of ongoing change and larger amounts of anticipated resistance resulted in higher resource needs.

5. **Benchmarking**
   Change management resources were allocated based on best practices research, consultant recommendations and lessons learned from past project experiences.

6. **Geographical distribution**
   Projects with global or widely distributed regional implementation required more change management resources.

7. **Phase of project**
   Participants reported that the number of resources needed for change management

could vary through the project life cycle. Many noted fewer requirements in the early stages and increasing needs as the project neared implementation. Additional resources were added to projects that fell behind or experienced a lack of progress.

8. **Established organizational guidelines**
   Organizations established enterprise-wide guidelines for making resourcing decisions. These were based on in-house change management methodologies or mandated by a central Project Management Office (PMO), Change Management Office (CMO) or Human Resources (HR) group.

9. **Strategic importance of the project**
   Participants responded that the project's impact to the business was considered in allocating resources. More resources were used in critical or urgent projects and projects with a high risk of failure.

10. **Project team's change management experience**
    The level of change management skill and expertise on the project team, coupled with the team's level of awareness of the importance of change management, factored into resourcing decisions.

Constraining factors:

1. **Budget**
   Nearly 20% of participants cited budget constraints as a primary factor limiting their ability to obtain change management resources. Sponsors and project team leaders were unwilling or unable to pay for change management resources. Many organizations had no formal budget for change management.

2. **Availability**
   Nearly 20% of participants indicated resource availability as a limiting factor in change management resource decisions. Time and workload constraints on employees, ongoing commitments and conflicting priorities limited the pool of resources available for change management.

3. **Skill set**
   Participants reported a lack of trained and experienced change management resources within their organizations. To be effective in a change management role, resources must not only have technical skills but also soft skills such as teamwork, flexibility and ability to engage a sponsor.

4. **Organizational maturity in change management**
   Resourcing decisions were impacted by the level of awareness of change management within the organization. Lack of buy-in and a low perceived value of change management, particularly at the sponsorship level, resulted in fewer resources.

5. **Confidentiality**
   In several cases, the sensitivity of the project inhibited the number of change management resources.

Team experience and expertise
Source date: 2009

Participants in the 2009 study evaluated the level of experience and expertise of the change management resources on the project. Nearly one half of participants indicated that the change management resources had less than adequate experience or expertise (Figure 12).

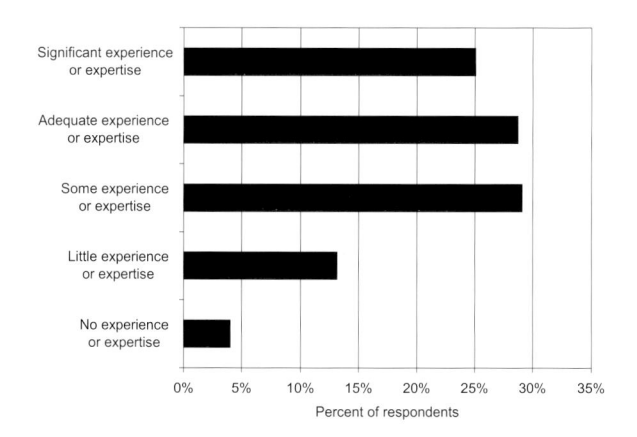

Figure 12 – Level of experience and expertise of change management resources

Building change management knowledge
Source date: 2009

Participants in the 2009 study were asked to identify how they overcame or addressed the lack of change management experience or knowledge in their project. They described the following top five tactics and methods used in overcoming or addressing the knowledge and experience gaps:

1. **Training in change management**
   Change leaders, project team members, managers and sponsors participated in training activities to learn about change management methodologies and strategies. Some attended formal training programs. Others received less formal training through internally developed programs, train-the-trainer programs or ongoing training in regular team meetings.

2. **Coaching and mentoring**
   Coaching and mentoring relationships allowed more experienced change management leaders to provide direction and support to their counterparts with less change management experience. Some organizations created a formal "buddy system" or shadowing opportunities to allow inexperienced individuals to work alongside experienced team members. Experienced team members took the lead in projects by setting a personal example and offering advice and guidance one-on-one.

3. **Self-study**
   Many participants sought out change management knowledge on their own through independent study and research that included reviewing training materials, books, published materials and benchmarking information. Internet-based resources such as online tutorials and webinars were referenced frequently. Participants also cited learning on the job through trial and error and addressing issues as they arose as a self-study tactic.

4. **Engaging consultants and external resources**
   Hiring external resources or consultants helped to fill gaps in expertise and supplement full-time employee knowledge. External resources provided support through delivery of training programs that emphasized competency building. Consultants worked to provide knowledge transfer through coaching and strategic advice and, in some cases, even built a change management methodology for the project.

5. **Peer-to-peer networking**
   Support groups and communities of practice provided avenues to communicate with other professionals in the field. These networking opportunities allowed for knowledge sharing, collecting of lessons learned and liaising with the leaders of similar projects. More informally, asking questions and fostering open dialogue with other departments that had relevant expertise (communications, training, etc.) helped to address gaps in change management knowledge.

Advice for new change management teams on resources and structure

Source date: 2007

Participants in the 2007 study cited a number of recommendations they would provide to new change management teams about team structure. The top recommendations provided by participants were:

- **Ensure appropriate sponsor access**
  Participants mentioned the need for more direct, unfiltered access to the primary sponsor. A number of participants cited the importance of having a team member with the time, credibility, level and respect to effectively coach sponsors.

- **Select the right team members**
  Participants provided a number of suggestions for team composition. They recommended a team that had:
  - A wide range of individual competencies, including communications and training skills
  - General experience on change projects
  - People directly impacted by the change
  - Cross-functional representation (representation from the business and not just from Human Resources)
  - Credibility within the organization
  - Members who were supportive and passionate about the change

- **Ensure budget and resources for change management**
  The change management effort and team must be resourced appropriately. This included allocating a budget for change management and providing dedicated resources.

- **Develop an effective relationship with the project team**
  While there were many variations on the suggested team structure, participants cited a structured and formal relationship with the project team. Some suggestions were to have all of the change management team on the project team, have a project team member on the change management team or create a liaison position. Participants also mentioned the importance of aligning objectives with the project team and integrating project management activities with change management.

- **Provide change management training**
  Change management training was suggested for the change management team and for project managers, senior leaders and front-line managers.

- **Understand the project details**
  The change management team should have a thorough understanding of the project itself to effectively create change management strategies and plans.

- **Start change management activities at the beginning of the project**
  Beginning change management activities at the start of a project enabled more proactive planning of change management efforts.

Resources and budget

Use of dedicated resources

Over three quarters of study participants (76%) reported having dedicated change management resources for the project on which they were reporting (Figure 13).

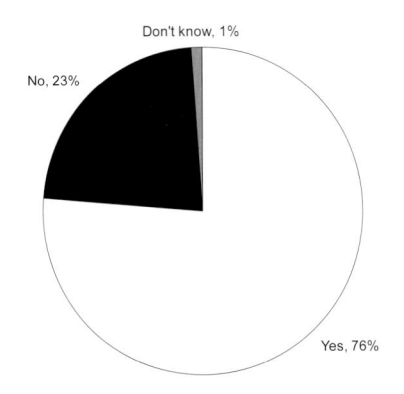

Figure 13 – Project had dedicated change management person or group

Advantages of a dedicated resource

Participants identified four main advantages to having a specific person or group dedicated to change management on the project. The most common response, having a dedicated person to provide focus and keep track of change management activities, was stated over twice as often as the second most common response.

1. **Provides focus and keeps track of change management activities**
   The primary advantage of having a dedicated resource was the focus that the resource could commit to the people side of change, including being responsible for change management activities and ensuring that the focus on change management is sustained. In addition, this person or group developed plans, prioritized activities and helped manage resistance.

2. **Acts as a single point of contact with clear responsibility and accountability**
   Participants indicated that having one person or group dedicated to change management was advantageous because they could offer credible and consistent communications regarding the change. Additionally, this person or group maintained ownership and accountability over the change management activities. "*One source for all change questions.*"

3. **Has the required knowledge, skills and experience**
   A dedicated change management individual or team had the necessary skills, experience, training and motivation to provide guidance throughout the change and educate others on effective change management processes. These individuals understood all of the key issues involved with the change, could see the change holistically and had a unique perspective on the change.

4. **Focuses on the change solely without distractions or other commitments**
   Distinct from the first response, the fourth advantage identified was having a dedicated resource without competing priorities and with fewer distractions. This resource could more effectively focus on and pursue change management activities. "*If it's not someone's job, it's no one's job.*"

Consequences of not having a dedicated resource

While participant responses indicated four main consequences of not having a dedicated change management resource, the most commonly cited response was cited almost three times as often as any other response.

1. **Neglected change management activities**
   Without a dedicated change management resource, key change management activities were neglected or not made a priority. Consequences included:

- The change management work was diluted and disjointed
- People were not engaged
- The end-user was not considered
- Staff morale was low
- The project was poorly supported
- People were not prepared for the change
- Priorities were conflicted
- Project management resources were spread too thin
- Change management did not receive adequate resources
- The project was driven by non-change-management-oriented objectives

Other consequences of not having a dedicated change management resource included:

2. **Increased risk of project failure**
   Research participants reported an increased risk of not meeting objectives, inadequate project outcomes or project failure as a consequence of not having a dedicated change management resource.

3. **Lack of coordination**
   Without a dedicated change management resource, there was a lack of direction, continuity and overall coordination of change management activities.

4. **Lack of ownership or accountability**
   A lack of ownership or accountability over the change management aspects of the project was identified as a consequence of not having a dedicated resource. As a result, research participants cited further consequences, such as a lack of plan, scope, structure and definition in regard to change management activities.

Correlating dedicated resources to effectiveness

The use of a dedicated resource for change management did impact the overall effectiveness of the change management program. The graph below shows the relationship between having a dedicated change management resource and the overall effectiveness of the change management program. 68% of participants reporting on a project without a dedicated change management resource evaluated their change management program as "Poor" or "Fair" compared to only 41% for those with a dedicated change management resource (Figure 14).

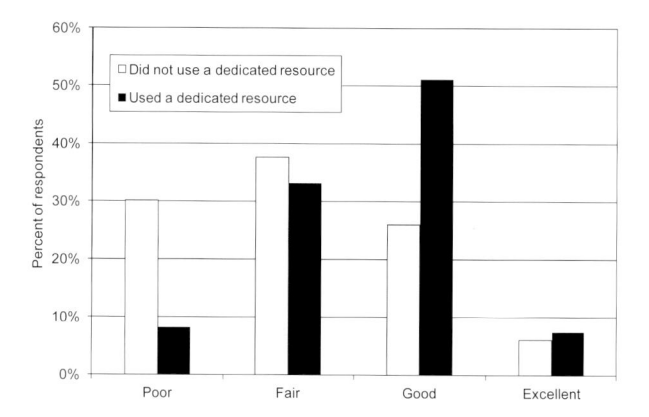

Figure 14 – Relationship between dedicated resources and overall effectiveness

Change management budget components

For the first time, participants in the 2011 benchmarking study provided details on the elements that were included in the budget for change management. The top elements were:

- **Change management resource costs**
  Compensation and salary for the change management practitioners or resources supporting the effort

- **Training costs**
  Design, development, delivery and materials for training, including costs for training specialists

- **Communications costs**
  Development and delivery of the communications approach, including costs for communications specialists; communications collateral including printed materials, brochures, posters, videos, promotional marketing materials, websites and intranet sites

Secondary budget components were:

- Consultant costs – fees for consultant support
- General expenses – including travel, food and refreshments
- Event costs – including workshops, group meetings, "lunch and learn" events, road shows and town hall meetings
- Change management materials – including change management training, plan development, supplies and licensing of materials
- Reinforcement and recognition costs – including celebration costs, rewards, gifts and team recognition events

Average FTE dedicated to change management

Study participants provided data on the number of full time equivalents (FTE) for the entire project team and the number of FTE dedicated specifically to change management. The following four graphs (Figures 15, 16, 17 and 18) show the average FTE dedicated to change management based on project investment, project scope, number of employees impacted and duration of the project.

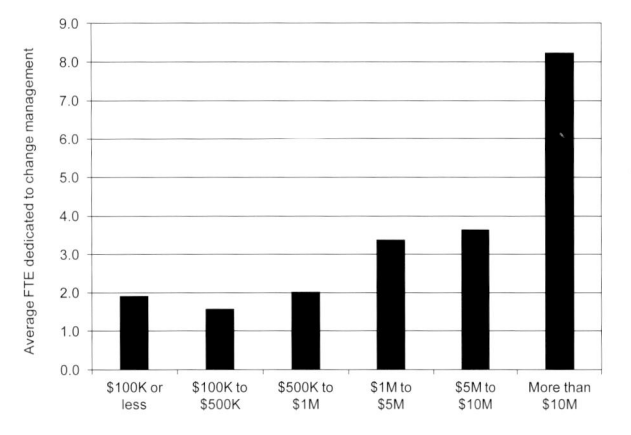

Figure 15 – Average FTE vs. project investment

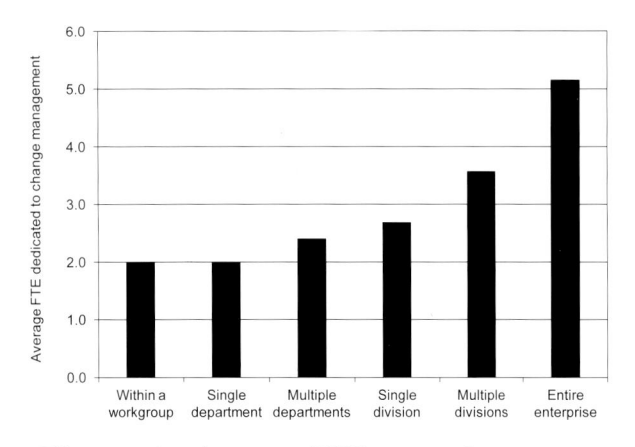

Figure 16 – Average FTE vs. project scope

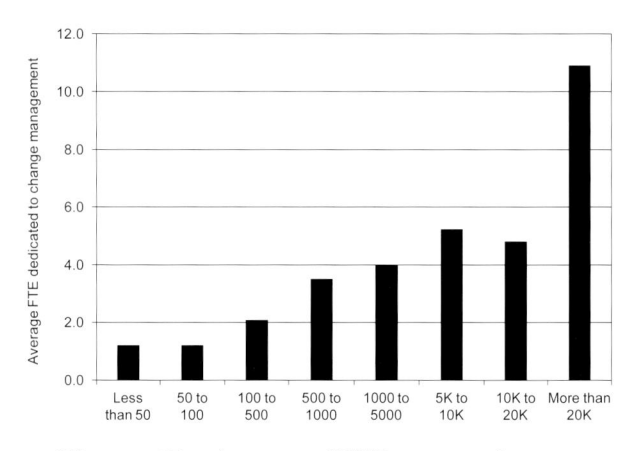

Figure 17 – Average FTE vs. employees impacted

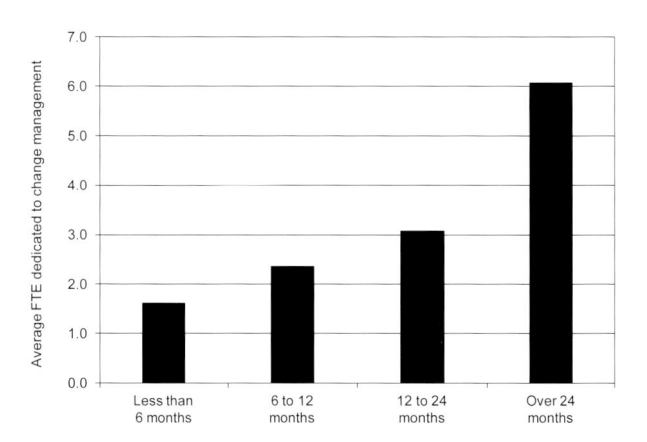

Figure 18 – Average FTE vs. duration

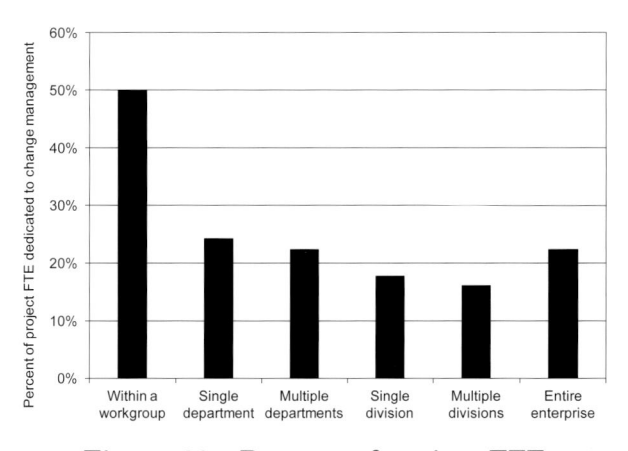

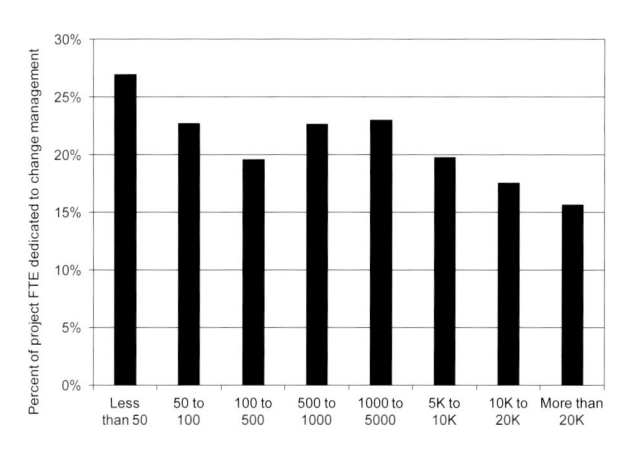

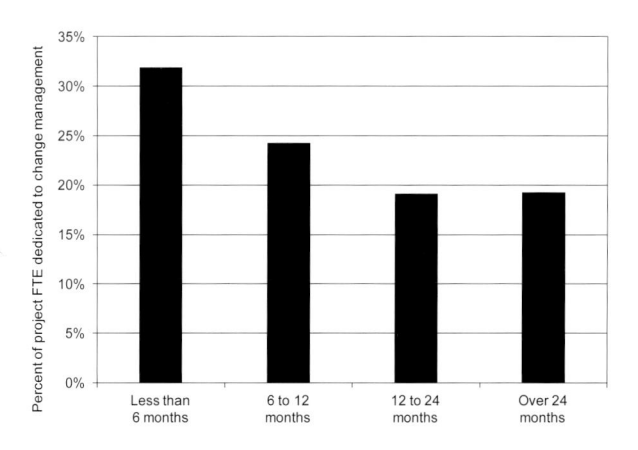

Percent of project FTE dedicated to change management

Figures 19, 20, 21 and 22 show the percent of total project FTE dedicated to change management based on project investment, project scope, number of employees impacted and duration of the project. 42% of participants indicated between 1% and 10% of project FTE were dedicated to change management, and 7% indicated that 0% of project FTE were dedicated to change management. The overall average of total project FTE allocated to change management was 21.1%.

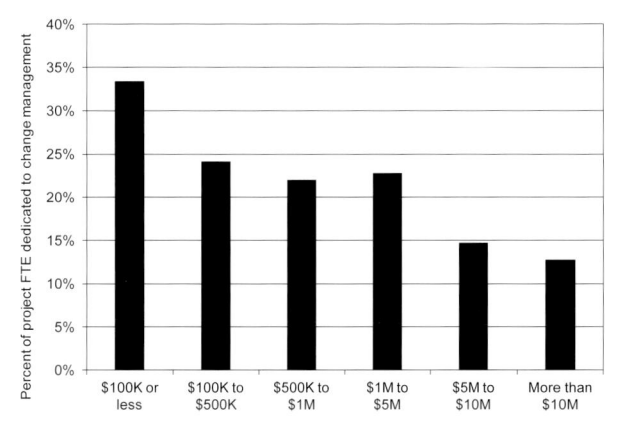

Figure 19 – Percent of project FTE dedicated to change management vs. project investment

Figure 20 – Percent of project FTE dedicated to change management vs. project scope

Figure 21 – Percent of project FTE dedicated to change management vs. employees impacted

Figure 22 – Percent of project FTE dedicated to change management vs. duration

Editor's note: While it may appear that allocation of FTE is lower for larger projects because of the slope of the bar graph, the data present the percentage of total project FTE allocated to change management, so actual FTE allocation may be larger for larger projects.

Average budget for change management

Study participants provided the budget for change management for the project on which they were reporting. The following four graphs (Figures 23, 24, 25 and 26) show the average change management budget based on project investment, project scope, number of employees impacted and duration of the project.

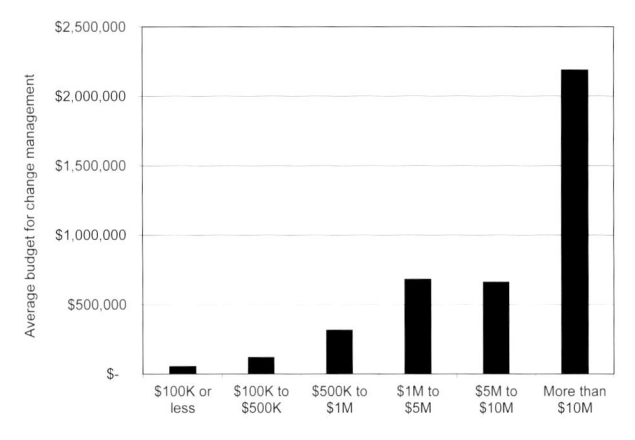

Figure 23 – Average budget vs. project investment

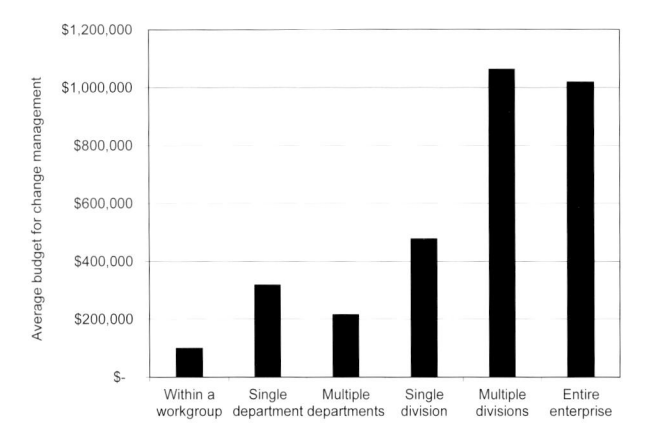

Figure 24 – Average budget vs. project scope

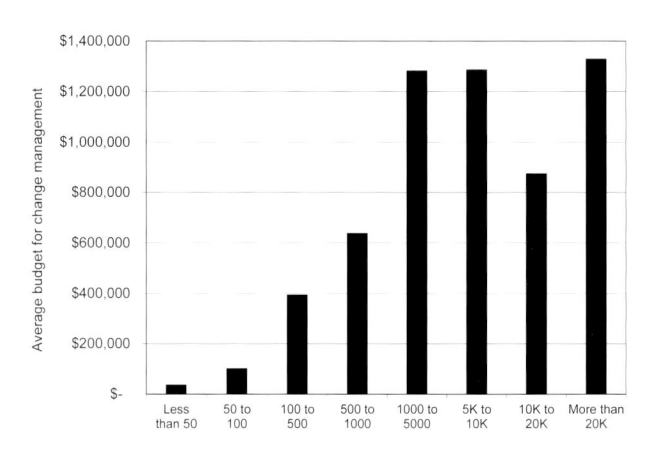

Figure 25 – Average budget vs. employees impacted

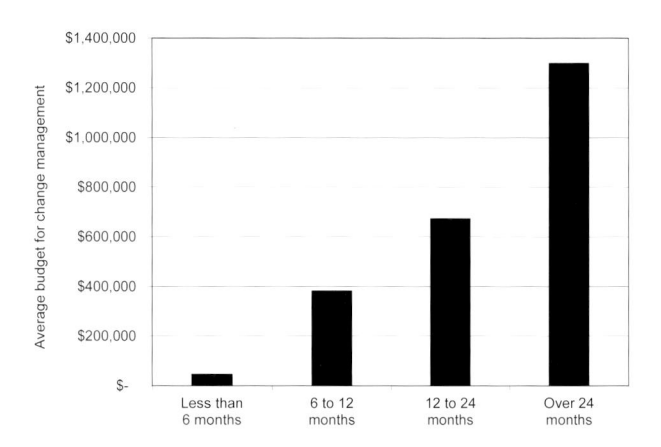

Figure 26 – Average budget vs. duration

Editor's note: The data on this question includes some variability since there is no common standard for which line items are considered part of the change management budget.

Percent of project budget allocated to change management

Figures 27, 28, 29 and 30 show the percent of total project budget allocated to change management based on project investment, project scope, number of employees impacted and duration of the project. The overall average was 12.5%. 17% indicated that none of the total project budget was allocated to change management, and 57% indicated between 1% and 10% of project budget was allocated to change management.

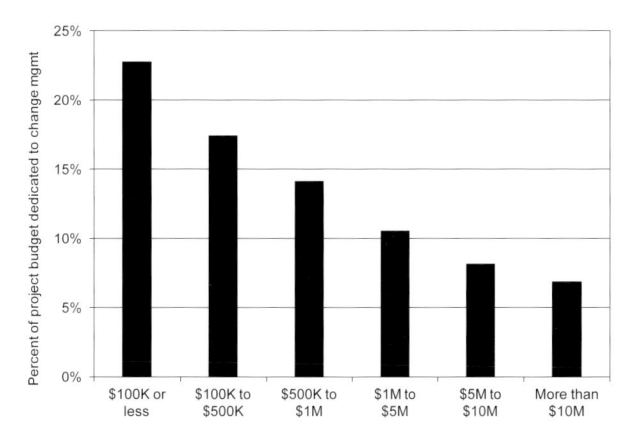

Figure 27 – Percent of project budget vs. project investment

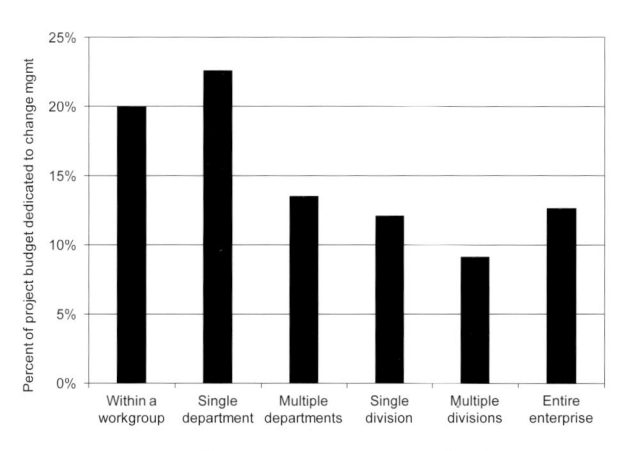

Figure 28 – Percent of project budget vs. project scope

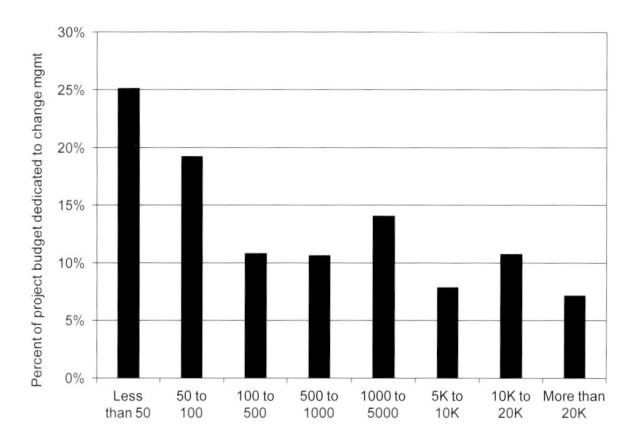

Figure 29 – Percent of project budget vs. employees impacted

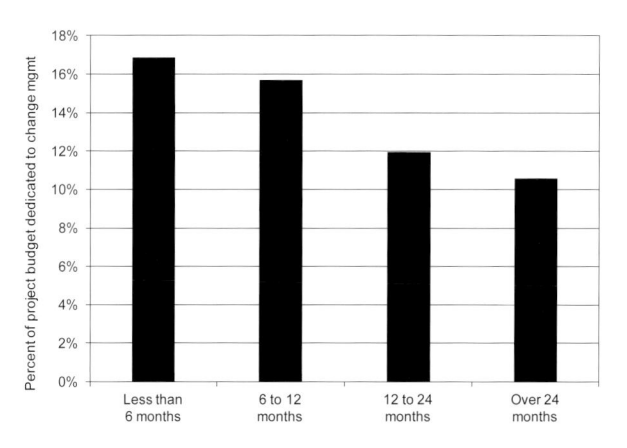

Figure 30 – Percent of project budget vs. duration

Editor's note: While it may appear that allocation of budget is lower for larger projects because of the slope of the bar graph, the data present the percentage of total project budget allocated to change management, so actual budget allocation may be larger for larger projects.

Project management and change management integration

Perception of change management by project teams
Source date: 2009

Overall, 58% of participants in the 2009 study reported that their project teams felt that change management was either critical or necessary (Figure 31). However, there were still over 40% of participants who indicated that their project team either viewed change management as just another activity to do (31%) or as a nuisance with no value (11%).

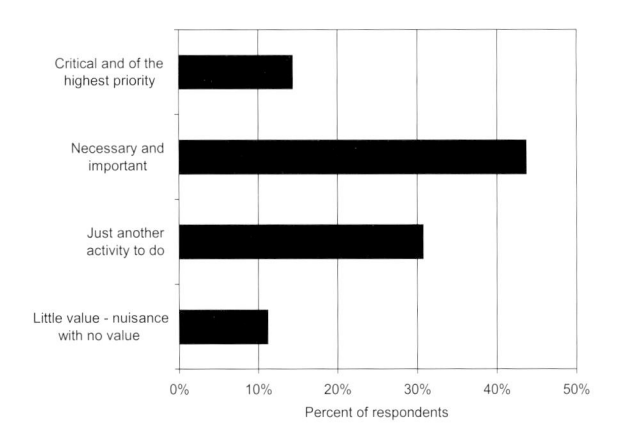

Figure 31 – Project teams' view of the role of change management

Steps to engage project team in change management
Source date: 2009

Participants in the 2009 study identified a number of effective steps taken to engage the project team in change management. The top eight tactics in rank order were:

1. **Working collaboratively with the project team**
   Participants cited numerous ways that the project team and change management team could work in collaboration. Responses included actions for the project team and actions for the change management team.

   - Actions for the project team included getting the project team involved in change management tasks, reviews and decisions; getting the project team to sign off on change management work and participating in workshops on the people-side issues of the project.
   - Actions for the change management team included taking part in project meetings; providing one-on-one coaching and mentoring to project team members; being involved in the development and planning work on the project; providing information to the project team from change management assessments and stakeholder evaluations; and participating in decision making.
   - A number of participants also cited the importance of team building and relationships so that the two groups worked as a single, cross-functional team sharing accountability and responsibility for project outcomes.

2. **Making a compelling case for why change management is necessary**
   An important approach for engaging the project team was to make a compelling case for why change management is needed. This included highlighting that change management is necessary for achieving results and is a valuable undertaking. Some participants focused on how change management would make the project team's job easier and remove some of the barriers and pain points they faced. Others focused on the role that behavioral and process changes would play in the project and the potential consequences, like increased resistance, that could happen if the people side of change was managed poorly. Looking at past changes and highlighting the role that change management played in successes, or pointing out the failures that resulted from ignoring change management, was another approach mentioned by participants.

3. **Providing training and education**
   Provide the project team with change management education and make them aware of the process that would be followed and the role and impact of change management.

4. **Making change management "real" to project teams**
   A number of participants said that change management had to be tied to the work the project team did to be successful. This included talking about change management using the language and terminology of the project team, directly linking it to project work, focusing on deliverables, and clarifying the outcomes and activities of change management.

5. **Integrating change management activities into the project plan**
   Project teams were more engaged when the change management activities could be integrated into the already existing project activities.

6. **Leveraging sponsor involvement**
   Senior leaders could encourage project team engagement by demonstrating their support for utilizing change management. In some cases, senior leaders insisted on change management for the project.

7. **Communicating**
   The change management team used deliberate communication efforts with the project team on key change management topics and issues.

8. **Documenting of roles and responsibilities**
   Clearly documenting the role of both the change management team and the project team helped facilitate engagement.

Project management integration on projects

Source date: 2009

While only 60% of participants in the 2009 study stated that they used a structured methodology for managing the people side of change, 86% reported applying a structured project management approach to the change (Figure 32).

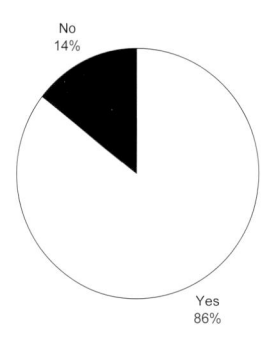

Figure 32 – Did the project you reported on for this study apply project management?

No 14%
Yes 86%

Over 80% of the participants in the 2009 study integrated change management activities into the project activities (Figure 33).

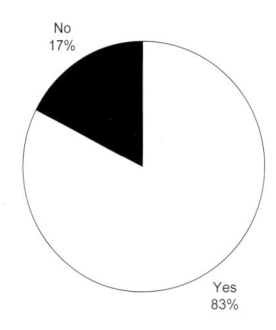

Figure 33 – Integrated change management activities into the project activities?

No 17%
Yes 83%

Obstacles with project team

Source date: 2009

Participants in the 2009 study were asked to identify the biggest obstacles they faced when introducing change management to the project team. The top five obstacles cited were:

1. **Did not see the importance of change management**
   The project team did not view change management as an important part of project success. They were not convinced change management was necessary and did not see the risk of ignoring the people side of change. They considered it the "soft" or "fuzzy" work and saw no real benefit. Change management was perceived as a waste of time or as a luxury.

2. **Lack of knowledge and understanding of change management**
   The project team did not understand what change management really was. In some cases, they equated change management with training or communications. Change management was viewed as simply an activity to "check off" upon completion.

3. **No budget, resources or time to do change management**
   Change management was seen as too costly and often no budget existed for change management activities. Resource constraints on the project team meant no one was available to focus on change management and the team found it difficult to make the time for change management activities.

4. **Role confusion**
   Role confusion existed around change management. In some cases, the team did not understand their role or the role change management would play in the project. In other cases, change management was seen as someone else's responsibility and not the responsibility of the project team.

5. **Assumption that change management slowed down the project**
   A number of participants indicated that the project team felt that using change management would hamper the progress of the project. Typically these concerns revolved around impeding progress, slowing down the project or causing changes in the timeline of the project. Several participants also noted that the project team saw change management as additional and burdensome work.

Other responses on obstacles with the project team included:

- Confusion on how to integrate change management and project activities
- Change management was a new and difficult concept to grasp
- The project team did not see or appreciate the people side of the change they were managing
- Change management was not a priority

What would you do differently on the next project regarding integrating change management into project activities?

Source date: 2009

Participants in the 2009 study provided a number of suggestions regarding what they would do differently in terms of change management and project activity integration. The top five suggestions were:

1. **Begin change management earlier**
   By a two-to-one margin, participants suggested starting change management at the onset of the project. By starting change management earlier, at the initiation of the project, change management and project activities were more easily integrated.

   "Have a CM person in the initiating phase of the program to have enough time to design a proper program instead of having to retro-fit and catch up."

2. **Provide training on change management**
   More change management training and educational workshops for project team members allowed for better partnership and integration. When project team members understood change management, they were in a better position to utilize and integrate the outputs into their work.

3. **Ensure adequate resources for change management**
   There were several suggestions regarding

resources. The first was the designation of a change management resource for the project, including the option of hiring a change manager. Participants also commented on the importance of having qualified, experienced practitioners doing the change management work. In addition to the human resource component, participants mentioned ensuring that time and budget were available for change management work.

4. **Engage senior leaders**
Senior leaders were important on two fronts. The first was engaging senior leaders in the importance and necessity of change management so they could support it during the project. The second aspect was ensuring adequate sponsorship and leadership involvement during the project itself. A number of participants indicated that they would have the change management resource report directly to senior leaders.

5. **Engage with project members**
Engaging the project team involved both building the case for change management and working in conjunction on the project. Participants indicated that they had to "sell" the story of change management to their project managers to ensure they understood the need for effectively managing the people side of change. Participants also provided tactical suggestions including having the project team work in partnership on change management issues, sitting in with the project team, being more involved in the technical side of the change and ensuring that the project leader takes accountability and ownership of change management issues like user adoption and acceptance.

Additional suggestions included:
- Fully integrate plans into a holistic, single project plan that included all change management and project management deliverables
- Clarify responsibilities for the change management group and the project team members regarding change management
- Utilize a formal change management approach and methodology

Change management training for project team

Source date: 2009

Participants in the 2009 study shared the percentage of the project team that had training in change management (Figure 34). Nearly two thirds of the study participants indicated that 25% or less of the project team had been trained in change management. About 10% of study participants said the entire project team had training in change management.

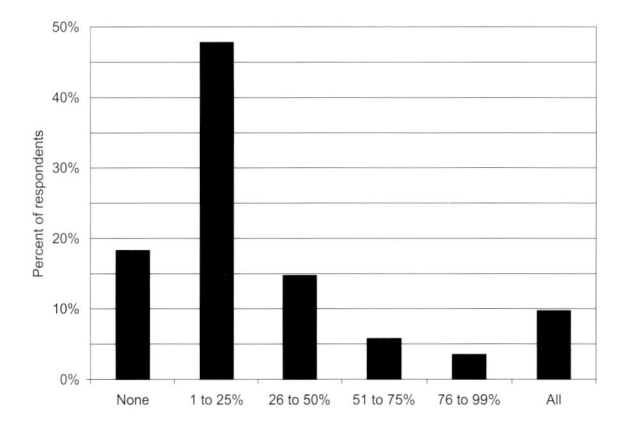

Figure 34 – Percent of project team with change management training

Change readiness

Identifying change readiness
Source date: 2009

Participants in the 2009 study used three primary methods to assess their organizations' readiness for change.

1. **Written assessments and surveys** were favored by half of all responding. They used a variety of tools to gather information, including a readiness assessment, business impact assessment, change characteristics and organizational attributes assessment, SWOT analysis, gap analysis, perception survey, stakeholder analysis and a change portfolio assessment.

2. **Interviews** with senior leaders, key stakeholders, managers and staff were mentioned by one fourth of the study participants. Some study participants referred to these as "alignment interviews." They also mentioned the benefit of having one-on-one interactions and being able to have discussions informally and confidentially to gain insight.

3. **Focus groups and meetings** were also cited as a means to identify the readiness of an organization to make a change.

"We have a very formal process for assessing results. We have focus groups, but then we run large full day workshops to review readiness starting 12 weeks out from go-live involving all project team members and operational representatives. Readiness of each functional area is rated on a traffic light system and risks and issues are identified and highlighted. The output from these sessions is reported up to the management team. This process is repeated at 8 weeks, 4 weeks, and 2 weeks [prior to the go-live date]."

Readiness assessment factors
Source date: 2009

When formally assessing organizational readiness for change, participants in the 2009 study were asked for the most important areas to consider. The top factors in rank order were:

1. **Assessing whether a clear and concise business need for change is understood at all levels of the organization**
   Do the employees know the risks of not changing, understand the challenges ahead and have the desire to move forward?

2. **Assessing the change legacy of the organization**
   Does past history indicate a culture of successful or failed change? Is the culture open to change or averse to change?

   "Change-agile as a core value."

3. **Assessing the style and ability of the sponsor to champion the change**
   Is the sponsor influential, engaging and trusted within the organization? Is the sponsor aware of the important role he or she will play in leading the change effort?

   "Leadership ability to shepherd the change."

4. **Assessing the amount of change occurring in the organization**
   Is the climate in constant flux, fatigued, saturated or enduring competing initiatives?

Additional factors mentioned included:
- Funding and resources
- Communication effectiveness
- Management involvement
- Change management knowledge
- Resistance
- Clearly defined future state
- Complexity of the change
- Training requirements of the workforce

- Processes to support the change
- Time
- Ability to change
- ROI

Readiness evaluation
Source date: 2009

Figure 35 shows that over 60% of participants in the 2009 study took steps to evaluate the readiness of the organization for their particular change.

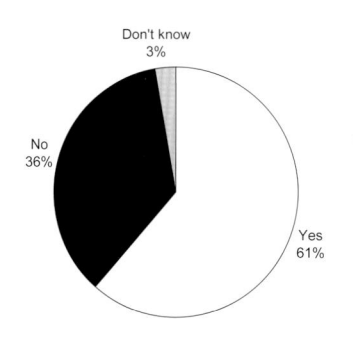

Figure 35 – Took steps to evaluate change readiness

Main organizational barriers or challenges
Source date: 2009

Participants in the 2009 study reported a variety of organizational barriers and challenges when implementing change. The top five barriers in rank order were:

1. **Lack of buy-in**
   Employees from all levels of the organization did not understand the business need for change and, as a result, were disinterested in the change, reluctant to take ownership and resistant to participating in the change. They wanted to know "what's in it for me?"

2. **Organizational culture**
   A culture of complacency, conservatism and laissez-faire attitudes created challenges. Many reported their organizations as being slow-movers accustomed to the same old way where change was counter-cultural.

   "100-year history of growth and success without change."

3. **The structure of the organization**
   Large organizations struggled with the sheer number of people involved; some organizations were bureaucratic and complex and others faced geographic or global spread, which created unique challenges.

4. **Lack of change management knowledge and expertise**
   Participants cited a need for a consistent approach, an internal change management competency and an overall change management strategy.

   "We don't know how to start. We don't have any experience on how to manage the change."

5. **Lack of an effective leader and sponsor of change**
   Study participants said they needed a decisive leader who was enthusiastic about the change. They needed a real sponsor willing to lead and visibly support the change.

Study participants shared other organizational barriers, including:

- A history of failed change
- Limited resources and funding
- Change fatigue and saturation
- Competing priorities
- "Siloed" departments/organizations

Change management activities

Participants described their change management approach by listing the specific actions and steps they completed. The data was divided into three major project phases: start-up (planning), design and implementation. The activities and steps were further categorized according to the primary target audiences:

- Project team
- Managers (including business leaders)
- Employees

The net result is that the activities and steps participants used can be shown in a 3 x 3 grid, with rows representing project timing (start-up, design and implementation) and columns representing the audience or group (Figure 36).

For each box in this grid, detailed lists of corresponding activities are provided. The labels for each box are intended to be general descriptions for the category and are not intended to stand alone from the activity lists in Tables 2, 3 and 4.

The lists (List A, List B, etc.) referred to in Tables 2, 3 and 4 can be found in the section titled "Supplemental change management activities lists" following the tables.

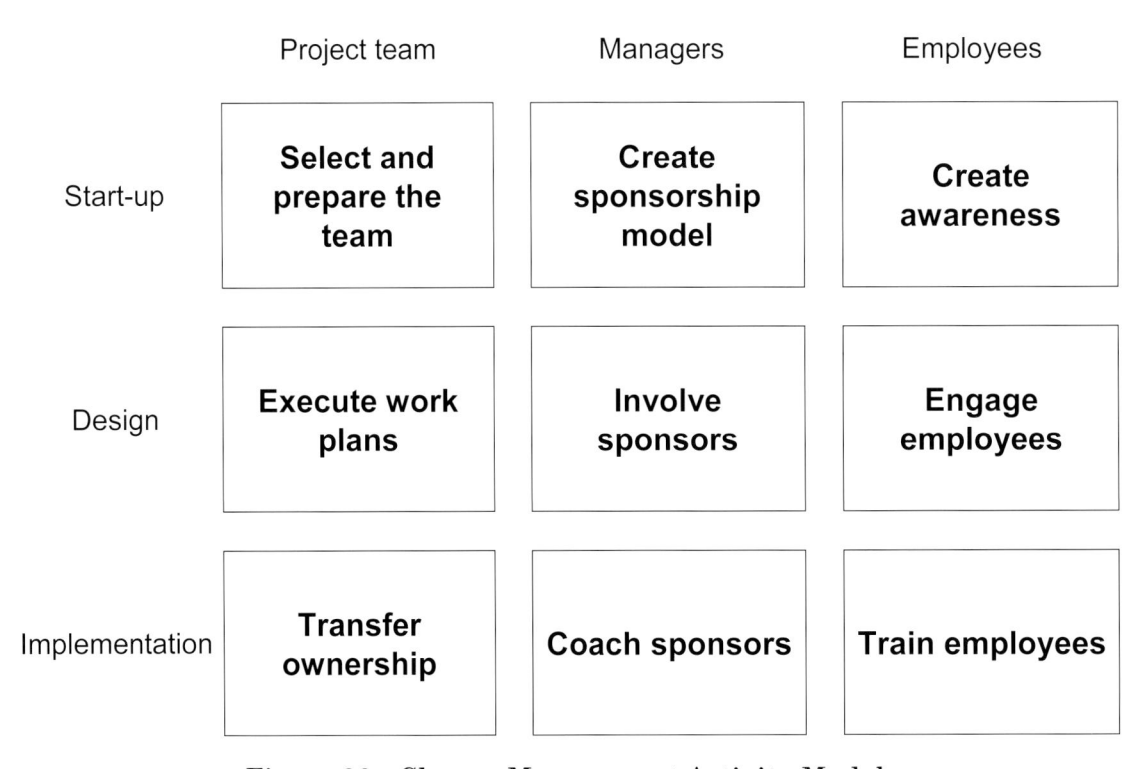

Editor's note: The Change Management Activity Model shown in Figure 36 was first developed in 2003 and now includes data from the 2003, 2005, 2007, 2009 and 2011 reports to create a comprehensive view of change management activities across multiple studies.

	Project team	Managers	Employees
Start-up	Select and prepare the team	Create sponsorship model	Create awareness
Design	Execute work plans	Involve sponsors	Engage employees
Implementation	Transfer ownership	Coach sponsors	Train employees

Figure 36 – Change Management Activity Model

Prosci® Best Practices in Change Management

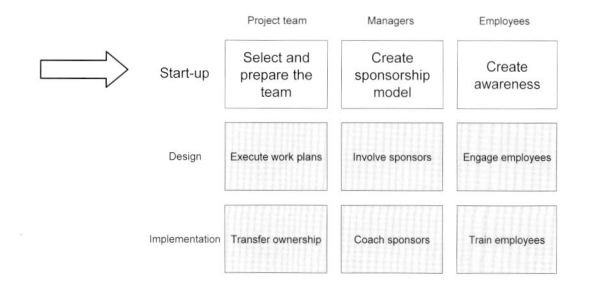

	with the Project team	with Managers	with Employees
	Select and prepare the team	**Create sponsorship model**	**Create awareness**
Start-up	• Identify the "right" change management team members; consider representation by location or function; use outside expertise when necessary • Establish a team structure • Train the team on change management methods and develop team principles and rules; secure the needed resources and budget for change management • Understand the nature of the change and the future state (see List A); assess the timing of the change; ensure clarity about why the change is being made • Define the impact of the change on specific groups; conduct a gap analysis • Assess and analyze the current organization (see List B), climate and culture (readiness for change) • Create a sponsorship model (see adjacent column) • Complete change management readiness assessments (assess culture, barriers and risks) • Create change strategies and plans (see List C); develop a schedule and budget; review these plans and get approval from the steering committee • Develop change management training for managers and supervisors • Integrate change management plans into project management plans; be an active part of the project team • Utilize a structured and proven change management methodology; customize or scale to fit the organization and the change • Identify critical success factors and potential obstacles	• Identify the required primary sponsor (at right level in the organization); directly engage his or her support • Identify key senior managers and stakeholders throughout the organization who are needed to sponsor the change; assess their current level of support for the change and their competency to manage change • With the direct involvement of the primary sponsor, begin building support among all key managers; engage them as active and visible sponsors of the change and ensure alignment with project objectives • Form a steering committee for the project (dependent on overall project size) • Show managers the current state versus the future state; create a common view of the nature of the change, why the change is being made and the organization's readiness for change • Train senior and mid-level managers on change management and their roles as sponsors of change • Help create key messages for managers to communicate to the organization (presentations and elevator conversations) • Create identifiable actions that senior managers can do to begin supporting the change (see "Sponsorship" section of this report) • Customize your change management strategy to address potential resistance from managers • Train managers and supervisors on change management and their role as coaches, including how to use change management tools, how to manage resistance and how to support employees through the transition • Provide managers with the tools and information needed to manage change with their employees	• Begin initial communications with employees to create awareness of the need for change and to share the nature of the change (see List D)

Table 2 – Change management start-up activities

Prosci® Best Practices in Change Management

	Start-up	Project team	Managers	Employees
		Select and prepare the team	Create sponsorship model	Create awareness
⇨	Design	Execute work plans	Involve sponsors	Engage employees
	Implementation	Transfer ownership	Coach sponsors	Train employees

	with the Project team	with Managers	with Employees
	Execute work plans	**Involve sponsors**	**Engage employees**
Design	<ul><li>Implement change management strategies (from start-up phase), including specific plans for communications, sponsorship, coaching and training</li><li>Conduct regular workshops with change agents</li><li>Identify pockets of resistance and develop special tactics with different groups to counter this resistance</li><li>Identify job roles impacted; begin to define future skills and competencies for employees; use as input for training requirements and curriculum design</li><li>Develop coaching and mentoring strategies for front-line supervisors, including development of change management competencies</li><li>Train the trainers; begin the process of developing internal competency around managing change throughout the organization</li><li>Hire external resources if necessary to support the change</li><li>Collect input from customers on how this change will impact them</li><li>Define measurable objectives (key performance indicators - KPIs)</li></ul>	<ul><li>Interview all critical senior managers to determine their expectations and desired outcomes; gather input on the change strategy and understand their concerns</li><li>Maintain regular contact with all senior managers; schedule and conduct frequent and regular meetings; seek their input on critical decisions</li><li>Conduct steering committee meetings on a regular basis (dependent on project size)</li><li>Work to develop sponsor capabilities: What do they need to be doing to support the change? How can they best accomplish those goals?</li><li>Coach sponsors; provide sponsors with a roadmap of sponsor activities and help them prepare key messages; provide coaching on how to share the business vision and the change with employees</li><li>Identify resistant managers; engage the primary sponsor and other senior managers to address this resistance</li><li>Seek approval from senior managers at key milestones in the process</li><li>Engage managers in the design process; gather input from managers and understand their concerns; ensure that key stakeholders are involved in the solution design</li><li>Create a close or "tight" relationship between the change team and sponsors</li><li>Collect feedback from managers about how employees are embracing the change, areas of resistance and potential issues with the change</li></ul>	<ul><li>Build awareness around the overall change and why the change is being made (see change messages in List D)</li><li>Engage employees in the design process; gather input from employees on the design and understand their concerns</li><li>Use pilots or models to test ideas with employees and to share the future state</li><li>Use face-to-face meetings to share the vision and strategy</li><li>Gather employee feedback on the vision and strategy using focus groups and interviews</li><li>Use question-and-answer sessions, interviews and memos to address employee concerns and share information on a regular basis</li><li>Demonstrate successes and early wins to employees</li><li>Share ongoing progress of the design team, including updates to the schedule, so that employees know what to expect and when</li><li>Continue to answer questions about the personal impact to employees: How will this impact me? How will this change my daily work? How will I benefit from this change?</li></ul>

Table 3 – Change management design activities

Prosci® Best Practices in Change Management

```
                Project team        Managers            Employees
Start-up    [Select and prepare] [Create sponsorship] [Create awareness]
             the team              model

Design      [Execute work plans]  [Involve sponsors]   [Engage employees]

Implementation [Transfer          [Coach               [Train
                ownership]         sponsors]            employees]
```

	with the Project team	with Managers	with Employees
	Transfer ownership	**Coach sponsors**	**Train employees**
Implementation	• Review project progress; monitor activities and measure performance (review KPIs); identify successes and demonstrate short-term wins • Adapt change management plans as necessary to address gaps in performance • Develop ways to celebrate successes with both managers and employees • Create feedback mechanisms • Create coaching aides for supervisors to enable them to help their employees through the transition (see List E for "Coaching aides") • Begin to migrate change leadership to operational managers • Extend team structure to involve local groups in change activities • Support local trainers within the organization to implement education and training about the new processes and systems • Identify lessons learned and update change management approach and tools	• Engage sponsors in managing resistance (encourage one-on-one intervention) • Continue regular and frequent meetings to review progress and performance; update business leaders and senior managers on the solution and implementation progress • Increase the level of senior manager communications with employees (e.g. leadership must stay active and visible throughout the implementation efforts) • Provide managers with concrete activities they can perform to support the implementation (provide upward coaching) • Report roadblocks to senior managers promptly; resolve critical issues quickly through effective use of the steering committee • Use senior managers effectively to manage resistance • Maintain frequent and honest communications with managers • Provide opportunities to voice resistance • Collect data from employees about the change (issues, concerns, resistance areas) and share with managers • Evaluate manager effectiveness at managing the change; create corrective action plans where needed	• Implement training on the new processes, systems and job roles; align this training with gap analysis completed by front-line supervisors for their employees (include one-on-one training) • Listen to employees and value their feedback; move quickly to adjust the design or resolve issues that surface during implementation • Provide one-on-one follow-up and coaching • Share the critical success factors with employees; audit compliance with the new processes and implement corrective action when needed • Assess employees (where are they in the change process?); measure effectiveness of the change management plans and adjust as necessary • Quickly identify and address pockets of resistance • Celebrate successes and achievement of significant milestones • Implement rewards and incentive systems for employees • Continue ongoing communications about project outcomes and progress, including specifics about what will happen, when and why • When appropriate, tie compensation to performance

Table 4 – Change management implementation activities

Supplemental change management activities lists

List A – Understanding the future state
- Nature and scope of the change
- Overall timeframe
- Alignment with the business strategy
- Goals of the change
- Reasons for changing
- Risk assessment (risk of not changing)
- The gap between the future state and today
- Who is impacted and how; who is most adversely impacted
- Future state design (if available at this phase) including sample models or scenarios
- What will change; what will stay the same

List B – Organizational assessment
- Change capacity (How much change has the organization made recently and how much more change can the organization absorb?)
- Change history (What was the effectiveness of past changes and what perceptions do employees have of past change projects?)
- Culture assessment (To what degree do the values and norms of the organization support or oppose change?)
- Change competency (What are the change management skills and abilities within the organization?)
- Authority and capability of primary sponsor (Does the primary sponsor have sufficient power to lead the change?)
- Strengths and weaknesses of the organization related to this change (Overall, what is working in favor of the change and what is working against the change?)

List C – Strategies and plans
- Change management plan (overall strategy)
- Communications plan
- Sponsor plan
- Training plan (including change management training)
- Coaching plan

List D – Employee messages
- The current situation and the rationale for the change (why the change is needed)
- A vision of the organization after the change takes place (alignment with the business strategy)
- The basics of what is changing, the nature of the change and when it will happen
- The goals or objectives for the change
- The expectation that change will happen and is not a choice (risk of not changing)
- The impact of the change on the day-to-day activities of the employee; "what's in it for me?" (WIIFM)
- Implications of the change on job security (will I have a job?)
- Specific behaviors and activities expected from the employee during the change
- Status updates on the performance of the change, including success stories
- Procedures for getting help and assistance during the change

List E – Coaching aids
- Concrete activities that front-line managers and supervisors can perform to support the change with their employees
- Tools to communicate the new roles and responsibilities to their employees
- Self-assessment guides for employees to assess skill and knowledge gaps
- Resistance assessments and mechanisms to collect feedback from employees during early implementation phases
- Tools to create individual development plans

Sponsorship

Most critical activities

Study participants identified three critical primary sponsor roles which are required for the success of a change project or initiative and cited activities that characterize each role. A complete list of concrete sponsor activities to support these three roles is included in the Sponsor Activity Model on page 67. The Sponsor Activity Model provides a more comprehensive list of the most important activities for sponsors to do with project teams, managers and employees at various phases of the project.

1. **Participate actively and visibly throughout the project**

    - Be accessible to the project team through all stages of the project
    - Clear calendar to be physically present at key events
    - Allocate the necessary resources and provide the necessary funding
    - Attend frequent project status meetings and actively track progress
    - Play an active role in critical decisions and make timely decisions
    - Remove roadblocks, obstacles and barriers
    - Advocate for the project and demonstrate commitment; model the change in your own behavior
    - Build excitement and enthusiasm for the project

2. **Communicate directly with employees**

    - Deliver messages in person; talk directly to impacted employees
    - Clearly articulate reasons why the change is being made and what created the need to change
    - Share the consequences and risks to the organization if change is not made
    - Reinforce and repeat key messages consistently and frequently, not just during project kickoff
    - Share goals and personal expectations for the project
    - Acknowledge challenges and obstacles honestly

3. **Build a coalition of sponsorship**

    - Create buy-in with peers and key stakeholder groups
    - Clarify roles and establish expectations with mid-level and front-line managers
    - Communicate change messages ("what, why and how") in person with front-line supervisors
    - Solicit and listen to management feedback
    - Advocate for the change with senior leadership; sponsor the change upward
    - Ensure alignment with organizational strategy and direction
    - Ensure change messages and support for the change are cascaded throughout the organization
    - Hold managers accountable for their support and address resistance from management

Biggest mistakes

Study participants identified the biggest mistakes that top-level sponsors made during a major change:

1. **Failed to remain visible and engaged throughout the project**
   Disappearing or invisible sponsorship was cited more frequently than any other sponsor mistake. Primary sponsors kicked off a project then walked away, acted as a sponsor in name only, or became unavailable and inaccessible to the project team during the project life cycle.

2. **Failed to demonstrate support for the project in words and actions**
   Participants reported that failing to be an active and genuine advocate for a project was the second most common mistake made by sponsors. Sponsors acted detached or disinterested, did not "walk the walk" and

sometimes even publicly questioned the project.

3. **Failed to effectively communicate messages about the need for change**
Sponsors who made this mistake did not communicate with sufficient frequency, repetition or consistency. They did not focus their messages on the business drivers and why the change was being made. Others failed to utilize a variety of communication vehicles and did not customize their messages for unique audiences.

4. **Ignored the people side of the change**
Participants indicated that failing to recognize or embrace the people side of the project was another common mistake sponsors made. Sponsors ignored the scale of employee impacts and assumed all impacted groups were immediately on board without allowing for individual change processes. In other cases sponsors focused only on project details such as installation and delivery timelines rather than ultimate benefit realization.

5. **Delegated or abdicated the sponsorship role and responsibilities**
Delegation of the sponsorship role was reported by participants as a major sponsor mistake. The responsibilities of sponsorship were assigned to individuals or groups without the necessary authority to effectively be a sponsor, including project teams, consultants or lower-level leaders.

Most effective tactics for creating active and visible sponsorship

Research participants identified five tactics for creating active and visible executive sponsorship.

1. **Provide behind-the-scenes assistance to the sponsor on his or her role**
The most effective tactic reported by respondents for creating active and visible sponsorship was assisting with action plans, scheduling activities and preparing materials for the executive sponsor. Efforts by the change management team included: developing a sponsor roadmap or action plan; involving the sponsor in hands-on work to show visible support; drafting communications (e.g. newsletters, emails); preparing talking points; scheduling or inviting the sponsor to meetings; and creating opportunities for the sponsor to be active and visible (e.g. town halls, roadshows, staff meetings, walk-arounds).

2. **Coach the sponsor on their role**
The second most common tactic for creating active and visible sponsorship was to explain the role of effective sponsorship, establish expectations for the role and equip the executive sponsor with tools, advice and coaching to make their job as sponsor easy to fulfill. Respondents also indicated that it was important to build trust and rapport with the sponsor to enact this coaching effectively.

3. **Hold regular meetings with the executive sponsor**
Engaging with the sponsor through regular meetings or communications was the third most common tactic. Activities during these meetings or correspondences included: discussing project updates and progress; reiterating key messages; asking and answering questions; sharing successes; and giving feedback on the sponsor's involvement on the project.

4. **Ensure the sponsor communicates directly with employees**
Research participants indicated that ensuring the sponsor communicates directly with employees (e.g. through face-to-face communications, live or recorded speeches, videos, written communication, etc.) was another tactic for having the sponsor actively and visibly engage in the change.

5. **Hold the sponsor accountable in their role**
Study participants indicated that holding the executive sponsor accountable and ensuring that he or she shows support for the change management efforts was a tactic for creating active and visible sponsorship. Suggestions included alignment to their personal interests, ties to key performance indicators or personal initiative.

Sponsor role understanding and fulfillment

Source date: 2009

Figure 37 shows participants' evaluation of how well their sponsors understood their roles and responsibilities. In both the 2009 and 2007 studies, more than one half of participants reported that their sponsors had a less than adequate understanding of the role of an effective change leader.

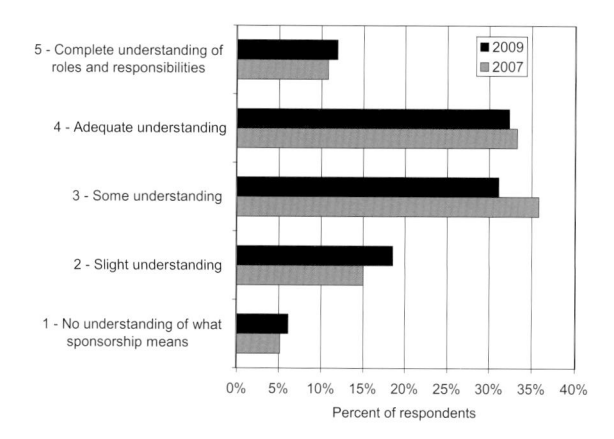

Figure 37 – Sponsors' understanding of roles and responsibilities

Participants also evaluated how effective their sponsors were at fulfilling each of the three primary roles (see "Most critical activities" section).

Figure 38 shows the percentage of participants who indicated their sponsors were "ineffective" or "extremely ineffective" in fulfilling each role. One fifth of participants reported their sponsors were ineffective at being active and visible throughout the project, while nearly one third of participants indicated that their sponsors were not effectively communicating directly with employees.

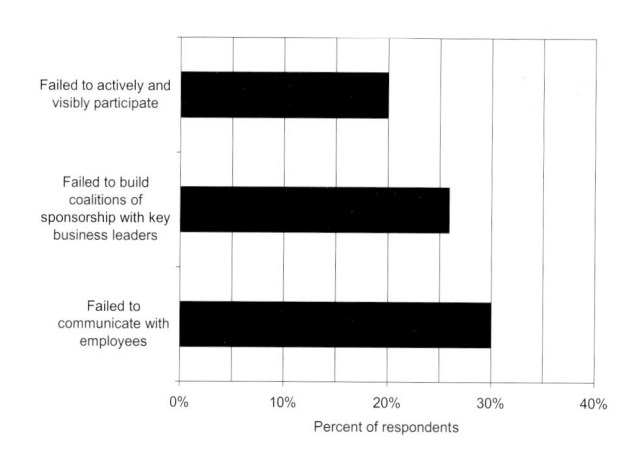

Figure 38 – Ineffective or extremely ineffective sponsor role fulfillment

There was a direct correlation between sponsor effectiveness and projects meeting or exceeding objectives (Figure 39). Projects with extremely effective sponsors met or exceeded objectives more than twice as often as those with ineffective sponsors.

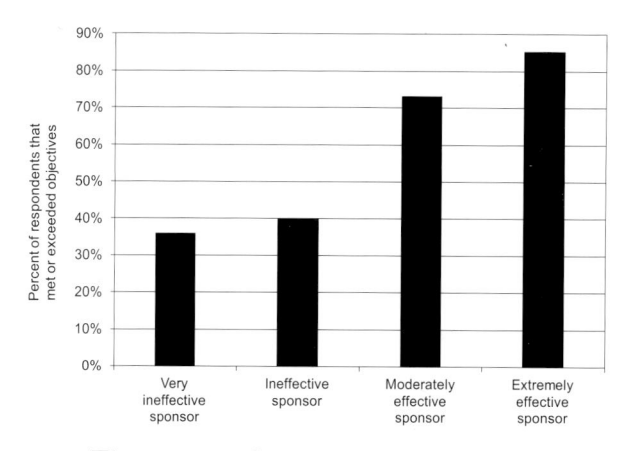

Figure 39 – Correlation of sponsor effectiveness to meeting objectives

Symptoms of ineffective sponsorship

Participants indicated the symptoms of ineffective sponsorship they had experienced (Figure 40). Inactive or invisible sponsors was the most cited symptom, followed by poor alignment among key stakeholders.

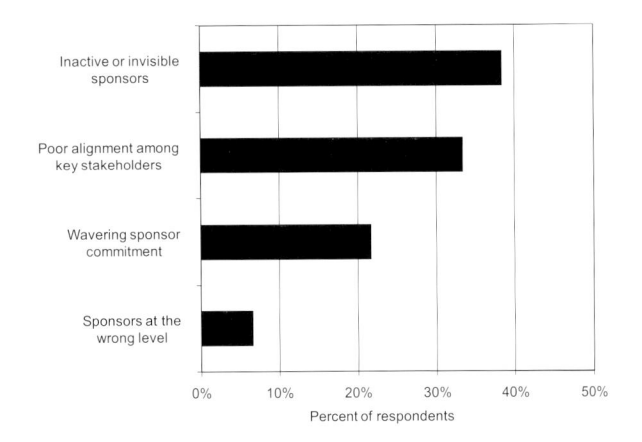

Figure 40 – Sponsor symptoms

Engaging reluctant senior leaders
Source date: 2009

Participants cited the most effective techniques to engage resistant or reluctant senior leaders. Results from both the 2007 and 2009 studies are combined below to provide a more complete set of recommendations from study participants.

1. **Clearly demonstrate the benefits of the change and the risks of not changing**
   Participants stated that benefits of the change should be communicated in language meaningful to that senior leader – "*speak their language.*" The business case should be clearly presented with a focus on the business outcomes and how the change aligns with the business strategy, as well as the risks to the business if this change is not made. Use financials and hard data, and include the results from early trials when available. These discussions should also include how the change will impact them and the "what's in it for me?" (WIIFM). Where possible, align the change with their goals.

2. **Direct intervention by the primary sponsor**
   Participants cited the need for direct intervention of the primary sponsor to manage resistance from other senior leaders. Participants indicated that the primary sponsor should:
   - Ensure alignment around the business strategy and associated changes
   - Set priorities and clearly communicate his or her expectations of each senior leader
   - Build an effective leadership coalition
   - Adjust the compensation and evaluation system to align with the change
   - Implement consequences for those unwilling to support the change

3. **Increase the level of involvement of resistant senior leaders**
   Participants suggested increasing the level of involvement and decision making of resistant senior leaders, including scheduling more frequent meetings, engaging them earlier in the process and gathering input from them on key design decisions. Participants indicated that senior leaders should be involved in the planning process up front and should have ownership in the final solution for changes impacting their areas.

4. **Identify the root cause of the resistance**
   Participants cited the need to clearly identify the root cause of the resistance by listening to the specific objections of senior leaders. Participants indicated that it was important to understand why the resistance was occurring and to explore the reasons in depth.

5. **Increase the level of one-on-one interactions**
   Participants stated that one-on-one interactions were essential to manage resistance from senior leaders. Participants encouraged face-to-face conversations that were candid and frequent.

6. **Provide coaching on their role as a sponsor**
   Many senior leaders were new to change management and needed more clearly defined responsibilities. Participants found it effective to coach them on their role, what it meant and how they were key to the success of the project. Special tactics such as developing a specific roadmap of activities or preparing communication messages were mentioned.

7. **Provide project details**
   Many "important" projects came across the

desks of senior leaders each day, so it was critical that they truly understood the meaning of the project they were being asked to support. Study participants said they engaged senior leaders by providing clear project details, benefits of the project (impact on the bottom line, meeting target audience needs) and risks of project failure.

8. **Regular communications**
Continued engagement of senior leaders was maintained through ongoing communications. Creating an open, one-on-one channel was a key success factor. Participants also found success in keeping senior leaders informed on progress through daily reports or updates on the status of risks and issues.

Losing a sponsor

Only 14% of study participants were involved in a project where the sponsor left during the course of the project (Figure 41).

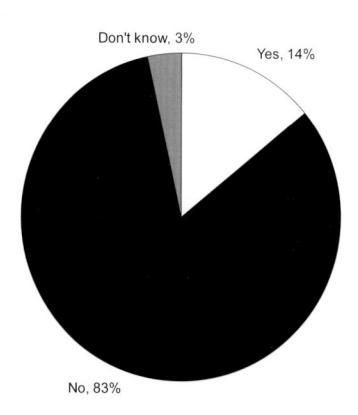

Figure 41 – Sponsor left during the course of the project

Consequences of losing a sponsor

Participants who lost a sponsor during the course of the project commented on the consequences. The most common consequences cited by participants in rank order were:

1. **Loss of or shift in direction**
The loss of a sponsor impacted direction, objectives, vision and expectations. These elements had to be reevaluated and decisions had to be made regarding the direction of the change.

2. **Employee disengagement**
The loss of a sponsor resulted in confusion, disillusionment and disengagement at the employee level.

3. **Loss of momentum**
The project fell into a period of stagnation and lost continuity.

4. **Time spent getting new sponsor up to speed**
The team had to invest time in getting the new sponsor up to speed about project details and developments that had occurred.

5. **Project timeframes altered**
The project was delayed or in some cases restarted.

6. **Instability**
The loss of a sponsor resulted in turbulence, disruption and general instability.

Tactics for dealing with losing a sponsor

Participants who had a sponsor leave during the course of the project commented on tactics they used to address losing a sponsor. The top four responses were:

1. **Get the new sponsor "up to speed" quickly**
Meet with the new sponsor face-to-face and regularly. Provide briefings and background on the project. Provide updates on the status of the project.

2. **Secure commitment**
Ensure that the new sponsor is supportive of the change and of their role in sponsoring the change.

3. **Maintain communications**
Continue to communicate about the change and keep the dialogue open. In some cases,

communicate about the reasons for a change in sponsorship.

4. **Focus on and work with the coalition**
When the top sponsor moved, the members of the coalition of managers and supervisors at lower levels were important allies. Efforts were focused on this group to keep them engaged and supporting the change with their employees.

Right level of sponsor

Participants indicated whether the change they were reporting on had the right level of sponsor. Figure 42 shows the responses, with 84% indicating that the change had the right level of sponsor. 11% indicated that their sponsor was too low in the organization.

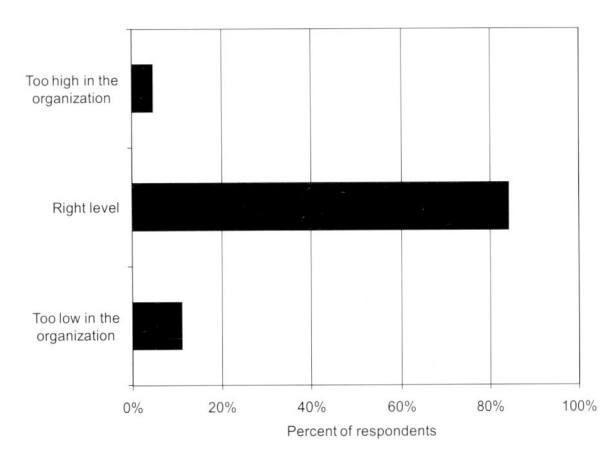

Figure 42 – Sponsor at right level in the organization

Recommendations for dealing with a sponsor at the wrong level

Research participants that provided recommendations for practitioners supporting a change that had the wrong level of sponsor identified two primary tactics: work with current sponsor or engage the correct level of sponsor.

The research participants who either recommended working with the current sponsor, or had to work with the current sponsor, identified four tactics:

1. **Build and leverage the coalition**
Of the four tactics proposed by respondents, building a coalition of change leaders throughout the organization was the most common suggestion. Respondents recommended creating a layer of change leadership with multiple sponsors from different levels to support the change.

2. **Enter into an open and honest dialogue with the current sponsor regarding his or her role**
Research participants proposed having a candid conversation with the current sponsor to address questions and concerns regarding the level of sponsorship, including raising awareness about his or her responsibilities. This conversation could include topics such as the impacts of the change to the current sponsor, the impacts of proper sponsorship on project success and how resistance will be managed and barriers removed.

3. **Offer coaching to the current sponsor**
The third most common recommendation from research participants was to coach the current sponsor on how to be effective. Topics for coaching included helping the sponsor network and build coalitions, offering training, providing recommendations on effective sponsorship and developing messages for the sponsor.

4. **Re-scope the project**
If the level of sponsorship provided was inadequate, research participants recommended restructuring or re-scoping the project to accommodate the level of the current sponsor.

Research participants who recommended engaging the correct level of sponsor provided three tactics for implementing a change in sponsorship.

1. **Elevate the issue and engage senior leadership to initiate a change**
Participants recommended escalating the issue to an executive steering committee, senior management or senior sponsor,

making the situation known and having a senior leader or leaders advocate for a change in sponsorship.

2. **Show the impacts of proper sponsorship on project success and show how the current sponsor is not appropriate**
Respondents who proposed engaging a different level of sponsor suggested showing the impacts of appropriate sponsorship on the project results and explaining the criteria for effective sponsorship. In addition, respondents recommended including reasons why the current sponsor was not a good fit for the role.

3. **Conduct a stakeholder analysis or sponsor assessment to indicate proper sponsor**
Participants suggested using a sponsor assessment diagram or stakeholder analysis to explain the need for a change in sponsorship or to show who would be better suited for the role.

How would you characterize your sponsor at the beginning of the project?
Source date: 2009

Participants characterized their sponsors at the beginning of the project (Figure 43).

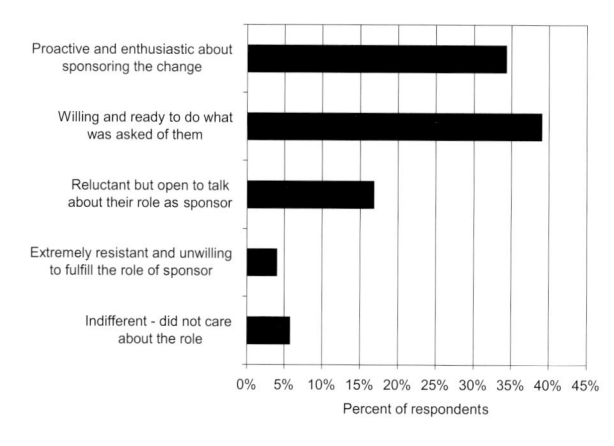

Figure 43 – Sponsor characterization at beginning of the project

Nearly three quarters of participants in the 2009 study characterized their sponsors positively at the beginning of the project – with 34% indicating sponsors were proactive and enthusiastic, and 39% indicating sponsors were willing and ready to do what was asked of them. Only 4% of study participants stated their sponsors were extremely resistant and unwilling to be a sponsor of change.

Sponsor access
Source date: 2009

Participants commented on the level of access they had to sponsors. Over one third of participants in the 2009 study indicated that they had inadequate or no access to sponsors throughout the project (Figure 44).

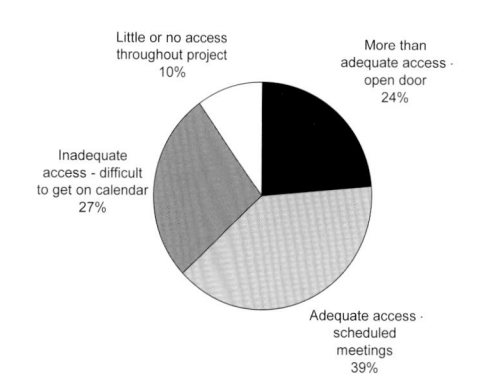

Figure 44 – Access to sponsor

The level of access to the sponsor directly correlated to whether the project met or exceeded objectives (Figure 45).

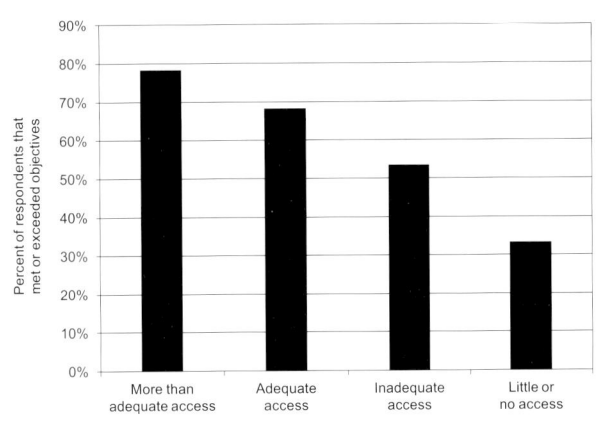

Figure 45 – Correlation of sponsor access to meeting objectives

In addition to overall sponsor access, participants indicated how frequently they met with sponsors during the project (Figure 46). Over half of participants reported meeting only monthly or quarterly with their sponsors. Conversely, over half of participants indicated that they would recommend weekly meetings with their sponsor.

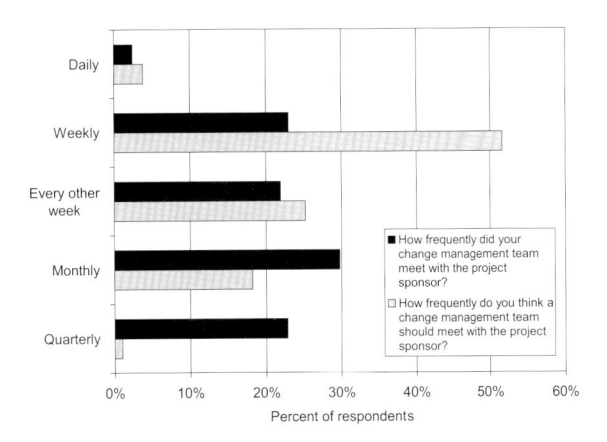

Figure 46 – Frequency of meeting with sponsors - actual and desired

Sponsor communication frequency

Source date: 2009

Participants in the 2009 study identified how many times per month their sponsor communicated to employees about a particular change. Figure 47 shows the data for direct communication frequency. Over one half of participants said that their sponsor communicated directly with employees only once per month or less.

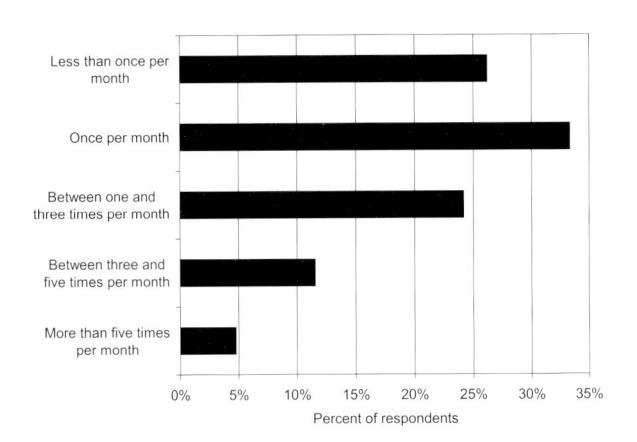

Figure 47 – Sponsor communication frequency

Sponsor Activity Model

Participants described the most important sponsor activities for managing change. The data was broken into three major project phases: start-up (planning), design and implementation. The activities and steps were further categorized by the primary target audiences:

- Project team
- Managers (including business leaders)
- Employees

Figure 48 below is a 3 x 3 diagram illustrating the responsibilities of the sponsor in each project phase (start-up, design and implementation). The activities required for each box in this figure are described in detail on the following pages.

Note: The labels for each box in Figure 48 are intended to be general descriptions for the category and are not intended to stand alone from the activity lists in Tables 5, 6 and 7.

Editor's note: The Sponsor Activity Model shown in Figure 48 was first developed in 2003 and now includes data from the 2003, 2005, 2007, 2009 and 2011 reports to create a comprehensive view of sponsor activities across multiple studies.

	Project team	Managers	Employees
Start-up	Acquire project resources	Build management support	Create awareness
Design	Provide direct support	Develop sponsorship	Educate
Implementation	Maintain momentum	Align leadership and manage resistance	Reinforce and reward

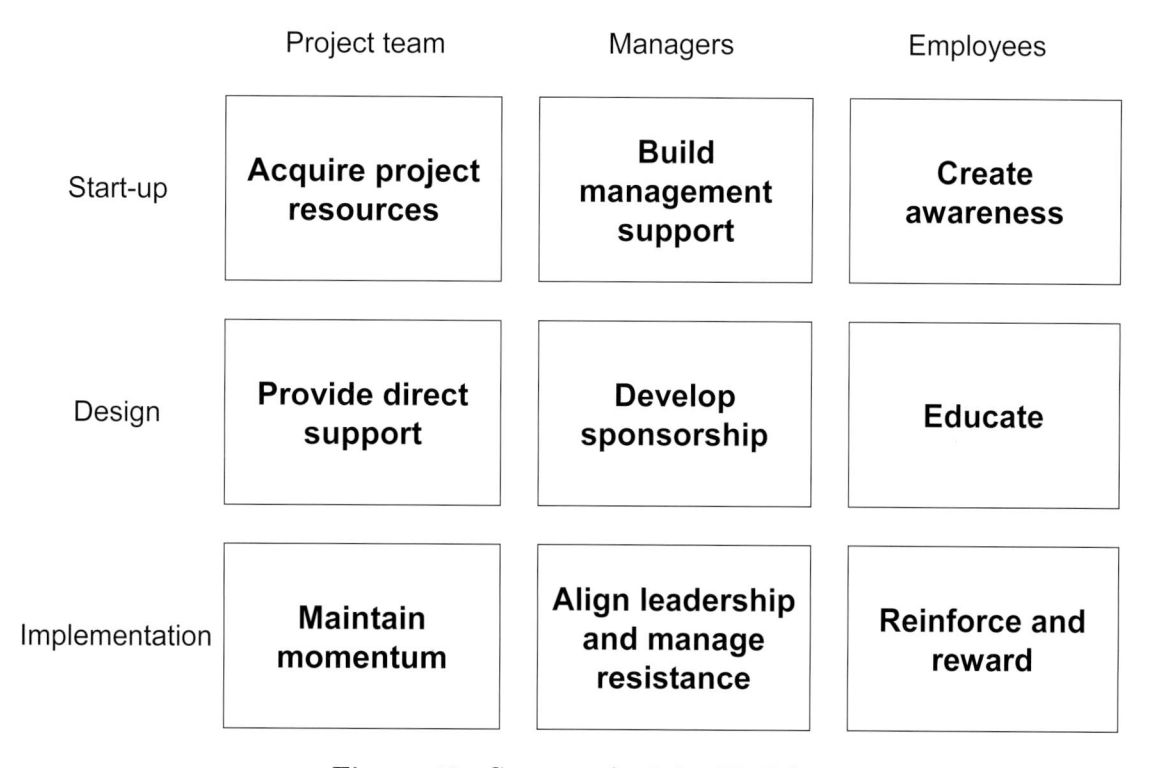

Figure 48 – Sponsor Activity Model

Prosci® Best Practices in Change Management

	Project team	Managers	Employees
Start-up	Acquire project resources	Build management support	Create awareness
Design	Provide direct support	Develop sponsorship	Educate
Implementation	Maintain momentum	Align leadership and manage resistance	Reinforce and reward

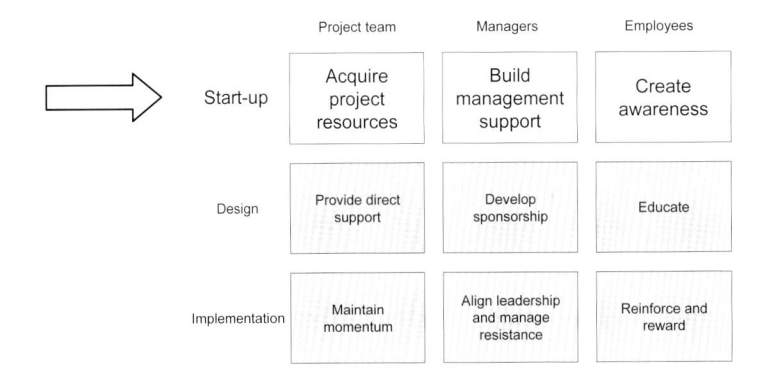

	with the Project team	with Managers	with Employees
	Acquire project resources	**Build management support**	**Create awareness**
Start-up	• Select the best project leader and team members; include resources with change management expertise • Provide necessary funding for the team, including training for all team members on change management • Set priorities related to day-to-day work versus project work to allow adequate team member participation • Help the team understand the critical business issues or opportunities that must be addressed • Provide clear direction and objectives for the project; describe what success will look like • Jointly develop a high-level view of the future and link the change to the business strategy • Be directly involved with the project team; set expectations; review key deliverables and remove obstacles • Take ownership for success of the project and hold the team accountable for results • Establish a commitment to change management; talk about change management and ensure required roles are filled	• Enlist the support of executive managers and create a support network (coalition of managers needed to support the change) • Create a steering committee of key managers to monitor progress (dependent on project size) • Educate senior managers about the business drivers for change and the risks of not changing • Work directly with managers who show early signs of resistance • Create change advocates within the leadership team; build support and enthusiasm for the change • Provide training on change management for senior managers • Establish change activities that the leadership group is responsible for completing • Define accountabilities for mid-level managers • Determine and communicate priorities between this change and other change initiatives • Resolve conflicting operational objectives with other senior leaders • Solicit and listen to management feedback • Connect project to organization's strategy and goals	• Describe the current state of the business and share the business issues or opportunities • Explain why a change is needed now; share the risks of not changing • Share a vision for the future; explain the nature of the change and show how the change will address the business problems or opportunities • Answer the questions: "How will this change affect me?" and "What's in it for me?" • Be proactive, vocal and visible; communicate frequently, including face-to-face • Listen and be open to dialogue and resistance • Tell employees what they can expect to happen and when • Understand the organizational culture and beliefs • Repeat key messages over and over • Share plans with customers and suppliers • Show project milestones and provide progress updates • Communicate clearly and honestly about aspects of the project that are still unknown

Table 5 – Sponsor start-up activities

	Start-up	Design	Implementation
Project team	Acquire project resources	Provide direct support	Maintain momentum
Managers	Build management support	Develop sponsorship	Align leadership and manage resistance
Employees	Create awareness	Educate	Reinforce and reward

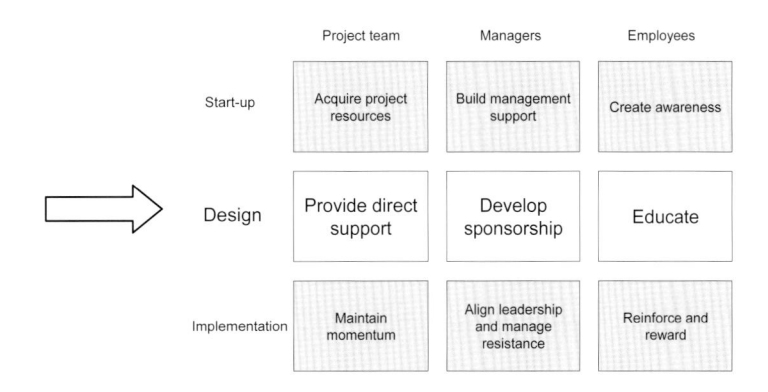

	with the Project team	with Managers	with Employees
	Provide direct support	**Develop sponsorship**	**Educate**
Design	<ul><li>Stay involved: attend key project meetings, review project status and hold the team accountable for results</li><li>Provide the necessary resources and funding, including ensuring that the right people are made available to support the design work</li><li>Be accessible to the team; be a sounding board; provide ideas and constructive criticism to the team; ask "What if?"</li><li>Remove roadblocks; make timely decisions on project issues and help manage conflicts and political issues</li><li>Communicate expectations and feedback from other managers</li><li>Keep the team on track and manage "scope creep"</li><li>Reward success stories and achievements</li><li>Take the time to understand the solution</li><li>Identify conflicts with other projects that may impact this team</li><li>Make sure the project team knows that your door is open and you are available to support their work</li><li>Play an active role in all critical decisions</li></ul>	<ul><li>Continue to build support and sponsorship among senior managers; reinforce the key messages; resolve differences in perception; address areas of resistance</li><li>Let senior managers know how they can proactively support the change; provide them with a clear roadmap for sponsoring the change with their direct reports</li><li>Conduct steering committee meetings; keep managers informed; use this forum to resolve critical issues</li><li>Use public and private conversations to reinforce leadership support; recognize outstanding managers</li><li>Communicate project progress to all executive managers</li><li>Hold mid-level managers accountable</li><li>Do not tolerate resistance from mid-level managers or allow managers to "opt out" of the change; be clear on expectations</li><li>Ensure that a consistent message is being sent by managers to impacted employees</li></ul>	<ul><li>Communicate frequently with employees; make your personal commitment visible, including face-to-face conversations</li><li>Reinforce the reason for change, the risk of not changing and the evolving details about the future state</li><li>Show employees how the change aligns with the direction and strategy for the business</li><li>Answer the question "What will this change mean to me?"</li><li>Listen to what employees have to say; take the pulse of the organization and collect feedback</li><li>Share project progress and provide updates on a regular basis; update employees on "what you can expect to happen and when"</li><li>Enable employee participation and involvement</li><li>Recognize the good work that employees have done</li><li>Involve customers and suppliers</li><li>Ensure adequate time is allocated for training and skill-building prior to implementation</li></ul>

Table 6 – Sponsor design activities

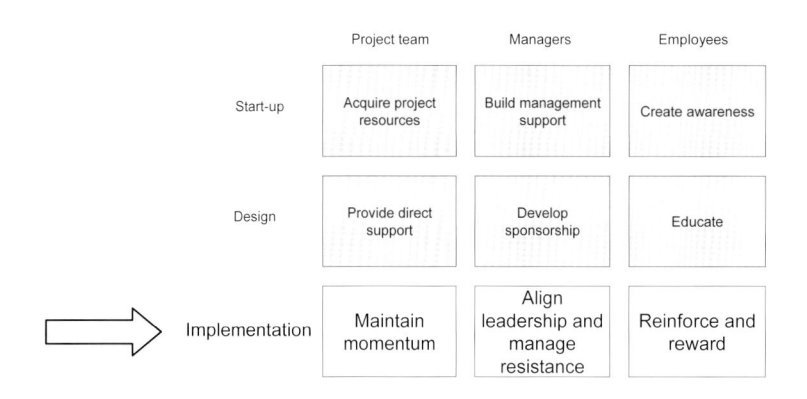

	with the Project team	with Managers	with Employees
	Maintain momentum	**Align leadership and manage resistance**	**Reinforce and reward**
Implementation	<ul><li>Secure resources necessary for implementation</li><li>Stay engaged with the team: attend meetings, reward successes, hold them accountable for results and build enthusiasm</li><li>Remove roadblocks and help the team overcome obstacles</li><li>Stay the course; avoid shifting priorities too early</li><li>Attend frequent project status meetings and actively track progress</li><li>Resolve issues and conflicts - respond to escalation</li></ul>	<ul><li>Continue to meet in public and private with business leaders and senior managers; align sponsorship; provide progress updates; resolve issues</li><li>Communicate expectations to senior managers for their support of the change; provide activities they can do and messages they can communicate to their organizations</li><li>Manage resistance from middle managers; correct or remove managers who will not support the change</li><li>Model the change through personal example and hands-on involvement</li><li>Stay involved throughout the entire project; stay visible</li><li>Hold managers accountable for their support</li></ul>	<ul><li>Reinforce key messages; align business strategy with project objectives; increase personal communications</li><li>Reinforce why the change is being made and the risk of not changing (some employees may be ready to hear this message only when the change is near implementation)</li><li>Listen to employees and encourage feedback; be willing to answer the tough questions</li><li>Set expectations for employees; clearly communicate consequences of not changing</li><li>Identify with the additional work and difficulties that may be experienced during implementation</li><li>Enforce application of new processes and behaviors</li><li>Look for quick wins; share successes and build enthusiasm for the change</li><li>Celebrate success stories in person; be present and visible</li><li>Acknowledge challenges and obstacles honestly</li></ul>

Table 7 – Sponsor implementation activities

Managers and supervisors

Most critical roles for managers and supervisors

Participants in the 2011 benchmarking study identified five critical roles of managers and supervisors in times of change.

1. **Communicate with direct reports about the change**
   Managers and supervisors should communicate about the change with direct reports, including information on why the change is happening, details about the change, expected impacts for the organization and the employee's job role, benefits of the change, answers to "what's in it for me?" (WIIFM), expectations and performance targets. Managers and supervisors should create two-way communication opportunities where they can answer questions, gather feedback and actively listen to employee concerns. Communications from managers should be consistent and provide a clear message about the change.

2. **Demonstrate support for the change**
   Managers and supervisors should be champions of the change, actively demonstrating their support and enthusiasm for the change. Managers should be role models for the change and advocate for the change with both their words and actions.

3. **Coach employees through the change process**
   Managers and supervisors should support their employees throughout the transition and act as coaches for direct reports. They should encourage employees with positive support. These actions build trust with the impacted employees. Participants also cited leadership, motivation and mentoring as keys to coaching success. Managers should ensure that their direct reports have the necessary time and resources to devote to the change.

4. **Identify and manage resistance**
   Because managers and supervisors are the closest to impacted employees, they are in the best position to identify and manage resistance. Managers and supervisors should remove or neutralize barriers to the change success.

5. **Engage with and provide support to the project team**
   Managers and supervisors should act as liaisons between impacted employees and the project and change management teams. Managers are in a unique position to provide input into the design phase of the change and to provide feedback on how employees are moving through the change process, including adoption and performance issues.

Participants also noted the importance of managers and supervisors understanding the change itself and their role. To effectively fulfill the five roles outlined above, managers and supervisors need timely and complete information to communicate to their direct reports. Managers need key talking points on the need for change, details about the change, benefits of the change and anticipated challenges. Managers and supervisors also need a foundational understanding of change management and the roles in leading the people side of change.

Most common mistakes

Participants in the 2011 study identified the most common mistakes made by managers and supervisors in times of change. The top five mistakes identified by participants were:

1. **Lack of visible support and involvement**
   Managers and supervisors failed to exhibit visible, consistent support and engagement in the change. Respondents noted causes including: assuming employees would automatically embrace and engage in the change without support or encouragement; failing to take accountability for the success of the change; and assuming that the project or change team was responsible for communication and engagement surrounding the change.

2. **Failing to understand or listen to employee concerns**
   Managers and supervisors did not engage with or actively listen to employees, or work to understand their concerns. Forums for employee questions, concerns and feedback were not instituted. In some instances, managers and supervisors failed to answer questions when they were posed, refused to find answers to employee questions, or simply ignored concerns and resistance from employees.

3. **Insufficient communication to impacted employees**
   Managers and supervisors failed to communicate information about the change downstream consistently. In cases where communication was present, messages presented to employees were ambiguous, unclear or dishonest. Communications were unclear regarding change details, context, drivers, impacts, business case and benefits.

4. **Resisting the change**
   Managers and supervisors actively resisted the change. Resistant behaviors noted included publicly expressing negative messages toward the change, indicating to employees that the change was not important or would not last, and deliberately withholding information.

5. **Poorly leading, coaching and supporting employees**
   Participants indicated poor and inconsistent leadership, coaching and support for employees through the change process. Bullying or bossing employees into engaging was viewed as ineffective.

Additional mistakes mentioned included:
- Failing to build a sufficient understanding of the change, specific details, impacts or benefits
- Not appropriating necessary resources, including time, training or funding
- Selling the change without believing in it, "paying lip service" to the change
- Not understanding change management or their role in change management
- Allowing work-arounds, failing to reinforce the change and failing to celebrate successes

Biggest skill, competency or tool gap

Study respondents were asked to identify the biggest gaps in terms of skills, competencies or tools that prevented managers and supervisors from becoming great leaders of change with their direct reports. Three particular gaps were named most frequently:

1. **Communication skills**
   Knowing when, how and what to communicate was the most common gap for managers and supervisors in becoming great change leaders. Respondents indicated a need for honest and respectful two-way communication effectively translated to the perspective of the employees without being too technical.

2. **Formal change management training**
   Training in the fundamentals and principles of change management was cited as a second significant gap. Managers and supervisors need to be trained on why change management is essential for successful projects, how it impacts return on investment (ROI), and tactics for managing the chaos of change as a standard, repeatable process. Training included an understanding of the ongoing individual change process and emotional cycle of employees experiencing change.

3. **Coaching skills**
   Study respondents identified a gap in the skills required for guiding and supporting employees through the transition and the process of change. Coaching tactics, such as critical listening, expectation setting and balancing positive and constructive feedback, were deemed necessary for managers and supervisors to be effective coaches. Coaching skills included the ability to identify and confront resistant behaviors and proactively

implement conflict resolution tactics with direct reports.

Other skill, competency or tool gaps identified in the study responses included:

- **General leadership skills**
  A lack of experience and confidence in managing people, particularly among managers who had been promoted based on technical skills

- **Resistance management skills**
  The ability to identify and confront resistant behaviors and proactively implement conflict resolution tactics with direct reports

- **Understanding the role of managers in change**
  A gap in understanding the importance of the manager's role and the full scope of manager's responsibilities to actively influence the transitions for their teams

- **Soft skills**
  Interpersonal traits such as trust, motivation, reading people, openness, emotional intelligence and active listening

- **Strategic perspective**
  A lack of orientation toward the organization's overall strategic direction and long term, cross-functional vision

- **Information about the change**
  Insufficient detail about the change itself, including the benefits, impact and technical components of what was being implemented

Preparation

Participants were asked to evaluate the following statement on a "strongly agree" to "strongly disagree" scale: *My organization adequately prepares managers/supervisors with the skills, training and tools they need to lead during change.* Over two thirds (69%) of participants either disagreed or strongly disagreed with the statement that their managers and supervisors were adequately prepared to manage change with their employees (Figure 49).

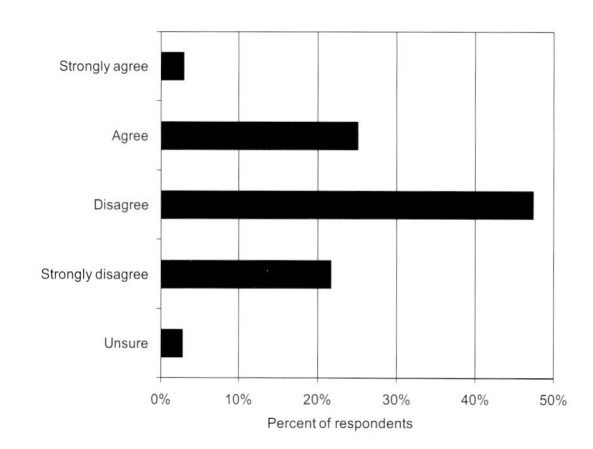

Figure 49 – Adequately prepared managers and supervisors

Coaching

Participants rated the effectiveness of managers and supervisors in their organization at coaching employees through the personal transitions associated with the change, one of the primary responsibilities of managers and supervisors in times of change. Over three quarters of study participants (77%) indicated that managers and supervisors were only somewhat effective or not effective at coaching employees through personal transitions (Figure 50).

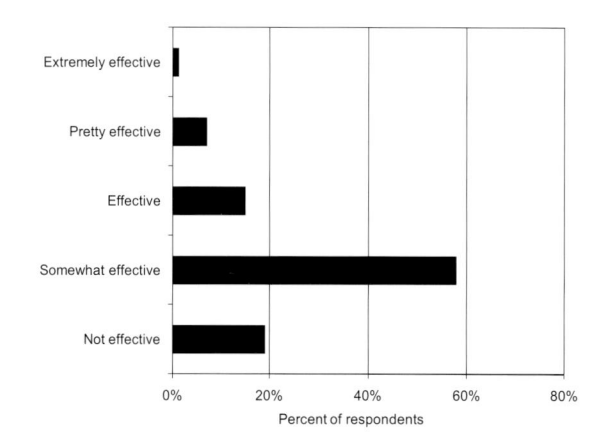

Figure 50 – Effectiveness at coaching employees through personal transitions

Participants identified specific steps taken to help managers and supervisors become more effective at coaching employees through their personal transitions associated with change. The top five activities identified were:

1. **Training on coaching**
   Respondents provided managers and supervisors with training specifically focused on coaching employees through the change process. Training programs varied from group workshops to individual training.

2. **General training in various competencies that included coaching**
   Managers and supervisors received some instruction on coaching during workshops and training for other competencies.

3. **Coaching tools and templates**
   Respondents provided managers and supervisors with tools and templates specific to coaching for reference. Common tools cited included toolkits, best practices, FAQs, shared successes and experiences with coaching.

4. **Feedback to target coaching activities**
   Respondents utilized feedback collected from surveys, forums, performance reviews and informal channels to identify where coaching efforts were needed. This focused support aided managers and supervisors in coaching their direct reports.

5. **Complete and timely information**
   To enable effective coaching, participants presented managers and supervisors with comprehensive information about the change, including why the change was needed, descriptions of the change, impact on employees, expectations of employees, goals, schedule, benefits and possible challenges. Talking point documents and communication aids ensured consistent messaging.

Managing resistance

Participants rated the effectiveness of managers and supervisors in their organizations at managing resistance to change (Figure 51). 80% of participants identified their managers and supervisors as only "somewhat effective" or "not effective" at managing resistance, with nearly one quarter of participants (22%) saying their managers were "not effective."

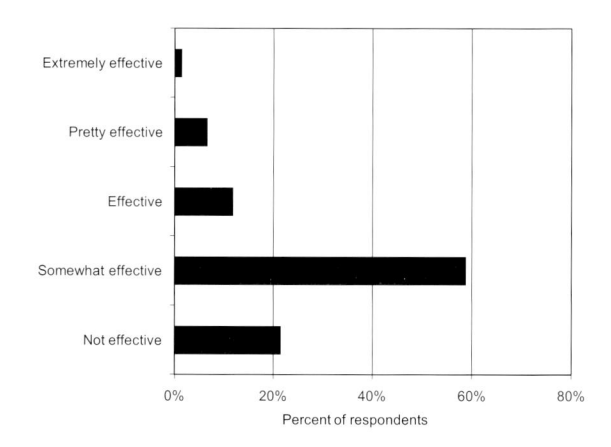

Figure 51 – Effectiveness at managing resistance

Participants identified specific steps taken to help managers and supervisors become better at managing resistance. The top six steps identified were:

1. **Training on resistance management**
   Training specifically on managing resistance was provided to managers and supervisors. Trainings included targeted tactics in resistance management, identifying resistance and overcoming individual resistance. Additional training topics included human reactions and behavioral aspects of change.

2. **Change management training that included resistance management**
   Change management training was provided to managers and supervisors that included components on resistance management. Change management trainings varied in focus, including comprehensive change management courses, lessons targeted specifically at leading personal change and sessions educating participants about the roles in change and expectations.

3. **Provide toolkits and templates focused on resistance management**
   Respondents provided managers with tools and templates to assist in resistance management. Commonly noted tools included

best practices, case studies, shared success stories, resistance FAQs and toolkits for managing resistance.

4. **Solicit feedback to further understand resistance**
   Soliciting feedback from employees to identify and understand resistance helped managers and supervisors become more effective at managing resistance. Multiple feedback channels were identified including forums, focus groups, surveys, involvement in design phases, direct feedback from prime resisters, and historical reactions to change.

5. **Providing information, briefings and messaging about the change**
   Providing information, briefings and messaging about the change to managers and supervisors helped them preemptively identify possible resistance and answer resisters queries in a prepared, coherent and consistent manner.

6. **Increased communication efforts**
   Respondents modified communications plans to increase communications. Proactive communications tailored to specific stakeholder groups that addressed possible objections were emphasized. Several participants noted specific training for managers and supervisors on communication.

Tactics for gaining support from managers

Source date: 2009

Participants in the 2009 study identified the tactics they used to gain support and engage with managers and supervisors. The most frequently cited tactics included:

1. **Involving managers and supervisors in the project**
   Managers and supervisors were engaged in project planning and solution design. This allowed them to have a voice and to take ownership in project success. Involvement occurred through two-way communications, focus groups, input on scheduling and assessments, and consultation on key decisions.

2. **Highlighting the benefits of the change**
   Creating awareness about the benefits of the future state, both for the individual managers and for their teams, occurred by showing measurable outcomes such as cost savings and return on investment, as well as by answering the questions: "what's in it for me?"; "what's in it for my team?" and "what's in it for the customers?"

3. **Maintaining frequent and honest communications**
   Managers were kept "in the loop" through ongoing communications that were open and honest. Status reports were provided frequently (bi-weekly, weekly or twice-per-week basis).

4. **Demonstrating active sponsorship**
   Participants leveraged project sponsors to gain support for the change among managers and supervisors. Both executive sponsors and middle managers demonstrated visible and clear support for the change by providing funding, facilitating meetings and being available to answer questions. Sponsorship provided accountability and helped to set priorities.

5. **Delivering training and workshops**
   Participants provided training and best practices information to managers that addressed skills, strategies and tools for leading change.

6. **Providing opportunities to voice resistance**
   Managers and supervisors were provided with opportunities to express their opinions and concerns to their supervisors and the change team. Participants listened carefully to understand the feedback and then took appropriate action to address concerns.

Other successful tactics for building support and engagement among managers included:

- Having one-on-one interaction
- Building open, transparent relationships

- Linking deliverables to performance objectives for accountability
- Building managers' awareness of their critical role in successful change
- Giving managers a role in communicating project information to their teams
- Providing a formal support network
- Reinforcing successes through rewards and celebrations
- Connecting the change to organizational goals and values

How to support managers and supervisors during change
Source date: 2009

Participants in the 2009 study offered a variety of suggestions on how to support managers and supervisors during change:

1. Designate a change champion or change team to coach and mentor managers. These subject matter experts could provide expertise and moral support while working through issues with managers. Some organizations established a help desk to put managers in touch with resources quickly.

2. Engage in constant dialogue and daily face-to-face communications with managers.

3. Provide tools for managers and supervisors to use while rolling out the change including: media kits, job aids, talking points, communication scripts, change management articles, case studies, reference materials and FAQs.

4. Collect information related to the change from employees via electronic or paper surveys, and share the feedback with managers and supervisors.

5. Share progress updates; keep managers and supervisors up-to-date and recognize when milestones have been achieved.

Other tactics to support managers and supervisors included:

- Offering formal change management training
- Creating awareness for change among all departments
- Conducting process/technology training
- Setting goals

Additional learning opportunities
Source date: 2009

In addition to formal classroom training, participants offered the following approaches for building change management skills and knowledge with managers and supervisors.

- **One-on-one discussions and coaching**
  These sessions provided safe interactions to help managers and supervisors lead change with their direct reports. Participants mentioned peer coaching, mentoring by senior leaders and support from change management specialists as useful skill-building methods.

- **Formal, regular communications**
  These one-to-many communications included emails, pamphlets, newsletters, bulletin boards and electronic forum messages.

- **Meetings**
  In some cases change management was added as an agenda item to normal meetings. Meetings focusing on change management specifically included short presentations, road shows, "lunch and learn" opportunities and forums covering a particular change management issue.

- **Workshops and seminars**
  The most effective sessions were interactive and included problem solving, question-and-answer facilitation and role playing.

- **Tools**
  Managers and supervisors were provided tip sheets, quick reference guides, workbooks and toolkits to support their change management efforts.

- **Articles and books**
  Managers and supervisors were provided with additional literature on leading change.

The content addressed in these additional training methods included:

- Specific roles and responsibilities of the manager or supervisor to support the change management effort
- Project-related information including details of the project plan, business case, key messages for communications and progress updates
- Stories and experiences including success stories from previous changes and examples of issues or concerns from the current change

Evaluating manager and supervisor change management effectiveness

Source date: 2009

More than 80% of participants in the 2009 study evaluated the effectiveness of managers and supervisors in fulfilling their change management roles. The methods used to evaluate the managers' change management skill level varied from informal and casual in nature to a formalized process to gather the data and appraise the effectiveness. The methods cited, in order of frequency, were:

- Employee surveys (specifically surveys assessing employee understanding of change messages communicated by their managers, as well as employee perceptions of the change overall)
- Informal face-to-face conversations with employees (to gain a sense of employee attitudes and their understanding of the change underway)
- Observations by change management team members (change management team members could join team meetings and listen to managers present the change to employees, thereby directly assessing the managers' ability to influence their employees and manage the change)
- Successful implementation of the business change

  "Adoption of [the] new process was our measure for success."

- Utilization of a formalized change management assessment tool implemented at periodic intervals throughout the life of the project

Communications

Preferred sender

Participants in the 2011 benchmarking study indicated the preferred senders of communications messages for both personal messages and organizational-level messages. Figure 52 shows the distinct preference for preferred senders of change messages. Overwhelmingly, the employee's supervisor was the preferred sender of personal messages while executives and senior leaders were preferred senders of the business messages. These findings reinforce findings from previous studies.

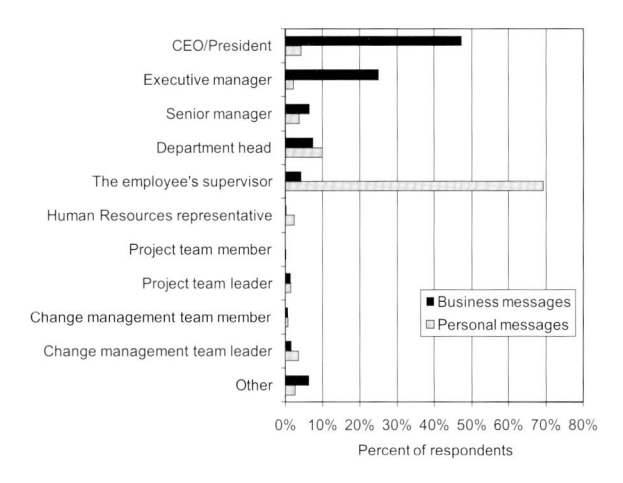

Figure 52 – Preferred senders of messages

Most important messages for employees

Participants identified the most important messages to communicate to employees regarding the change. While participants identified five important messages communicated to employees regarding the change, responses surrounding the business reasons for the change were stated twice as often as the next most frequent response.

1. **Business reasons for the change**
   Messages communicated to employees conveyed the reasons why the organization was changing, including:

   - The necessity of the change to ensure organizational success and sustainability in the future
   - The benefits of the change, including strategic objectives, potential return on investment (ROI), improved performance, and increase in business value
   - The risks of not changing and the negative impacts and consequences if the change was not pursued
   - The necessity of the change to remain competitive in the market
   - Improvements to processes, operations and design enhancements
   - The role of the change in support of business initiatives and business strategy

2. **Why the employees should want to participate**
   Messages communicated to employees built desire to participate in the change, or answered "what's in it for me" (WIIFM) from the employee's perspective, such as:

   - Demonstrating how the change will make their jobs easier, more efficient, more productive, more rewarding and less redundant
   - Normalizing the change or the occurrence of change
   - Indicating potential opportunities for new jobs or advancements
   - Explaining how the change aligns with employee priorities
   - Sharing how the change would increase the quality of their work life and work environment
   - Transferring ownership of the change to the employees with phrases such as "this is your change" or "innovation is the right and fun thing to do"

- Providing testimonials and examples of where the change was successful elsewhere

3. **Impact of the change on employees**
These messages identified how the change would impact employees including:
   - Changes to the way employees did work or changes to their job roles
   - Behavior changes that would be required
   - Who specifically was impacted
   - The tradeoffs and the downsides of the change
   - Potential for job loss
   - Employees' new roles and what needs to be done
   - What the change meant for the employee, including what they could expect, what their new role would entail and how the change applied to them
   - How they were expected to perform
   - What was needed from employees in terms of involvement, commitment, support and contribution
   - Emphasis that the employee's assimilation had a direct impact on the success of the project

4. **How the change was happening**
These messages included information regarding the specifics of how the change was occurring within the organization including:
   - The dates of implementation, the rollout schedule or timeline, the timeframe for adoption and the go-live date
   - Project status, including progress updates and milestones
   - The change plan or phases of the change
   - The next steps of the change
   - Who was leading or managing the change
   - Where the change was happening
   - Celebration of short term successes

5. **Details about the change**
These messages explained the specifics of the change, such as:
   - What the change was and the accompanying project objectives
   - The new processes, activities or procedures
   - What was not changing (e.g. ensuring job security)
   - Specifics about the difference between the future state and the current state (i.e. how tomorrow will be different from today)
   - Acknowledgement that not all the answers were available, "*what we don't know*"
   - The scope of the change
   - The challenges of the change
   - What the change meant for the organization

Additional key messages to employees included:
- How employees would be supported through the change
- To whom or where they could go for more information, such as training resources, updates, job aids or requests for additional support
- Information pertaining to how and when employees would be trained and the necessity and importance of training
- What they would need to be prepared and how they could best prepare
- The resources that would be made available to them to help with the transition
- Encouraging statements that emphasized the importance of the individual or reassurances that the transition would be made as a group, such as: "*the change is a journey we will accomplish as a team from the start to the end*" or "*this will be tough but together we'll get through it*"

Most important messages for managers and supervisors

Participants identified six important messages to communicate to managers and supervisors regarding the change.

1. **Roles and expectations for managers and supervisors**
   Most messages regarding role and expectations emphasized the importance of the role, responsibilities and the expectations of managers and supervisors during change. These messages conveyed how imperative their role was as change advocates, ambassadors and role models of the change. For example, *"your participation in the change as an adopter/champion increases the likelihood of the change's success."* Expectations of managers also included:

   - How to communicate change to staff
   - How to answer questions
   - The key messages to pass on to employees
   - How often communication should take place and the importance of keeping employees informed about the change
   - Identifying and managing resistance, including identifying areas of potential resistance
   - Helping staff adapt to the change through coaching, preparation and guidance
   - Managing questions and facilitating a smooth transition

2. **Business reasons for change**
   Similar to messages communicated to employees, participants listed the business reasons for the change as one of the most important messages communicated to managers and supervisors, including:

   - The need for change
   - The alignment of the change with the direction of the organization
   - The risks of not changing
   - The benefits to the organization

3. **Impact of the change on managers and supervisors**
   Participants identified the importance of communicating the impacts of the change on managers and supervisors, such as:

   - Impacts to their job roles and behavior in the work place
   - Impacts to their employees in terms of the type of work employees were expected to perform, employee behavior in the work place and new job roles for their employees
   - Impacts to their team or line of business
   - Potential or expected delays or disturbances to their work area

4. **Details about the change**
   These messages explained the change in terms of the change objectives and the specifics of the change. Other points included:

   - The change vision
   - What was not changing
   - Challenges of the change
   - Today versus tomorrow

5. **How the change was being implemented**
   Participants communicated how the change was happening within the organization to managers and supervisors, including:

   - Timelines for change implementation
   - How employees were being trained and prepared for the change
   - Progress, status and updates
   - Project plans and next steps
   - What was being done to minimize risk

6. **How managers and supervisors would be prepared and supported**
   These messages included details pertaining to the ways the organization was providing support for managers and supervisors, and also how managers and supervisors were being prepared to support their employees. Main points included:

   - Where to go for support

- How support would be provided
- Who to contact with concerns
- Where to get more information
- What managers and supervisors needed to be prepared
- How to lead people through change; how to be "the mirror of change"
- How to manage change

Most important messages for senior managers and executives

Participants identified five key messages to communicate to senior managers and executives regarding the change.

1. **Roles and responsibilities of senior managers and executives**
   The primary message communicated to senior managers and executives regarding the change emphasized their roles and responsibilities as sponsors of change, such as:
   - The necessity of their help in preparing for, leading and supporting the change, *"Your leadership, wisdom and active support are vital to success"*
   - The expectations of them in terms of what they need to do and their responsibilities – such as staying up-to-date on the project and managing the change with their reports
   - Their role in communicating with their staff in an open and timely manner, including messages that reflected the reasons for the change and messages that "sell the vision" of the change
   - The need for them to be active, visible and engaged in the change

2. **Business reasons for the change**
   The second most important message communicated to senior managers and executives included the reasons why the change was occurring, including:
   - The necessity of the change from the organization's perspective
   - The benefits to the organization upon completion of a successful change, such as increased competitiveness and proficiency
   - Alignment with other business objectives, priorities, organizational strategies or long term goals
   - The change drivers

3. **How the change was happening and progressing**
   These messages included information regarding how the change was taking place and how well the change was being adopted within the organization, including:
   - Status updates and milestones reached
   - Timelines of the project, including project schedules and deadlines
   - The planned approach for the change, implementation process and next steps
   - Challenges that arose during the change process, such as unforeseen issues, problems, increased workloads and strain on resources
   - How change management was being utilized and applied during the change
   - Reactions from staff

4. **The impacts of the change**
   These messages identified the impacts of the change, including:
   - Impacts to the organization in terms of who would be impacted, the costs of the change, performance dips and potential declines in productivity during the change process
   - Impacts to senior managers and executives specifically, such as what they could expect from the change and its impacts to their area or group
   - Impacts to employees in terms of job role changes, required behavioral changes and new expectations

5. **Details about the change**
   These messages identified the specifics of the change by addressing what was changing, such as:

   - The change objectives, expected results and scope of the change
   - The change vision and desired outcomes
   - What would not be changing, what would be new and what would be different

Attributes of a successful change message

Source date: 2009

Participants in the 2009 study identified three attributes of a successful change message when communicating to employees.

1. **Shares what the change will mean to the employee**
   Employees want to hear about how the change will impact them personally, including:

   - How will this change impact me?
   - What will I do differently?
   - What's in it for me? (WIIFM)

   Employees want to know how the change will affect their job, including the impact on day-to-day job duties, reporting responsibilities and changes in compensation.

2. **Explains the business reasons for why the change is happening**
   Employees want to know why the change is important and necessary for the success of the business, as well as the specific benefits to the business as a whole. Employees need to understand the business reasons for the change and how the change aligns with the organization's goals, vision and strategy. Employees also want to know what would happen to the business if the change was not made (essentially, the consequence of inaction).

3. **Is honest and clear**
   Employees want to hear a message that is sincere, truthful and accurate. The message should include the good and the bad as well as honest answers about what the communicator does and does not know.

   "Say what you know and admit what you don't know."

Additional attributes of an effective change message from the 2007 Best Practices report include:

- **Shares what is changing**
  The message should define the overall nature of the change and what specifically is changing in the organization. Information about the transition from the current state to the future state, and what is expected of the employees during this transition period, should also be included.

- **Conveys the impact on the organization**
  Employees should know how the organization and specific departments will be affected by the change, as well as any benefits or negative impacts that may result.

- **Prepares employees for the change**
  Employees should be assured they are not alone when moving into the future state. They should have a clear picture of the training and support they will receive to enable them to make the transition. This may include help desks, ongoing training or online resources.

Attributes of successful communicators

Source date: 2009

In addition to commenting on effective messages, participants in the 2009 study also shared feedback on effective communicators. The most successful and effective communicators demonstrated the following ten attributes, in rank order.

1. **Committed, engaged and passionate about the change**
   Successful communicators were positive, enthusiastic and passionate about the change – they believed in it. They were committed to

and engaged in the change and showed their support actively and visibly. They were champions of the change and led by example.

2. **Credible**
Effective communicators were trusted and respected, and had the ability to influence all levels in the organization. They had experience and authority.

3. **Able to deliver a clear message**
Delivering a clear message meant one that was simple, focused and concise. Effective and successful communicators were able to deliver clear messages in non-technical language that could be understood by all receivers.

4. **Knowledgeable about the change and its impact on the organization**
Successful communicators understood why the change was needed, the purpose and benefits of the change, and its impacts on the people. They were also knowledgeable about the organization, internal processes and the organization's history. They connected this knowledge with their ability to see the "big picture" vision and future state. Their communications shared this perspective and context.

"Explained clearly the organizational reason for the change and the personal impact on the individual; did this in an informative and respectful way."

5. **Consistent and timely in their messages**
Communicators delivered frequent messages on a regular schedule. These messages remained consistent and were repeated often.

6. **Open and honest**
Open and honest meant the communicators and their messages were genuine and delivered with truth and transparency.

7. **Two-way communicators**
The most important element for communicators in two-way communications was the ability to listen. Two-way communicators were open to conversations and feedback.

8. **Fluent in the "language" of their audience**
Effective communicators created a message that was tailored and relevant to their receivers. They always included the answer to "what's in it for me?" for the intended audience.

"Taking the broad message and making it meaningful for the group being communicated with."

9. **Personable**
Personable communicators were patient, confident and compassionate. They had excellent interpersonal skills, communicated with empathy and were approachable.

10. **Choosing the right channel**
Choosing the right channel meant the ability to offer communications in a variety of ways while ensuring that face-to-face communication was one of those channels.

Tactics for correcting misinformation and misunderstandings
Source date: 2009

There were six different tactics used for correcting misunderstandings resulting from background conversations or the "rumor mill" identified by participants in the 2009 study.

1. **Enabling open discussion time**
Open discussion time included events that allowed people to exchange information freely, present questions and provide feedback. Open discussions happened in many different formats including: town halls, brown bag lunches, road show presentations, conference calls, site visits, forums, small group meetings and focus groups.

2. **Identifying current rumors and addressing them immediately**
It was important that the identification of current rumors be done anonymously. Participants cited the following ways to collect rumors anonymously: telephone hotlines, designated email addresses, help desks and collection boxes. Participants also noted that it was best to address those

rumors, when possible, in a face-to-face format.

3. **Engaging sponsors**
Participants cited many different methods of engaging leadership. No matter how sponsors were engaged, sponsors were recognized as the most effective group to address and correct background conversations resulting from misinformation.

"National leadership team traveled to each location and allowed an opportunity for Q&A."

4. **Providing regular communications**
Regular communications were a source of consistency and provided updated information on the change. The most common interval of regular communications among participants was weekly, followed by monthly.

5. **Updating "frequently asked questions"**
Frequently asked questions (FAQs) answered common questions and addressed misinformation spreading through background conversations. FAQs were updated on a regular basis and circulated among employees in various ways including newsletters, electronic postings and written documentation.

6. **Providing electronic sources of information**
A source of information that could be accessed electronically at any time by employees and could be updated by the team was a useful tool for keeping employees up-to-date. This source of information was available to everyone in the organization to provide a sense of transparency and openness. Participants also cited the value of interactions through an electronic source including blogs, discussion boards and postings.

"Set up a 'rumor busters' website and fed it with both real and manufactured rumors and corrections."

What would you do differently regarding communications?

Participants provided five suggestions for what they would have done differently regarding communications. The most commonly cited response, more communication, was cited twice as often as the next response.

1. **More communication**
Participant responses indicated that they would communicate more, to more people, more often and to all levels within the organization. Responses also indicated that these communications should be more targeted, more face-to-face, more interactive and more relevant to the audience.

2. **Have a communication strategy**
The second most common response reflected the need for a more detailed communication strategy, including a succinct, consistent and accurate core set of messages. A strategy would also include a more robust implementation timeline for communication activities.

3. **Communicate earlier**
Participants indicated they would begin communication earlier. These efforts included syncing to other communication networks, connecting to the project sooner and beginning in-person meetings earlier, even if only partial information was available.

4. **More attention to senior leadership**
The fourth recommendation from participants involved more attention, interaction and involvement with senior leadership. Participants reported that they would have evoked more support and ownership from senior leadership.

5. **More dedicated people working on communication**
Study results revealed that communication efforts needed to have more people dedicated to them, including having more dedicated and expert resources assigned to producing and implementing communications.

Use of social media and Web 2.0 in communications

A new set of questions was added to the 2011 study regarding the use of Web 2.0 and social networking applications in communications. Overall, less than one in five participants utilized these new communication tools (Figure 53).

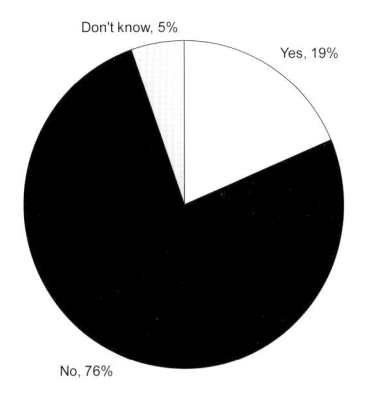

Don't know, 5%
Yes, 19%
No, 76%

Figure 53 – Use of social media and Web 2.0

Social media and Web 2.0 tools used

Participants who reported using Web 2.0 or social networking tools identified four categories of applications that they used. The respondents reported using internal group information sharing and discussion media twice as often as any other response.

1. **Internal group information sharing and discussion media**
   This most common response indicated that exclusive, internally used networking applications were the most common application of Web 2.0. Examples of tools that were identified by participants included blogs, wikis, discussion boards and internally created project portals.

2. **Public web-based tools**
   The second most commonly used tools were applications for sharing information and prompting dialogue in a public forum in the form of "conventional" social networking tools.

3. **Outward communication tools**
   In utilizing Web 2.0 tools, participant responses indicated the use of one-way information delivery, such as message boards, email, podcasts and video on demand.

4. **Collaboration tools**
   Tools designed for collaboration were a fourth application of Web 2.0 and social networking tools identified by participants. Examples included poll and vote technology and questionnaires.

Benefits of social media and Web 2.0 tools in communications

Three primary benefits were identified by participants who used Web 2.0 or social networking applications.

1. **Get messages out**
   The most commonly cited reason for using Web 2.0 and social networking applications was to communicate messages to a broader audience, faster and more efficiently.

2. **Engage the organization**
   Respondents reported that Web 2.0 and social networking tools were used to create a more inclusive and supportive work environment by encouraging a more open dialogue within the organization. Additionally, these newer methods of communication were used to engage all generations.

3. **Informal feedback and tracking**
   A third benefit identified by participants was the availability of informal feedback and monitoring of staff's perceptions regarding the change. This ability helped to identify and manage resistance or potential resistance and solve misconceptions or problems early on in the change process.

Recommendations regarding social media and Web 2.0 tools

Five primary recommendations for others who were looking to use the new communication media offered by Web 2.0 were provided by participants who had used social networking applications:

1. *"If it works for you, use it."*
2. Consider the culture of your company and the audience you are trying to reach before considering the use of Web 2.0 and social networking tools.
3. Dedicate someone to be responsible for monitoring and responding to postings, email or other communication media.
4. Determine how you want to use the application before using it.
5. Use a variety of tools and methods.

Communication vehicles

Participants used a variety of communication methods during their change projects. The list below contains a comprehensive list of communications vehicles identified by study participants in the 2003, 2005, 2007 and 2011 benchmarking studies.

Articles in industry journals

Banners

Billboards

Blogs

Booklets

Branded promotional materials

Briefings

Brochures

Brown bag meetings

Bulletin boards

Bulletins

Café meetings

Cafeteria postings

Calendar of events

Cascading communications

Celebration events

Change agent networks

Charts/graphs to show progress

Circulars

Coffee mornings

Communication toolkits

Conversations

Demonstrations

Department meetings

Desk drops

Documents

Electronic billboards/plasma screens

Email

Executive messages

Executive presentations

Face-to-face interactions

Fact sheets

Faxes

Fliers

Focus groups

Forums

Frequently asked questions (FAQs)

Gallery walks

Giveaways

Group meetings

Hallway conversations

Help desk

Industrial theater

Information fairs

Informational meetings

Internal messaging systems

Interviews

Intranet sites

Intranet pop-ups

Kick-off events

Leadership meetings

Leaflets

Lectures

Letters

Lunch and learns

Magazines

Mailers

Memos

Newsletters (corporate)

Newsletters (project)

One-on-one meetings

Online content management systems

Online training

Organizational meetings

Pamphlets

Pay stub inserts

Performance reviews

Physical mailings

Podcasts

Posters

Presentation aides and outlines

Presentations

Project fairs

Question and answer sessions (Q&A)

Rallies

Reader boards

Recognition packages

Road shows

Roundtables

Site visits

Skits

Social media / networks

Stakeholder meetings

Status reports

Storyboards

Success stories

Surveys

Targeted emails

Team meetings

Teleconferences

Testimonials

Text messages

Town hall meetings

Tradeshows

Training courses

TV displays

Video conferences

Videos

Virtual meetings

Voicemail messages

Walk-arounds

Webcasts

Webinars

Websites

Wikis

Word of mouth

Workshops

Training

Training for employees on the new processes, skills and behaviors required by the project, as well as the role the change management team played in project-related training were addressed in the 2009 study.

Primary methods used to train employees

Source date: 2009

The top five methods used to train employees on the new processes, skills and behaviors required by the change were:

- Classroom training (nearly half of all study participants utilized classroom education to train their employees on the new skills required)
- One-on-one coaching or mentoring
- Self-paced, web-based training
- Hands-on training (gave employees an opportunity to try the tools and have support available for immediate feedback)
- Job aids (hard-copy aids for the new tools and processes, including reference cards, user manuals, FAQs or cheat sheets)

Participants shared the following insights related to the most effective training techniques:

- Hands-on training was overwhelmingly the most effective training method. Participants found it to be the most beneficial because there was an opportunity to try out the new system in a safe environment and receive immediate feedback. Some examples of hands-on training included live demonstrations, role plays and simulations.
- One-on-one coaching was an important element of the participants' training efforts. During the coaching sessions, managers were able to answer the employees' questions as well as assess their ability to use the new tool.
- While classroom-style training was found to be beneficial to address large groups, small group discussions were also utilized as a training technique. The small group setting allowed for open discussions and addressed the "what" and "why" as well as what was in it for the employee.

Follow-up support was an important element of training to aid in reinforcement. It was also beneficial to assess the comfort level of the employees with the new processes.

Role of change management team

Source date: 2009

The role the change management team played in project-related training included:

- **The creation, planning and delivery of training**
  62% of all study participants said their change management team planned, created and delivered the training.

  "Change management led the entire training effort, from development to leading sessions."

- **To support, coach and oversee the training**
  The change management team's role was to support and oversee the training program. Change managers were responsible for *"providing ongoing consultation and support to the trainers."*

- **Communications**
  Change managers were responsible for communicating the when, what and how related to the project training as well as ensuring key messages were present during the training program.

Resistance

How resistance was identified

Participants in the 2011 study shared tactics for identifying resistance. The top responses were:

1. **Observing behavior showing a lack of adoption or buy-in**
   Recipients of the change did not visibly adopt or commit to the desired change. Behaviors that indicated a lack of buy-in included absenteeism, limited feedback, withholding requested information, workarounds and the use of old systems. Resistance was recognized by monitoring informal communications throughout the organization (e.g. "the grapevine," discussions in hallways, water cooler conversations, lunch discussions, etc.) and by observing body language and physical cues for feedback on the change.

2. **Using feedback tools including readiness assessments, stakeholder analyses, email and social media**
   Respondents identified resistance using metrics and feedback systems to solicit responses to the change from various levels of the organization. While surveys were utilized most often, stakeholder analyses and readiness assessments were commonly used as well. Respondents also mentioned the use of social media, online drop-boxes and the creation of distinct email accounts for feedback.

3. **Seeking feedback through organizational channels and informal networks**
   Resistance to change was identified using leadership networks and other distinct communication channels to filter feedback from different levels and perspectives in the organization. Change agent networks were noted most commonly among respondents, but networks of key users and stakeholders were also prominent channels.

4. **Conducting meetings, interviews, focus groups and training workshops**
   Resistance was identified when it surfaced openly in face-to-face encounters such as meetings, interviews, focus groups and training workshops about the change.

5. **Defining resistant behaviors and monitoring occurrences**
   Respondents defined specific, change resistant and non-resistant behaviors such as complaining, asking negative, loaded questions and asking redundant questions. Monitoring these behaviors allowed respondents to gauge the extent of resistance to the change.

Most resistant group

Participants in the 2011 benchmarking study identified the groups they experienced the most resistance from for the change (Figure 54). Middle-level managers were identified as the most resistant group by over one third of participants, followed by front-line employees and front-line supervisors.

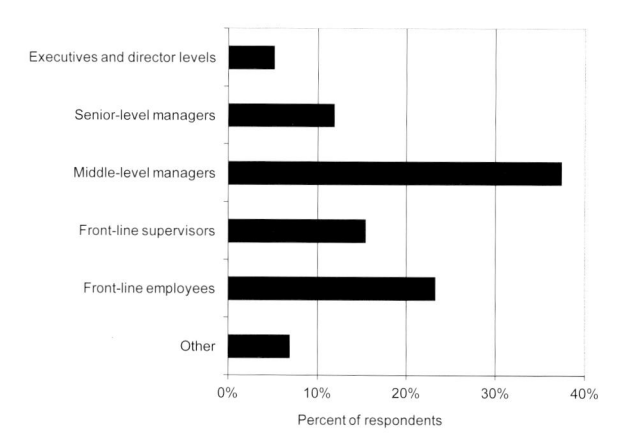

Figure 54 – Most resistant groups

Primary reasons employees resisted change

Source date: 2009

Data from Prosci's 2007 and 2009 reports reveal consistent themes for why employees resisted change. Specifically, participants cited five top reasons that front-line employees resisted change in their organizations, including:

1. **Lack of awareness**
   Employees resisted change because they lacked awareness of why the change was being made or did not understand the nature of the change. They did not know the business reasons for making a change or the consequences of not changing. Study participants stated that employees resisted more when they did not have the answer to the question "what's in it for me?" or WIIFM. Participants also said that employees lacked awareness because their managers were uninformed or were sending mixed messages.

2. **Impact on current job role**
   Many employees resisted change when they believed there would be a negative impact on their job role or workload. Specifically, employees were resistant to changes that:

   - Increased the amount of work they would be required to perform (too busy already)
   - Did not allow for current process "work-arounds"
   - Would cause a loss of position or power when the change was implemented (employees feared that the change and the associated performance measures would "work against them")

3. **Organization's past performance with change**
   Participants cited the organization's past failure to implement changes as a factor in employee lack of commitment to a current change. Some participants cited a culture of non-compliance or "serial resisters" as factors contributing to employee resistance. Many participants also stated that front-line employees were resistant to any type of change because these employees were comfortable or "entrenched" in the old way of doing things.

4. **Lack of visible support and commitment from managers**
   Participants cited a lack of support from employees when the employees' managers did not stress the importance of making the change or did not show a personal commitment to making the change themselves (when managers were not involved in the change or were showing resistance or uncertainty). Participants also stated that a lack of visible support from senior management contributed to employee resistance, especially when business leaders failed to communicate directly with employees or when employees lacked trust in their leaders.

5. **Job loss**
   Employees were especially fearful of any changes that could possibly affect their employment during difficult economic times.

Other notable responses were:

- Some employees were resistant to change because they were not given the opportunity to actively participate in the change. Lack of involvement and engagement early in the design resulted in employees resisting change simply because they were not part of the process.

- Study participants also cited change saturation (too much change already underway) as another factor for employee resistance.

Steps for dealing with employee resistance

Source date: 2009

Participants in the 2009 study suggested two main focus areas for managing employee resistance.

- Awareness of why the change is needed
- How the change would directly impact employees

Building awareness of the business need for the change, and the intended results, was an important step to reducing resistance. Specifically, participants recommended communicating to employees about:

- The goals of the change
- Why the change was being made
- Personal and organizational risks if no change was made

Sharing how the change would impact and benefit employees, including how they fit into the change, was the second area for reducing resistance. Explaining "what's in it for me" and engaging employees in conversations about the personal impact of the change were viewed as significant steps toward reducing resistance to the change. Where applicable, this included sharing the associated personal benefits or rewards.

To accomplish these objectives, study participants made recommendations in three areas.

1. **Communications**
   Open and honest two-way communications targeted toward specific groups was reported as the most effective communication method. Face-to-face sessions allowed for employee comments and interactions, and increased employee buy-in and ownership of the change. Participants noted that these communications only worked if employees felt that their concerns were being acted upon. The timing of communications was also important, as participants stated that early, timely and accurate communications worked best.

2. **Leadership involvement**
   Increased sponsor involvement, along with direct communications to employees, dramatically increased employee buy-in and support for the change. Having leadership address employee concerns swiftly and directly decreased resistance among employees. Results from the 2007 report support this tactic. In that study, participants recommended that executive sponsors provide candid, proactive and consistent messages when supporting the change and dealing with resistance. Executives and senior managers mitigated resistance by demonstrating their alignment with the change in an active and visible way while engaging subordinates in discussions about the change.

3. **The role of managers**
   Supervisors and managers were needed to provide employees with key messages about the change, to coach them through the transition and to equip them to be successful after the change was in place. Managers were critical for sharing why the change was happening and how an employee would be impacted personally. Immediate supervisors were in the best position to talk about expectations for each employee, including performance expectations that would be part of future evaluations or performance reviews. Supervisors could also discuss the consequences of not engaging in the change. This method of managing resistance was the most effective if the direct supervisor was trusted by those they were coaching. Employee resistance was also lower if their manager already supported or "bought into" the change.

Additional methods for managing employee resistance included:

- **Employee involvement and participation**
  Participants stated that resistance was less when employees were engaged in the process and when they had the opportunity to provide feedback. Direct involvement of employees increased their buy-in to the solution, and resulted in "positive word-of-mouth" about the change.

- **Training and mentoring programs**
  Employees felt more comfortable with a change and demonstrated less resistance when they were given the skills necessary to effectively make the change. One training method used frequently by participants was a mentoring program or the creation of networks of change agents who demonstrated the necessary skills to other employees. Another popular information sharing and training method was the use of virtual "help desks" that employees could visit to see the

answers to FAQs or to see what a new process looked like before it went live.

Avoidable employee resistance

Participants in the 2011 study indicated how much employee resistance they experienced could have been avoided with effective change management (Figure 55). Results from the 2011 study paralleled the findings from the 2009 study. 44% of study participants indicated that more than half of the resistance they experienced could have been avoided, compared to 42% in the 2009 study.

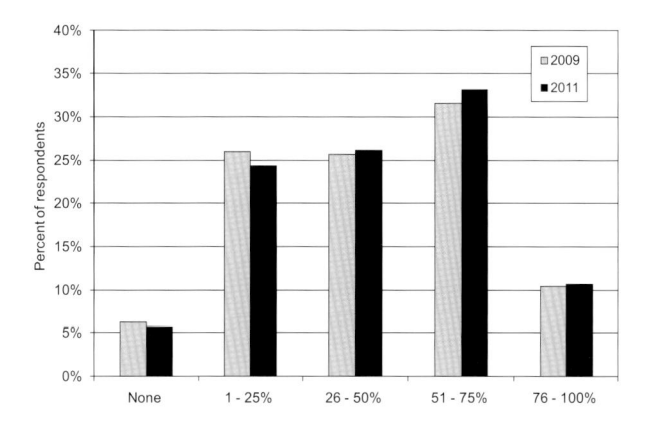

Figure 55 – Percent of employee resistance seen as avoidable

Proactive steps for avoiding or preventing resistance from employees
Source date: 2009

There were three main courses of action that participants in the 2009 study identified to proactively reduce employee resistance.

1. **Clear, honest, two-way communications**
   Participants cited early, regular and detailed communications with all levels of employees as a way to reduce resistance. These communications should be face-to-face from supervisors and managers with consistent and structured messages, and should begin at the project's inception and continue until project completion. This approach provided a forum for employees to share their ideas and concerns. Employees wanted to give feedback about the project and wanted to receive regular updates on the project's progress.

   Participants stated that employees were interested in a detailed discussion of goals, risks and business needs of the change project to help them understand the nature of and reason for the change. Resistance would have been decreased if employees had a better understanding of how the change would impact them personally and what the benefits would be when they made the change (WIIFM). One important part in the discussion about benefits was to manage expectations so that front-line employees had a "realistic" view of what was going to happen.

2. **Early involvement of end-users in all phases of project development**
   Participants said they involved front-line employees in all steps of the process from planning to rollout. They involved employees earlier as a way to identify pockets of resistance and address pain points. They also included front-line employees in the planning phase so that the change was not presented as a "done deal" in which employees had limited input. This involvement gave employees a sense of control and empowered them to become active participants in the change. With this early involvement, participants said they started training programs early in the project to allow employees to familiarize themselves with the future state. This early involvement also allowed for the roles at all levels in the organization to be identified and understood from the onset.

3. **Manager and supervisor engagement**
   Participants stated that the early participation of managers and supervisors helped to reduce employee resistance and the likelihood that the managers and supervisors themselves would be resistant. Participants also stated that coaching managers to be change role models, or "agents of change," made them more accountable in the success of the change project. To establish this role,

managers needed training in both the details of the change and in change management. Lastly, giving managers and supervisors the necessary authority to motivate the front-line employees through incentive programs and performance reviews helped mitigate resistance.

Primary reasons managers resisted change

Source date: 2009

Participants in the 2009 study cited four top reasons why managers resisted change.

1. **Lack of awareness about and involvement in the change**
   By far, the largest contributor to resistance from managers was a lack of understanding of the scope, timeline and impact of the change on them and on their employees. Study participants stated that managers felt left out of the project planning phase, and that their expertise and proximity to the end-users was not utilized. This lack of awareness and involvement in the specifics of the project caused a lack of clarity in their roles and responsibilities in the change, and they were unsure of what was expected of them. The impression from managers was that a lack of information about the change suggested a negative impact on them and their employees. Managers were also resistant when the benefits of the project were not clearly defined for them, especially when these benefits were only identified at the corporate level.

2. **Loss of control or negative impact on job role**
   Many managers felt that the change reduced the dependence on their personal knowledge and contribution, thereby making them redundant (less needed). They felt this redundancy would cause them to lose their positions of power or lose their jobs completely. If the change was not going to result in management job loss, then managers felt that the change would cause them to fail or look incompetent because it took them out of their comfort zones or changed the way they did their jobs. They were also often afraid that the changes would have a negative impact on their job titles, wages and performance reviews for themselves and their staff.

3. **Increased workload and lack of time**
   A lack of time to manage the change successfully was also a source of resistance from managers. Study participants reported that managers felt that the change itself was too cumbersome and time consuming or that they had competing priorities and had reached a point of change saturation for themselves and their employees. Managers also believed that the change would result in a decrease in productivity and an increase in workload for which they would be held accountable. At the very least, many managers saw the addition of the change as an "annoying interruption" to their day-to-day tasks.

4. **Culture of change resistance and past failures**
   Another source of resistance from managers dealt with the particular culture of their organizations and the history of past change projects. Managers distrusted a particular change due to a feeling that it was "the flavor of the month" and that it would fail like past changes had failed. Another aspect of this distrust was a sense that maintaining the status quo was the safest way to prevent any of the adverse effects of a failed change. This inertia was often due to a lack of management accountability in past initiatives.

Steps for dealing with manager resistance

Source date: 2009

Participants in the 2009 study suggested four main ways of mitigating resistance from managers.

1. **Open a two-way dialogue about the "what and why" of the change**
   Participants cited an open, two-way dialogue

as the most effective way to manage resistance from managers. These targeted communications with managers were most effective when they were detailed, timely, candid and face-to-face. Participants stated that managers were interested in:

- Reasons for the change and risks of not making the change
- The personal and professional benefits of the change
- A clear understanding of the goals of the project
- A picture of the "future state"
- Status of the project's progress
- Information about his or her individual roles and responsibilities during the change

Resistance was also reduced when the managers were given the opportunity to provide feedback about the change.

2. **Give managers the necessary tools and time to succeed at the change**
Managers' resistance was reduced when they understood the change and had the necessary skills and tools to succeed at the change. Skill building included role plays and demonstrating the new processes or tools as a way to build confidence with managers. Another important factor in mitigating resistance was the timing of the change and understanding the managers' competing priorities with regard to the change. Breaking the change down into small, actionable steps and giving the managers enough time to prepare their teams helped decrease resistance. Many participants also said that the inclusion of change management training was helpful in mitigating resistance.

3. **Engage senior leadership**
Managers were less resistant when there was active support from leadership and when they were granted the resources necessary to make the change effectively. This high level sponsorship came in the form of communications and workshops between management and the sponsors, as well as discussions about the business case for the change. Managers were more responsive in meetings with the sponsor because they felt that *"they could talk to someone who was in the position to take action on the manager's concerns."*

4. **Involve managers in all stages of the project**
Engaging managers in all stages of the process gave them ownership of the change and reduced the likelihood and strength of resistance. Early involvement allowed the managers to become agents of the change and made them part of the solution, not the problem. Managers were also less likely to be resistant when their subject matter expertise was tapped in the development of the change project. It made them feel like the change was happening with them, not to them.

Avoidable manager resistance

Participants in the 2011 study indicated how much resistance from managers could have been avoided with effective change management (Figure 56). The percentage of participants indicating that more than half of the resistance they experienced could have been avoided increased from 40% in the 2009 study to 49% in the 2011 study.

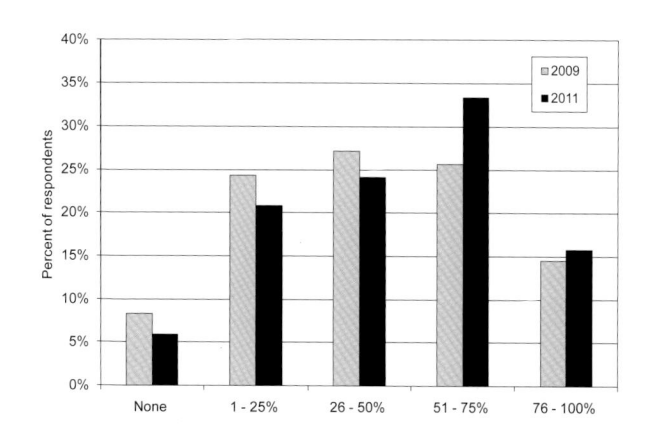

Figure 56 – Percent of manager resistance seen as avoidable

Proactive steps for avoiding or preventing resistance from managers and supervisors

Source date: 2009

Participants in the 2009 study provided three main action steps for proactively addressing manager and supervisor resistance.

1. **Management involvement in all phases of the project**
   Participants cited the early engagement of managers in the development and planning stages of the project as the number one proactive step they could have taken to prevent management resistance. This involvement included:

   - Asking for and using their feedback in the project plan
   - Creating an understanding of their role in the change from the onset
   - Making them part of the "communication cascade" to inform their employees of the change

   This early involvement would have made the managers "change agents" and also would have made them responsible for the success of the change.

2. **Early awareness building**
   Another factor that participants cited as a proactive step for avoiding managers' resistance was building managers' awareness of the benefits of the change and the overall strategy. They recommended detailed and frequent communications, even when all the details were not known, to keep the managers "in the loop." These communications would make the case for the change and explain the impact of the change on managers and their employees.

3. **Executive support**
   Participants cited active executive support as another important factor in preventing management resistance. This support came in several forms:

   - Detailed explanation of the strategy and business case for making the change
   - Consistent focus on the project and making the project's priority clear to managers
   - Understanding of, and help dealing with, competing workload issues

Ineffective methods for dealing with resistance

Source date: 2007

Participants in the 2007 study cited the top five mistakes to avoid when managing resistance.

1. **Ignoring resistance and expecting it to go away on its own**
   Participants overwhelmingly cited ignoring resistance as the biggest mistake. Ignoring or avoiding resistance did not make it go away and in some cases made it worse.

2. **Not listening to and understanding the concerns of those impacted**
   Participants said that not understanding the root cause of resistance prevented them from responding to the real issues and led to the conclusion that all resistance is the same. This led to an ineffective "one-size-fits-all" approach to managing resistance. Next time, participants said they would not assume all behavior was a result of resistance, but instead would work to listen to impacted employees and ask questions to understand the root causes and reasons for their behavior.

   "Not fully understanding the nature of the resistance and the factors leading to it, and trying to apply a 'one approach fits all' mindset."

3. **Not gaining input from those impacted**
   Participants stated that applying force and pressure from the top down to implement a change was a mistake for managing resistance. This approach did not build the buy-in and engagement of those impacted and therefore made it difficult to manage resistance.

   "Shutting resisters out – they may have some valuable contributions despite the resistance."

4. **Underestimating the resistance**
Underestimating the resistance to change was cited as a significant mistake by participants because it resulted in a lack of planning for the change. This lack of planning was felt most significantly in the areas of building executive sponsorship and securing their involvement.

5. **Poor communications**
Poor communications made managing resistance very difficult. Poor communications included inconsistent messages, incorrect messages, incorrect senders, bad timing and dishonest information. Participants also stated that using a public forum to confront a resister was a mistake.

Impacts of using pain or fear to manage change

Source date: 2007

Participants in the 2007 study overwhelmingly agreed that using fear or pain to manage change was not sustainable in the long term. Some participants acknowledged that using fear or pain may catalyze change or create "movement," but that this effect was short-lived. They stated that if fear was used as part of the awareness message to employees, the threat to the organization must be real and visible. Participants also stated that if fear or pain was used repeatedly as a tool to drive change, employees began to lose trust in the message (the "boy who cried wolf" scenario) and lose confidence in the organization's leadership. Study participants listed a number of likely consequences from managing change with fear or pain, including:

- Increased employee turnover (including losing the best employees)
- Lower productivity
- Higher resistance
- Slower adoption of the change

For the most part, study participants agreed that fear or pain as a resistance management tool alienated employees and created resentment. Employee morale was impacted and people became cynical toward the organization, leadership and the change.

Editor's note: A distinction should be made by the reader between using fear or pain on a personal level to motivate a person to change, and the natural worry or fear that can result from building awareness about the seriousness of a situation that is present in an organization. The distinction being made here is whether fear is being used as an intentional tool or weapon to manage resistance, as compared to a natural response to a real and observable condition.

Reinforcement and feedback

Determining if employees are engaging in the change

Participants in the 2011 study shared the most effective methods they used to determine if employees were engaging in the change. The top methods cited were:

1. **Using surveys, assessments and feedback systems to measure engagement**
   Participants used a number of vehicles to collect direct feedback from impacted employees to monitor engagement, including surveys, engagement assessments and formal feedback mechanisms (dedicated email inboxes, comment drop boxes, FAQ forums).

2. **Observing and interacting informally with change recipients**
   Respondents suggested observing change recipients' reactions and responses to change through informal interaction to determine engagement. The informal nature of this method encouraged an open, honest view of change engagement.

3. **Monitoring engagement through feedback channels and networks**
   Participants utilized communication networks and organizational channels including managers, change agents, trainers and Human Resources to determine overall employee engagement throughout the organization.

4. **Soliciting feedback by creating deliberate opportunities**
   Allotting dedicated opportunities for input and questions from change recipients during events and meetings related to the change motivated open, continuous feedback on employee engagement in the change.

5. **Tracking fluctuations in performance**
   Defining and tracking key performance indicators offered evidence of productive engagement in the change and comparison with benchmarks and projected outcomes.

6. **Tracking general use of and proficiency with implemented changes**
   Monitoring the use of changes and associated procedures measured engagement in a concrete, evident manner. Including metrics for proficient use of change systems in tracking and documentation clarified the extent of engagement.

Best provider of reinforcement and recognition

Figure 57 shows the groups that participants identified as the best providers of reinforcement and recognition at both the individual level and the group level.

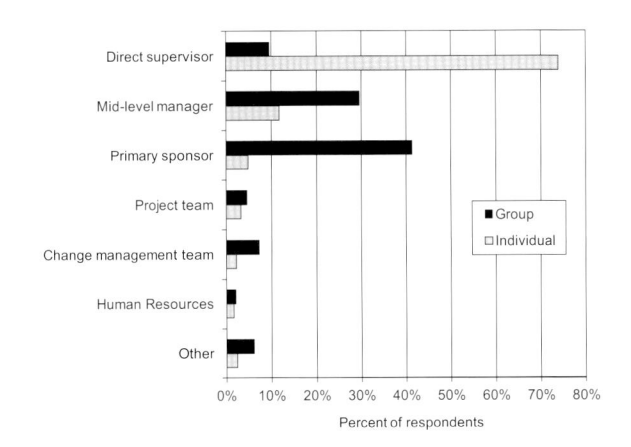

Figure 57 – Best provider of reinforcement and recognition

While participants leaned toward the direct supervisor for providing individual reinforcement and recognition, the primary sponsor or mid-level manager was identified as the best provider of group reinforcement and recognition.

Individual reinforcement

Study participants were asked to identify the most effective ways to reinforce and sustain change at the individual level. Study participants identified the four most effective ways as:

1. **Communicating success**
   Communicate consistently and continuously, including progress and short-term successes. Use positive and consistent communications, in both one-on-one situations between a supervisor and a direct report and with peers in informal settings. Communicate through post-implementation of the project to drive sustained change.

2. **Providing and collecting feedback**
   Ensure feedback is collected at all levels and demonstrate that the feedback was heard. Address both positive and negative feedback, utilizing one-on-one and team meeting settings. Provide honest and helpful feedback to end-users during implementation and post-implementation.

3. **Recognizing and rewarding adoption**
   Provide a variety of channels for recognition through both one-on-one and team meetings with direct reports. Acknowledge success of both short-term wins and long-term goal achievement. Show appreciation for the efforts made by each individual. Celebrate success and offer incentives throughout each phase of the change.

4. **Providing on-the-job support mechanisms**
   Make support mechanisms available during each phase of the change. Support from super-users, change champions, leaders and early adopters each offer technical and moral support. Allow for practicing and trial experiences with the future state. Provide job aids, help desks and updated process documentation.

Group reinforcement

Study participants were asked to identify the most effective ways to reinforce and sustain change at the group level. Participants identified the five most effective ways as:

1. **Communication**
   Communicate key messages consistently with each group to share status updates and success stories. Share lessons learned, frequently asked questions and success within the team. Make multiple forms of communication available to each group or division.

2. **Recognition**
   Recognize wins at the group level publicly, informally and face-to-face. Acknowledge the efforts of each team and celebrate positive outcomes. Include recognition and acknowledgement from leadership.

3. **Workshops**
   Workshops, training and group activities provide a strong, fun learning environment where individuals can learn from each other while supporting the team as a whole. Offer pre- and post-implementation workshops, providing support and follow up. Allow groups to participate, share success, voice opinions and better their collective efforts.

4. **Key performance indicators (KPIs)**
   Use key performance indicators (KPIs) to track and report progress. Record metrics and publish organizational results. Include accountability in job descriptions and create ownership.

5. **Sponsorship**
   Sponsors should share the bigger picture vision and strategy of the company, while being visible at the group level. Executive leaders and the steering committee sharing status updates and offering feedback reinforce change at the group level.

Mistakes to avoid when reinforcing change

Study participants were asked to provide recommendations on mistakes to avoid when reinforcing change. The three primary areas of recommendations were:

1. **Avoid ineffective or not meaningful reinforcement**
   - Focus on reinforcement activities aligned with project and organizational success

and the desired outcomes, delivered consistently across the organization. *"Do not underestimate the importance of reinforcement."*

- Ensure positive reinforcement delivered from the immediate supervisor.
- Utilize multiple channels of reinforcement employed throughout the change process. *"Don't wait until the end to start reinforcing the correct behavior."*
- Deliver meaningful and genuine reinforcement for true, significant wins. *"Do not provide a blanket reinforcement approach."*

2. **Avoid a lack of communication with impacted groups**
   - Ensure consistent communication with every individual involved through multiple channels.
   - Provide true success stories from within the organization communicated throughout the project life cycle.
   - Encourage open, honest two-way communications that engage impacted employee groups; *"take time to listen."*

3. **Do not avoid recognition of new behavior**
   - Provide direct recognition for specific behaviors aligned with the desired outcomes.
   - Acknowledge and reward demonstrated ability at the individual level.
   - Celebrate milestones aligned with the project.

Other notable recommendations include:

- Align key performance indicators (KPIs) with the new actions.
- Instill the "big picture" strategic vision within each employee.

How can performance appraisals and measures encourage change adoption?
Source date: 2007

Participants in the 2007 study indicated that performance appraisals, which link the business goals to individual performance, can enhance change adoption by:

- **Clarifying roles and expectations for every employee**
  Goals that are specific and focused on individual contributions remove uncertainty and provide the necessary structure for employees to support new business objectives.

  "Structure drives behavior, so make sure how people are measured and rewarded supports the strategy and expected behaviors of the company."

- **Rewarding change adopters in an equitable manner**
  Employees quickly recognize the value placed on change when it is tied to pay. Incentives that go hand-in-hand with performance increase the likelihood of enhanced outcomes.

- **Creating an accountability model**
  Goals tied to performance and business objectives allow managers to check, correct and celebrate wins along the way.

- **Identifying and managing resistance**
  Performance appraisals can effectively address and offer consequences for non-compliance.

In addition to using performance appraisals to reinforce change, more than one half of participants cited using new job descriptions as an additional mechanism to reinforce change.

Consultants

Did you use an external consultant?

Of the 2011 study participants, there was a fairly even split for those who used an external consultant to support their change management program and those who did not (Figure 58).

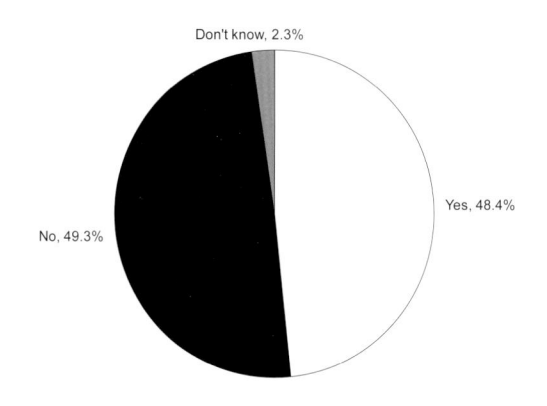

Figure 58 – Used consultant

Pie chart: Yes, 48.4%; No, 49.3%; Don't know, 2.3%

Why did you use a consultant?

Participants who used an external consultant to support their change management effort identified six reasons for hiring a consultant.

1. **Lack of internal competency or resources**
   Respondents hired a consultant based on a lack of internal change management knowledge or competency. In addition, a number of respondents cited a lack of resources and dedicated positions within their organizations.

2. **Knowledge, expertise and experience provided by consultants**
   Participants valued the knowledge, expertise and experience in change management provided by consultants.

3. **Support for the change management team or project team**
   Consultants were chosen to provide support to internal change management resources and project management teams, particularly citing duties such as daily tasks and work resulting from abnormally large changes.

4. **Proven results**
   Consultants were chosen because of a proven track record of success, outside recommendation or because the consultant had a certification in a desired change management methodology or process.

5. **Part of project proposal or contract**
   In some cases, change management consulting was a condition or element of a project plan or contracted as part of the initiative.

6. **Training to increase internal change management capacity**
   Consultants were chosen to train internal employees on change management and increase the organization's internal change management capability.

Why did you choose not to use a consultant?

Those participants who did not hire a consultant provided four reasons. By a two-to-one margin, the top reason was sufficient existing internal capability.

1. **Sufficient, existing internal capability and resources**
   The organization had existing capabilities in change management, including dedicated change management positions and certification, trained practitioners or training available for internal resources.

2. **Budgetary constraints**
   Due to limitations of project budget, an external consultant could not be hired.

3. **Need for change management was not identified or addressed on the project**
   The need for change management itself was not acknowledged, so no external support was sought.

4. **Lack of support from management**
   Senior management did not support the use of external consultants for change management activities.

Primary role played by consultants
Source date: 2009

Participants in the 2009 benchmarking study identified the top five roles played by consultants supporting change management activities as:

1. **Training provider**
   More than any other role, consultants were hired to provide change management training and impart their own change management expertise. They were asked to educate employees, management and executives on topics such as change management methodology, change strategy, resistance management and changing an organization's "state of mind."

2. **Change management lead**
   The second most common role consultants were asked to fill was that of change management lead. They were asked to create the change management plan(s) and take responsibility for any and all change management activities.

3. **Mentor and coach**
   A number of consultants were asked to fill the role of a mentor or coach. Responses implied a close connection with the people involved with the change. During planning and execution, the consultants were expected to provide support and feedback, often at what seemed to be a more emotional level, such as being a "cheerleader" or "keeping fire under their toes." Other aspects of these consultants' roles were sponsor alignment and coaching and addressing human resources-type issues, like mediation and conflict resolution.

4. **Advisor to the change management team**
   A number of consultants acted as advisors during change initiatives. Study participants relied on these consultants to apply readiness and present-state assessments as well as long term assessments and recommendations during the course of an initiative. A few scheduled only weekly visits with an organization. Although less connected to the people involved in the change initiative, these consultants were aware of what was going on and knowledgeable in change management and its processes.

5. **Resource for communications regarding the change and change management**
   Consultants were relied on for creating and disseminating communications regarding a change initiative. It was noted that they assisted with the communication between executives, managers and employees alike.

Criteria for choosing a change management consultant
Source date: 2009

Participants in the 2009 study identified the primary criteria used for selecting the change management consultant they hired. The top four responses were:

- **Consulting company's qualifications**
  These included both tangible and intangible qualities. Participants looked at the company's longevity, experience and references. However, intangible qualities also came into play. These included a consulting firm's ability to work as part of a team in the existing company culture, their interpersonal skills, work ethic and being judged a "good fit" for the organization.

- **Project management skills and knowledge, or experience in subject area**
  Some organizations placed priority on a consulting firm's experience with similar projects or technical expertise in the area of the change. Often, consultants were already involved in the technical side of the change or the project management aspect of the change, so they were asked to follow through with the people side of the change.

- **Change management expertise and use of a certain methodology**
  Many organizations gave weight to a consulting company's expertise in change management and its use of a proven change management methodology. One participant commented, *"I was told by my client that she didn't know what she wanted or needed but when I began to talk about change management processes and ideas in the interview, she knew that was it!"*

- **Existing relationship**
  Some change leaders did not have to select a consulting company. Their organizations already had an established relationship, or even a contract, with a consultant. If they were happy with the consultant's past performance, they were content to retain that firm for change management support.

Consultants used

The list below includes consultants referenced by participants in the 2011 and 2009 benchmarking studies. Those mentioned by more than one participant are indicated with an asterisk (*).

- 2.5 consulting
- 3rd i Consulting
- A.C.T. Advanced Consulting & Training *
- Abreon
- Acache
- Accelare
- Accenture *
- Accomplish Business Solutions Pty Ltd
- Accretive Solutions
- Acquiro
- Adams-Gabbert and Associates, LLC
- Adaptive Management Consultants
- African Synergies
- Agility Factor Inc.
- Alex Apouchtine
- Al-Musaned
- Altran
- Anson Consulting
- APlus Transition *
- Archstone
- ARGOS Consulting Group *
- Artis Rei
- Astral Consulting
- AT Kearney *
- Atos-Origin *
- Axis People Management
- Axon *
- Baglietto and Partners
- Bain
- Barclays
- Bartecko Consulting Ltd.
- Bartholomew Corporate Solutions
- BDM Directions
- Bearing Point *
- Being Human *
- BES consultants
- Bevington Group *
- Beyond Philosophy
- BlessingWhite
- Blue Heron Consulting *
- Blue Seed Consulting
- BMA GRUPO ALIANZA
- Booz Allen Hamilton *
- Boston Consulting Group *
- BPI Poland
- Breeze Consulting
- BRIDGES, Inc.
- Brighton Leadership Group
- Business Solutions - The Positive Way
- Cal y Mayor y Asociados
- California Manufacturing Technology Consulting
- Canadian Management Centre
- Cap Gemini *
- Capacity Development Africa
- Capita
- CARA
- Carbon Group *
- Carla Carter & Associates Inc *
- Carus Consulting Group
- CCHPO
- Cegedim
- Cegos
- Centna Consulting Limited
- Cepeda Systems & Software Analysis, Inc
- CGI *
- Chameleon Adventure Academy
- Chan
- Change Consultoria
- Change Elements
- Change Factory

- Change Guides LLC *
- Change Logic
- Change Success
- Change Worx
- Changemethod
- Changeworks Consulting
- Changewright Consulting *
- Chaucer Consulting
- Chebais Consulting
- CIBER *
- Clarkston Consulting
- CMTC
- Collective Next
- COMED IT
- Competitive Capabilities International
- Comunicación y Cambio S.A.S. (Medellín - Colombia)
- Conner Partners*
- Courtyard Group
- Croken Enterprises
- Crystalmount Solutions Inc. *
- CSC *
- Cue 7 Consortium
- David White
- Dawit Giorgis/African Crisis team
- DDI
- De Adviespraktijk *
- Delegata
- Deloitte *
- Delta Health
- Destin
- Development Strategies Plus
- Diversified Consulting (South Africa)
- DOXA Cambios Inteligentes
- Dreamhouse Consulting, LLC
- DSD Laboratories, Inc
- Eclipsys
- Edelman
- Edmondson Consulting
- EduServe
- Emerson Human Capital *
- Enaxis Consulting LP
- Enmasse services
- Enterprise Transformation Group Ltd.
- EQE Bulgaria AD
- Ermelbauer Consulting Ltd
- Ernest and Young *
- Ernst & Young *
- ETGL - Denver, Colorado
- Ethier Associates *
- Ethiopian Management Institute *
- Euro-praxis
- Evans and Peck
- evolve! People and Process Management
- Expressworks
- Fever Tree
- FINEST BUSSINES CONSULTING
- Firestone International Associates, Inc
- FMA Process Engineering
- Focusphera Consulting
- Francine Durivage
- Frank McGrath Change Management Ltd
- Freehills
- Fujitsu *
- GAR Organizational Solutions
- GEP Business Solutions
- German Agency for International development - GIZ
- GFIA
- GSS Holdings
- Halkjær Human Univerz
- Harriss Wagner Management Consultants *
- Hay Group
- HCL-Axon *
- Hewitt
- Highveld PFS
- Hitachi Consulting *
- HO team
- Holland & Davis (now Endeavor)
- Hong Kong Productivity Council
- HP *
- Humadyn
- iB4e
- IBM *
- IHI
- implementation dynamics
- Implementation Services
- Incahoots Consultancy
- Indra
- Infosys Consulting *
- Ink Business Development Services Ltd.
- Innovapost
- Insightrix
- Integral Insights
- Interlinks consult
- Investor IQ
- IUTUM
- Jalellpea Television
- John Dorris
- John Mant

- Keane Inc
- Kenya Water Institute
- Kirsten Sandberg
- KMAC
- Knowhouse consulting
- KPMG
- KPMG *
- Krauthammer International
- Kuziva Huni (Independent Consultant)
- La Société conseil Lambda *
- LaMarsh and Associates *
- Lambda
- Langford and Oliver Consulting
- Leadership Education And Development
- LECG
- Leftfield Consulting
- LeftField Project Solutions
- Leonardo Schvarstein
- Lifeline Education Resource Development Centre
- Lighthouse Institute
- Linium
- LM Dulye and Co
- Logica *
- Mac Consulting
- Make Change Positive
- Management Effect
- MAP Consulting
- MARSH Risk Consulting
- McDougall Smith
- McKinsey *
- Mdb Consulting
- Mercer
- Meridian Consulting
- MindPeace Consulting
- MNP
- Modal
- Momentum Inc
- MRC Group in Poland
- NCS Pte Ltd *
- Necron Benchmarking Consultants
- Nelson Consulting Group *
- Neoris
- next level consulting
- North Highland *
- northern exposure
- NouvEON
- Oakton *
- Onirik
- Online Business Systems Inc. *
- Oracle
- P2
- Paradigma Consultores Asociados *
- PCGI Consulting Inc.
- Pearce Delport
- People and Process Management
- People First
- PEOPLE ISSUES LIMITED
- PeopleFirm, LLC *
- PeopleNRG *
- PeopleSense
- Performance Path
- Performance republic international
- Perot Systems
- Point B
- POLITEC
- Possibility to Reality
- PriceWaterHouseCoopers *
- proacteur *
- ProFitness Advisors
- Progressor Consulting
- Project SI
- Projector Communications
- Protegra Consulting Group
- PSTG
- Pulse Development Services
- Purple Apple
- Qedis Consulting
- QMS
- QMSI
- Quatum West
- Ramse Consulting *
- REI Solutions
- Resources Global Professionals *
- Results Consulting
- Revere Froup
- Rhythm Consulting Inc.
- Robert Ayling Incorporated
- rSet
- Ruth McKenzie - independent consultant
- RWD Technologies *
- S1 Consulting
- SAIC *
- SAJE Consulting *
- Salalah College of Technology
- SAP
- Satreno Change Management
- Satyam Computer Systems *
- See Results, Inc.
- Sep Serfontein Consulting

- Serco Consulting
- Shape Consulting
- SHL Group
- SHMA
- Siemens
- SINFIC
- Sirius Solutions LLP
- Slalom Consulting
- SMS Consulting
- SMS M&T *
- Software and Systems Institute *
- Soltius Indonesia
- Solution Dynamics
- Solvera Solutions
- Son Systems
- SPIGIT
- Starfish Consulting
- Stegmeier Consulting Group
- Successworks
- Sunrise Acute Care
- Suntiva
- Superior Directions
- TASC Management Consulting *
- Tata Consulting Services
- TC LLP
- TCS
- TechProse
- The 5 Forces of Change
- The Carey Group
- The Centre for Personnel Transformation
- The Change Experience
- The Hackett Group
- The Litmus Group
- The Revere Group *
- The Synthetic Family
- The Taligens Group *
- The Urwick Group
- Thiago Lelis ME
- TMA
- Totem Consulting
- Towers Perrin
- Towers Watson
- Trexia
- UCS Solutions
- Ultima Consulting Firm
- Umtha Management Services Pty Ltd
- University of Tennessee Center for Industrial Services
- VeriScope, Inc.
- Vicky Coates and Associates
- WDScott
- West Monroe Partners
- Western Management Consultants *
- Wilson Learning *
- Wipro

Training on change management

The 2011 benchmarking study included a new section about training specifically on change management. Data was collected for five groups:

1. Change management resources
2. Project teams
3. Impacted executives and senior leaders
4. Impacted managers and supervisors
5. Impacted employees

For each group, participants indicated whether or not formal training on change management was provided (Figure 59).

	Actual (days)	Recommended (days)
Change management resources	3.73	5.06
Project teams	2.41	3.44
Executives and senior leaders	1.22	2.13
Managers and supervisors	2.04	2.95
Impacted employees	1.70	2.52

Table 8 – Average days of change management training

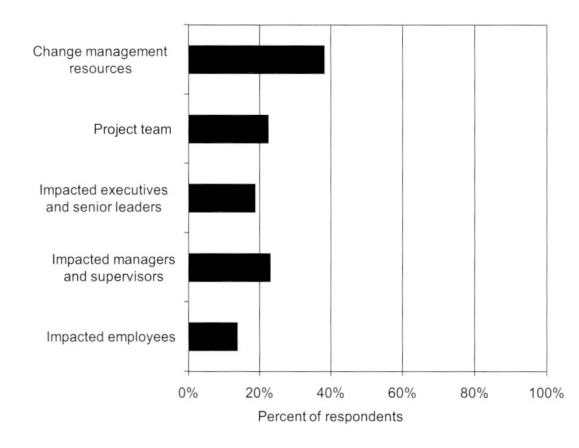

Figure 59 – Provision of training on change management

Change management resource training

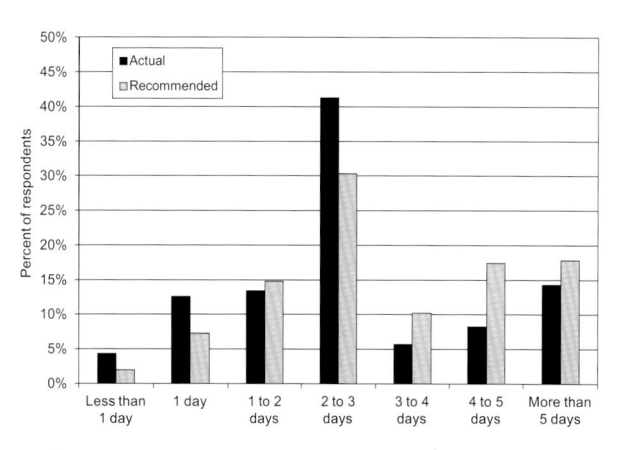

Figure 60 – Days of training for change management resources

Length of training

Participants shared the number of days of change management training provided for each of the five groups and the number of days they would recommend for each group. Table 8 contains averages for the actual number of days of change management training provided and the recommended number of days of change management training for each of the groups.

Participants were asked to identify the key learning objectives or topics for change management training for change management resources. The top four responses were:

1. Change management methodologies and processes
2. An overview of the basics of change management
3. Change management tools
4. Communication plans and skills

Project team training

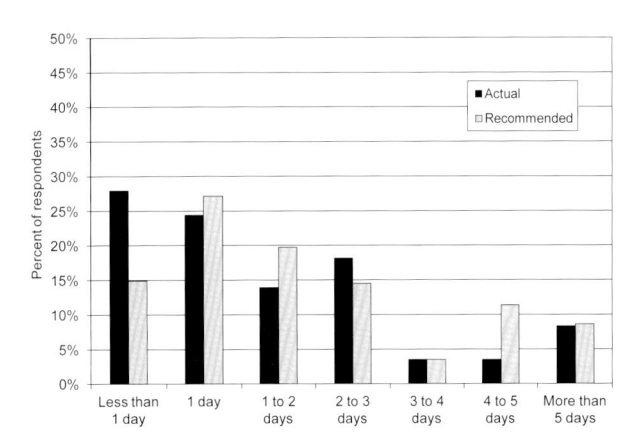

Figure 61 – Days of training for project team members

Participants were asked to identify the key learning objectives or topics for change management training for project team members. The top five responses were:

1. Awareness of the need for change management
2. Change management processes and methodologies
3. Roles in change management
4. The individual change experience
5. Support tools

Executive and senior leader training

Participants were asked to identify the key learning objectives or topics for change management training for executives and senior leaders. The top two responses were:

1. The roles and responsibilities of the sponsor during the project were cited more than twice as often as the next key training topic. The critical nature of their role was cited specifically.
2. A greater understanding of the change management methodology selected.

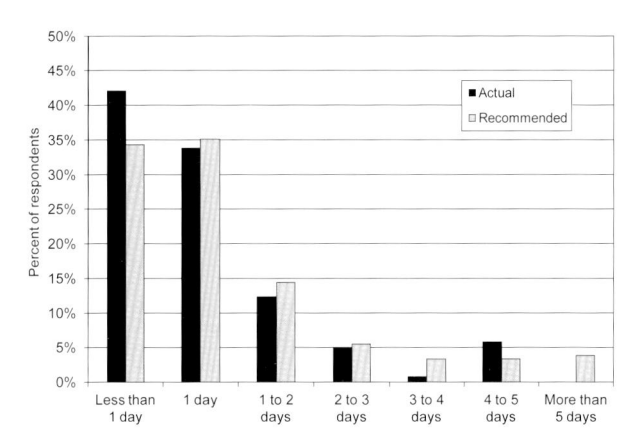

Figure 62 – Days of training for executives and senior leaders

Manager and supervisor training

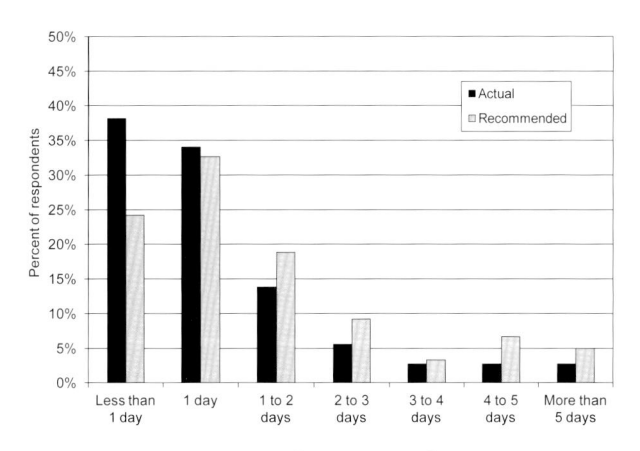

Figure 63 – Days of training for managers and supervisors

Participants were asked to identify the key learning objectives or topics for change management training for managers and supervisors. The top five responses were:

1. Leading and managing change
2. Roles in change management
3. Awareness of the need for change management
4. The change experience for individuals
5. Methodology and process

Employee training

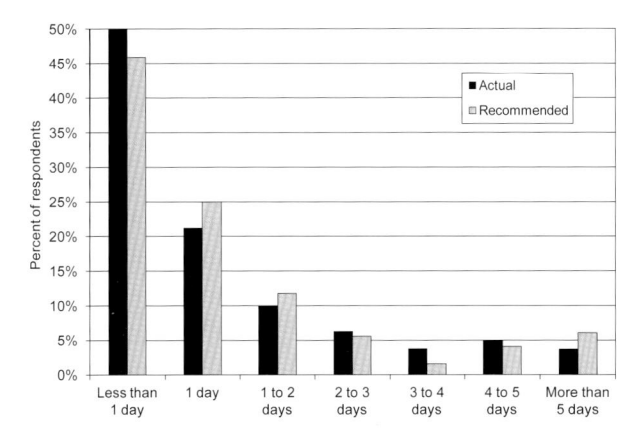

Figure 64 – Days of training for impacted employees

Participants were asked to identify the key learning objectives or topics for change management training for impacted employees. The top five responses were:

1. How individuals move through change
2. What change management is
3. Specifics on how to operate in the new environment
4. Roles in change management
5. Why the change is happening

Change management capability and competency

Prosci Change Management Maturity Model

Figure 65 shows how 2011 study participants rated their organizations (or for consultants, their client organizations) on the Prosci Change Management Maturity Model (see Appendix C for a full description). The levels of the Prosci Change Management Maturity Model describe the overall deployment and maturity of change management within an organization:

- Level 5: Organizational competency
- Level 4: Organizational standards
- Level 3: Multiple projects
- Level 2: Isolated projects
- Level 1: Absent or ad hoc

The percentage of participants in Level 1 (absent or ad hoc) or Level 2 (isolated projects) increased slightly in the 2011 study from 53% in 2007 to 58% in 2009 to 62% in 2011.

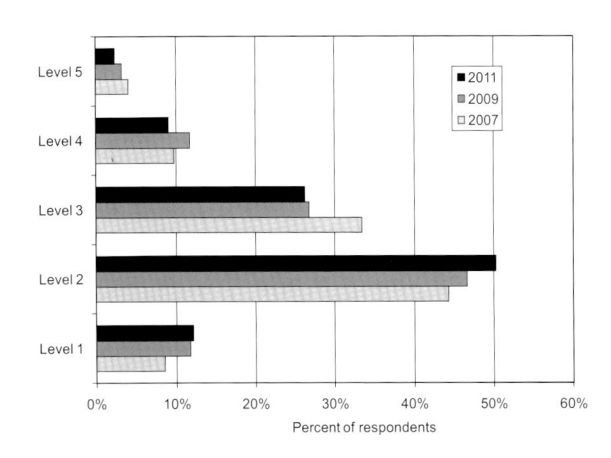

Figure 65 – Prosci Change Management Maturity Model

Data segmentation by region

The Prosci Change Management Maturity Model data provided by participants in the 2011 study was further segmented by region. Table 9 below shows the averages and standard deviations for each level in the Prosci Change Management Maturity Model, along with the percent of study participants represented by that region.

Region (percent of study participants from that region)	Average Maturity Model level	Standard deviation
All regions (100%)	2.39	0.90
United States (37.9%)	2.41	0.86
Australia and New Zealand (21.1%)	2.16	0.82
Canada (13.2%)	2.43	0.90
Europe (12.1%)	2.47	0.82
Africa (6.5%)	2.56	1.18
Asia and Pacific Islands (5.0%)	2.78	1.04
Latin America (3.1%)	2.10	0.85
Middle East (1.1%)	2.57	0.98

Table 9 – Maturity Model results by region

Editor's note: The distributions should not be interpreted as fully representative of change management maturity in each region, given that in regions with fewer respondents, data would more likely be provided by organizations with higher maturity and interest in change management than by other organizations in that region that did not participate in the 2011 benchmarking study.

The graphs that follow (Figures 66 – 73) show the distribution of Level 1, Level 2, Level 3, Level 4 and Level 5 for each region (order of regions based on largest representation in the study to smallest representation in the study).

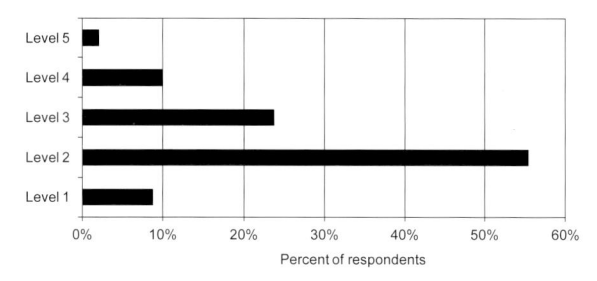

Figure 66 – Maturity Model data for the United States

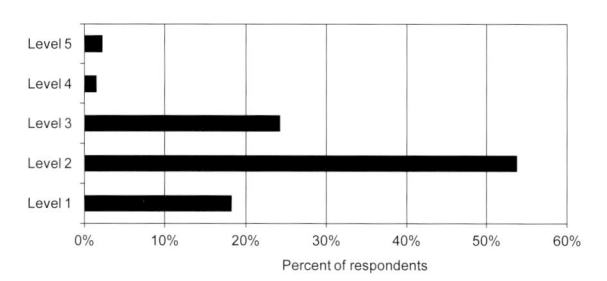

Figure 67 – Maturity Model data for Australia and New Zealand

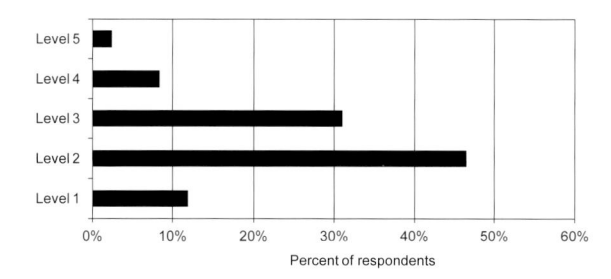

Figure 68 – Maturity Model data for Canada

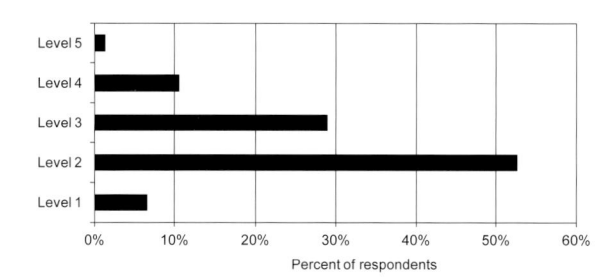

Figure 69 – Maturity Model data for Europe

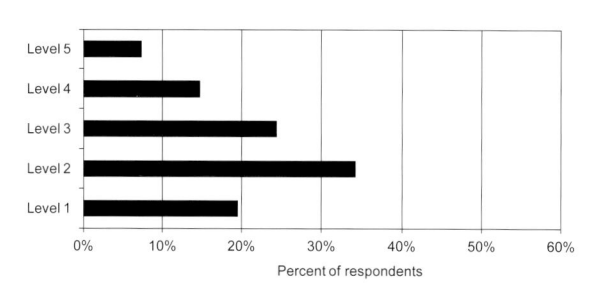

Figure 70 – Maturity Model data for Africa

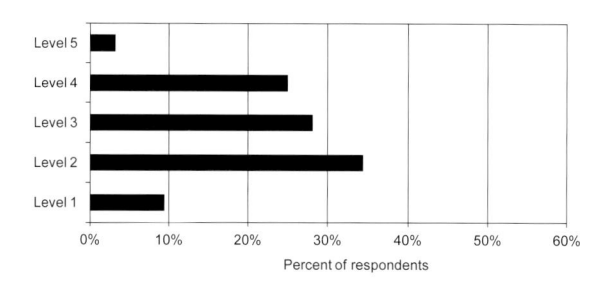

Figure 71 – Maturity Model data for Asia and Pacific Islands

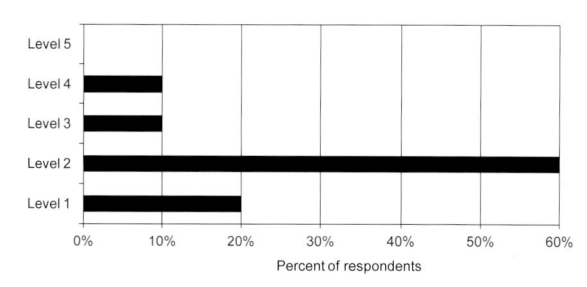

Figure 72 – Maturity Model data for Latin America

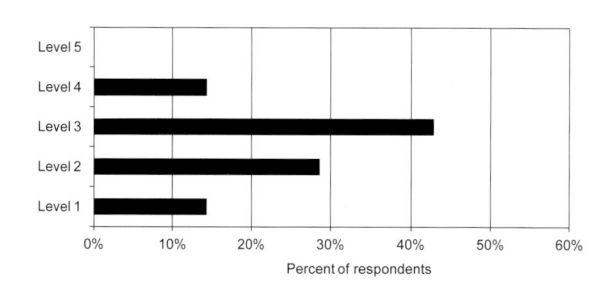

Figure 73 – Maturity Model data for Middle East

Data segmentation by industry

The table below shows the Prosci Change Management Maturity Model data for those industries representing more than 2% of total study participants. The table includes the average Prosci Change Management Maturity Model level and the standard deviation for each industry. The industries are ordered based on largest representation in the study to smallest representation in the study.

Industry (percentage of study participants from that industry)	Average Maturity Model level	Standard deviation
All industries (100%)	2.39	0.90
Finance/Banking (12.5%)	2.43	0.91
Government – State or Local (9.0%)	2.25	0.83
Health Care (8.0%)	2.10	0.70
Utilities (6.1%)	2.38	0.78
Insurance (5.0%)	2.63	0.94
Government – Civilian (4.4%)	2.11	0.79
Oil and Gas (4.2%)	2.52	0.89
Education (3.9%)	2.48	1.05
Telecommunications (3.6%)	2.65	0.93
Pharmaceutical (3.3%)	2.70	0.92
Food/Beverage (3.1%)	2.60	0.94
Information Systems (2.8%)	2.17	0.71
Consulting (2.7%)	2.65	1.17
Development and Manufacturing (2.5%)	2.38	0.72
Retail (2.5%)	2.31	0.95
Consumer Goods (2.3%)	2.29	0.99
Government – Defense (2.3%)	2.27	1.03
Aerospace (2.2%)	2.38	1.26
Service Industry (2.2%)	2.29	0.83
Mining (2.0%)	2.50	0.52

Table 10 – Maturity Model results by industry

Actively working to deploy change management

Just under half of study participants (46%) were actively working to deploy change management throughout their organizations (Figure 74).

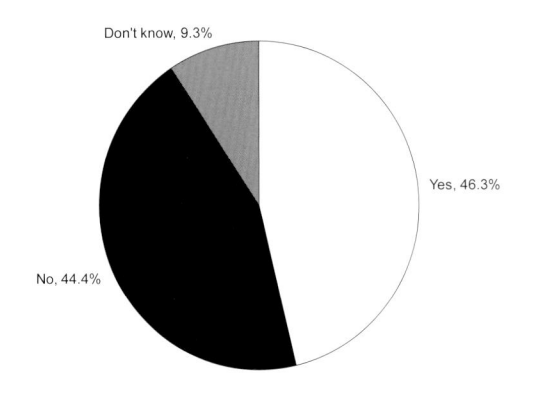

Figure 74 – Actively working to deploy change management

Those organizations that were actively working to deploy change management scored higher in the Prosci Change Management Maturity Model (Table 11). 48% of organizations working to actively deploy change management rated their organization as a Level 5, Level 4 or Level 3 in the Change Management Maturity Model, compared to 27% of those not actively working to deploy change management. Only 4% of those actively working to deploy change management rated their organization as a Level 1, compared to nearly one fifth of organizations not actively working to deploy change management.

Prosci Change Management Maturity Model Level	Actively working to deploy	Not actively working to deploy
Level 5	3.7%	1.4%
Level 4	11.6%	6.7%
Level 3	33.0%	18.8%
Level 2	47.6%	53.2%
Level 1	4.1%	19.9%
Total	100%	100%

Table 11 – Maturity Model ranking for those actively working to deploy

Data on organizations actively working to deploy change management was further segmented by region, industry and organization size. Figures 75, 76 and 77 below show the percentage of respondents who were actively working to deploy change management for these segments. The grey bar in each graph represents the entire study population average of 46%.

Canada, Africa, and Australia and New Zealand had a higher percentage of participants working to actively deploy change management than the overall study population. The regions of Latin America and Asia and the Pacific Islands had significantly lower percentages of participants working to actively deploy than the overall study population (Figure 75).

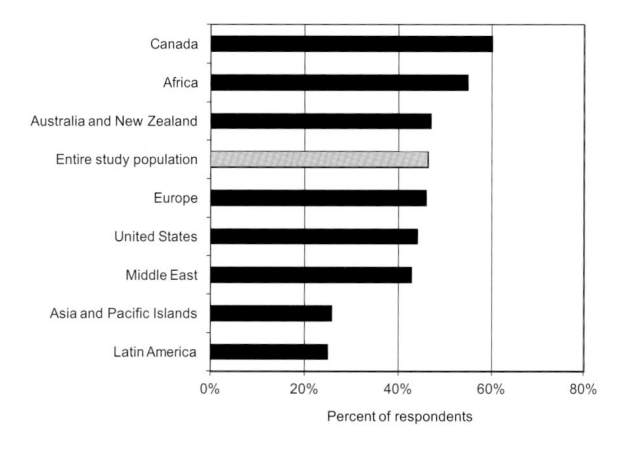

Figure 75 – Participants actively working to deploy by region

In terms of industry, respondents from Development and Manufacturing, Food/Beverage, Telecommunications, Finance/Banking and Insurance all reported higher levels of active deployment of change management than the overall study population (Figure 76).

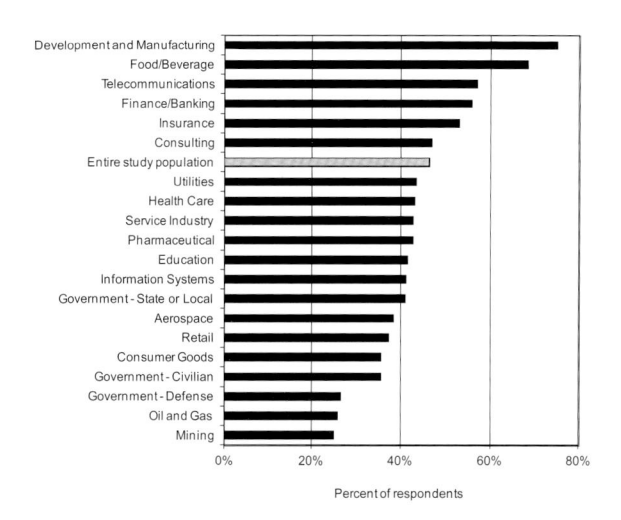

Figure 76 – Participants actively working to deploy by industry

Relative to organization size based on annual revenue, the most active organizations deploying change management were in the $10M to $25M range and over $1B. The least active organizations by size were $251M to $500M, less than $10M, and $501M to $1B (Figure 77).

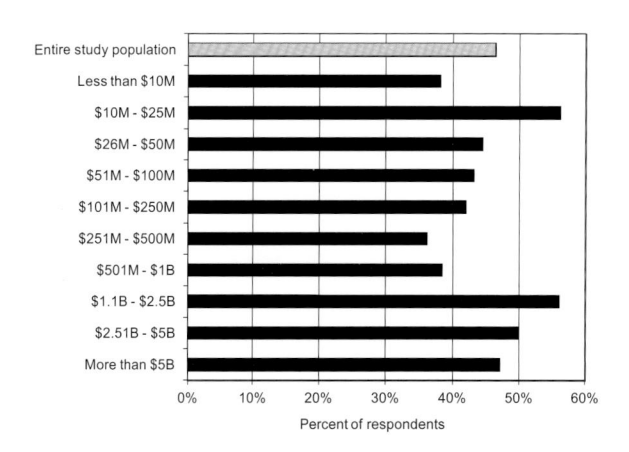

Figure 77 – Participants actively working to deploy by organization size

Editor's note: The distributions should not be interpreted as fully representative of change management deployment activity in each region, industry or organization size. For example, in regions with lower representation, data would more likely be provided by organizations with higher interest and activity in change management than by other organizations in that region that did not participate in the 2011 benchmarking study.

Length of effort

Of those working to deploy change management, 55% were within the first year of their deployment with 23% just beginning the effort. 14% of participants were over three years into their deployment efforts (Figure 78).

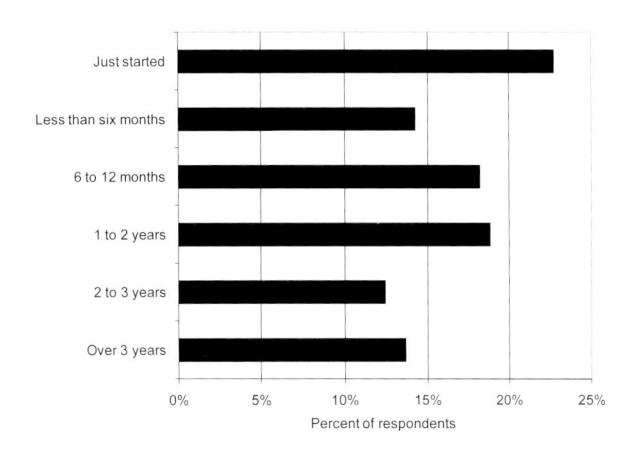

Figure 78 – How long has deployment been underway?

Originator of the effort

The Human Resources (HR) or Organization Development (OD) group was identified by over one quarter of participants as the originator of the effort to build organizational change management capability and competency, making it the most frequent source. The other top originators were: Executives/Leadership, Information Technology (IT), and the Project Management Office (PMO) or Project Delivery group (Figure 79).

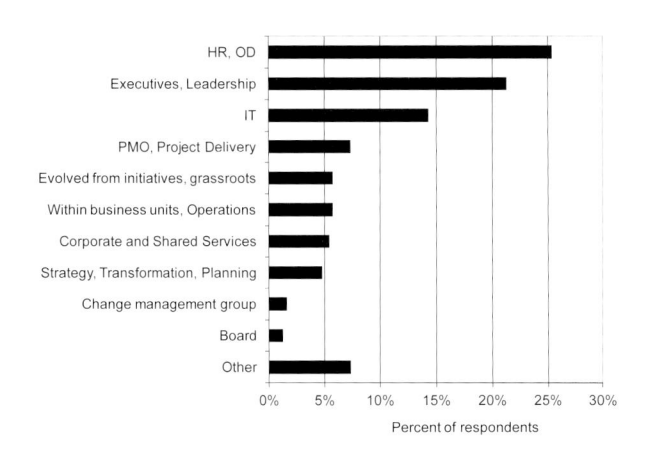

Figure 79 – Originator of the effort

Steps taken to deploy change management

Participants who were working to deploy change management throughout their organizations identified the specific steps they had taken in their deployment effort. The ten most frequently cited steps for change management deployment were:

1. **Provide change management training**
   Provide change management education and training to all levels in the organization. Train change agents and change management practitioners. Train managers and supervisors on their role as change leaders. Train executives on their role as sponsors and include change management in leadership development curricula. Train project managers and educate them on change management through briefings. Incorporate change management education into existing training programs where possible.

2. **Provide a common model**
   Provide a common and standard model for change management. Conduct due diligence and an informed search to identify an appropriate methodology. Select a methodology for wide-scale adoption or develop an approach in-house through documentation of methods and tools already in use. Create a common set of tools, templates and deliverables and make them

accessible and available. Create an intranet site or resource center for accessing change management tools. Continuously improve the change management process, adapting and adjusting the approach to more wide-scale use. Share best practices between practitioners.

3. **Work on projects**
   Search out and identify projects where the change management approach can be applied. Provide change management services and support on these projects. Assign change management resources to projects and ensure resources are available. Work to identify visible and key projects that can be referenced during the deployment effort.

4. **Treat change management deployment as a project**
   Create a deployment plan for rolling out change management, viewing the deployment as a project that can be managed. Create a vision and mission for the effort and clearly articulate it throughout the effort. Create a business case for change management deployment. Assign a leader and form a team to manage the deployment, preferably cross-functional with representation from various levels and units or functional groups. Monitor the change management deployment effort. Track progress and work being done. Capture and report issues as they emerge.

5. **Ensure sufficient sponsorship**
   Locate and engage an executive sponsor to drive the change management deployment effort. Build a coalition of support and actively recruit senior leadership support in various parts of the organization. Present the need for change management to management teams, including recommendations and requests for support. Encourage senior leaders to set the expectation that all projects utilize change management.

6. **Create functional group and staff positions**
   Create a Change Management Office, change management functional group or change management unit in the organization. Create and fund dedicated change management positions. Create job descriptions and roles for change management practitioners. Create a lead team of subject matter experts that can act as an advisory group for other change management practitioners in the organization. Build a pool of trained or certified change management practitioners that can be assigned to projects.

7. **Build buy-in for change management**
   Build awareness of the need for change management and buy-in to support change management by showing the value and importance. Connect change management to project, initiative and organizational success. Show the risk of not applying change management. Create a common and shared definition for change management throughout the organization.

8. **Integrate change management into project delivery processes**
   Embed change management into project delivery approaches and project management methodologies. Integrate project and change management activities and deliverables. Include change management considerations in governance processes and mechanisms already used in the organization. Tie change management into the business case process. Embed change management into the strategic planning process.

9. **Create change management networks**
   Create a network of change agents throughout the organization; the networks can be both formal and informal. Change agents should be created throughout various sites and business units or functional groups. Additional network options include: a user group, a Community of Practice or a Center of Excellence. Encourage periodic meetings of change agents.

10. **Communicate about the deployment effort and successes**
    Communicate about change management and the model being introduced as the organizational standard. Communication vehicles include: presentations, town hall meetings, emails, brown bag lunches, etc. Publicize the change management work done on projects and the outcomes. Share success stories and the role change management

played in enabling successful change. Show the value of change management in real terms. Create case studies capturing successes and impacts.

Activities with biggest impact

Participants identified four primary activities with the greatest impact on the change management deployment effort:

1. **Leadership commitment**
   Senior leaders actively demonstrated their commitment to change management. These leaders understood the importance of change management to the organization's success. They spoke about change management to others, including other senior leaders. They engaged in the effort to deploy change management and set expectations.

2. **Demonstrated success**
   Showing the impact of effective change management through application on real projects and documenting the results had an impact on the deployment effort. Proof of success improved the reputation, credibility and visibility of change management. Example projects where change management was applied were used as references and often resulted in additional advocates outside of the core change management team.

3. **Involvement on projects**
   Application of change management on particular projects built momentum for the change management deployment effort. Supporting specific initiatives gave change management practitioners the opportunity to engage project leaders and allowed them to experience change management in action. Other suggestions for increasing involvement on projects included embedding change management in the project delivery process, placing change management resources on projects and persistently applying change management processes and tools when possible.

4. **Training**
   A number of participants commented on the contribution of training to the deployment effort. This training was often endorsed or made mandatory for key resources. The regularity and availability of training was viewed as critical.

Additional activities referenced included:

- **Communications**
  Participants identified creating awareness about the importance of change management, making a compelling case for the need for change management and sharing details about the deployment effort and its intended outcomes.

- **Common and standard methodology and toolset**
  Participants identified having a common, shared and standard methodology and toolset as having an impact on deployment efforts.

- **Managing the deployment effort as a project**
  Participants identified treating the deployment effort as a project as a key contributor to successful efforts, including planning the change management deployment effort, using change management on the effort (i.e. change management takes change management), securing dedicated resources and funding and building a strong change management team.

Most important activities at launch

Participants identified those activities they felt were most important at the launch of the effort. The most important activities at the launch of the change management deployment effort, in rank order, were:

- **Sponsorship support**
  Senior leaders needed to communicate their support of change management both verbally and in action. In some cases this included a mandate to use change management on projects.

- **Communicating about the effort**
  Constant and consistent communications

about change management and the effort to deploy change management more broadly was the second most important activity. Face-to-face communications, including briefings and road shows, were mentioned specifically.

- **Creating clear expectations and vision**
  Clearly share the vision, purpose, expectations and objectives of the change management deployment effort. This included positioning the effort as a "business necessity" and building buy-in, trust, credibility and relevance.

- **Delivering training**
  Provide training on change management that is targeted and provides for immediate application. In some cases this training also served as an introduction to change management.

- **Providing a framework or methodology**
  Have a framework in place with usable tools. Participants also commented on the importance of having a common methodology.

- **Encouraging involvement**
  It was important to encourage involvement with project managers and leaders at the launch of the change management deployment effort to build buy-in, engagement and ownership.

- **Applying change management to projects**
  Getting involved and providing support on particular projects was important at the launch of the effort. This included assignment of resources, use of processes and tools, and being available and open to discuss change management impacts on projects.

- **Staffing change management**
  A number of participants commented on the importance of having change management resources available, including dedicated resources and trained practitioners with experience and expertise.

- **Managing the deployment project**
  Managing the effort as a project, including effective planning, was viewed as important during the launch of the change management deployment effort.

- **Demonstrating results**
  Make the case for change management through highlighting successes and the financial impacts.

Change Management Office or functional group

Just over one third of participants (36%) indicated having a Change Management Office or functional group (Figure 80). The group was most commonly named with:

- A title using the words "Change Management" including Change Management, Change Management Office, Change Management Department, Change Management Team, Enterprise Change Management, Organizational Change Management

- A title using the word "Change" including Business Change, Change Team, Change Group, Change Unit or Change Leadership

- A title using one of the following words related to change: Transition, Improvement, Transformation, Performance or Strategy

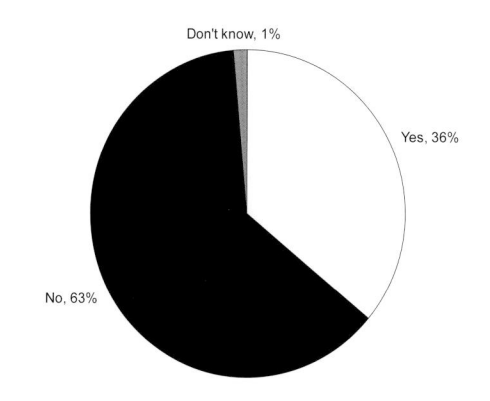

Figure 80 – Have Change Management Office or functional group

Location of functional group

Participants with a functional group dedicated to change management provided data on where the group resided within the organization (Figure 81). The top two responses were:

- Human Resources (HR) and Organization Development (OD)
- Information Technology (IT)

These results paralleled findings in the previous studies.

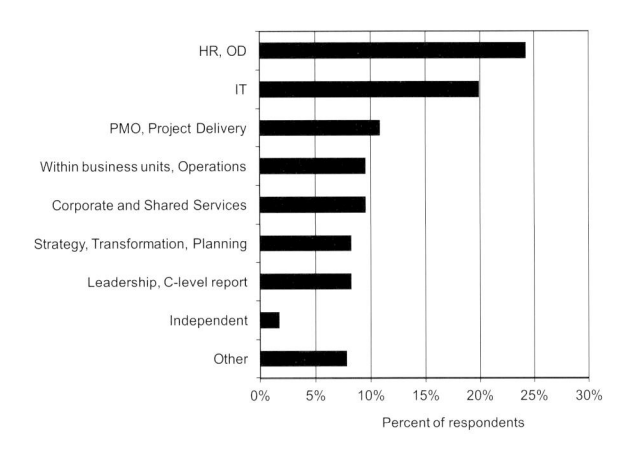

Figure 81 – Location of Change Management Office or functional group

Size of functional group

Participants with a functional group dedicated to change management indicated the number of employees in the group (Figure 82). Half of study participants indicated a functional group of five or fewer employees. The most frequent response was two employees, indicated by 13% of those providing data.

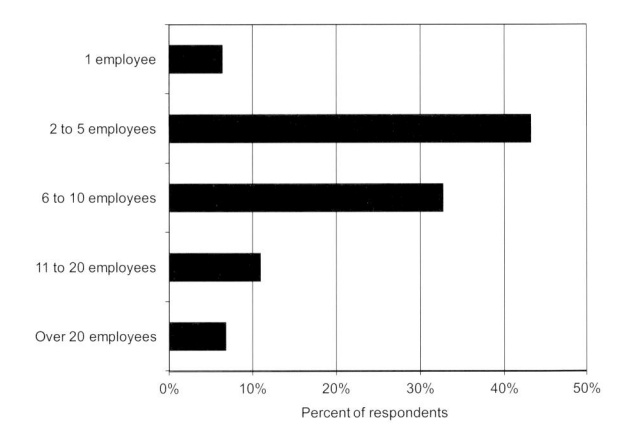

Figure 82 – Number of employees in the functional group

Advantages of particular locations

Source date: 2009

Participants in the 2009 benchmarking study provided data on their preference for location and the reasons why. Below are findings from the 2009 study on the advantages of having the Change Management Office residing in:

- Project Management Office
- Human Resources
- Independent
- Reporting to the highest level
- Cross-functional model
- Strategy or planning group
- Organization Development

Participants offered up a number of reasons why the **Project Management Office** was the best place for change management. The most commonly cited reasons included:

1. Alignment with and visibility into a majority of the change efforts underway
2. Change management could be easily integrated into the project activities and the project methodology
3. The group was already familiar with using methodologies and processes in relation to change efforts

4. The PMO had clout, credibility and influence in the organization
5. Change management could be more easily engaged early in the project life cycle
6. The PMO offered some independence from the operational issues that may divert focus from the given change

The second most frequently cited location for change management was in **Human Resources** for the following reasons:

1. HR and change management both focus on the people side of the organization
2. Typically, HR touched the entire enterprise and reached across multiple divisions or business units
3. Other activities and knowledge that closely aligned with change management resided in HR, including Organization Development, training and communications
4. Staff were more easily influenced by HR
5. HR already had a good "pulse" of the workforce

The third most frequently cited location for change management was an **independent office or group**, sometimes referred to as the Change Management Office. Participants cited the following benefits:

1. No biases to particular changes, departments or divisions
2. Effort on change management was focused
3. Executive buy-in and commitment was demonstrated by having an independent office
4. More easily took an enterprise view of the changes underway
5. Enabled application to both project and non-project changes

Many participants who indicated an independent office did comment on the importance of staying connected with other groups working on change, including HR, the PMO and the IT organization.

Number four on the list was a change management group reporting directly to the **highest level** in the organization. The reasons for this location included:

1. Visible sponsorship and commitment to change management
2. Built-in access to sponsors on key initiatives
3. Not being "bogged down" by operational issues and departmental resistance
4. Ability to connect to strategy

Some participants suggested a **cross-functional model** or multiple owners. They commented on the importance of a network dedicated to change management throughout the organization. Typically, the owners included some combination of HR, PMO, OD and IT.

Participants who indicated a **strategy or planning group**, such as Strategic Planning or Corporate Strategy, felt that this location provided the change management group with the best access to the most important projects in the organization. This group also typically reported to a very senior manager.

The participants that indicated **Organization Development (OD)** said that this group had broad visibility across much of the organization and had credibility and history working with large scale changes.

"Other" responses included:

- Internal consulting group
- Information Technology (IT)
- Centralized core team with representation in the business
- Operations
- Groups dedicated to performance improvement
- Training or Leadership Development

Success of deployment efforts

Participants who were working to deploy change management evaluated their overall level of success at deployment (Figure 83).

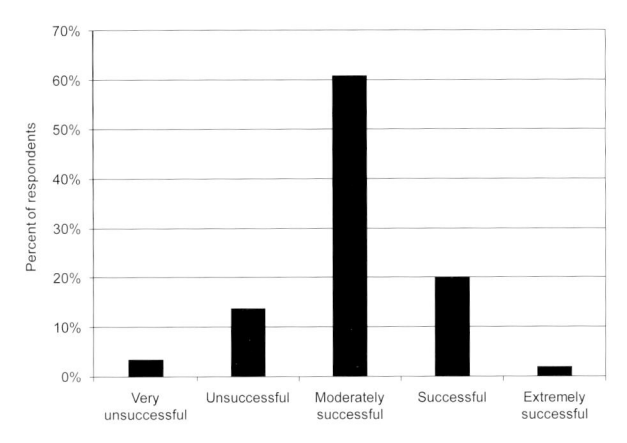

Figure 83 – Success of deployment effort

Contributors to successful deployments

The greatest contributors to deployment success identified by study participants who classified their deployment as successful or extremely successful were:

1. **Sponsorship and leadership commitment**
   Participants noted a strong sponsor presence, executive support for the effort and senior leadership support of change management. In addition, a clear vision created by senior leaders contributed to the effort.

2. **Proof of success**
   Many participants highlighted the impact of showing the value of change management on deployment success. Documenting and sharing proven successes on key projects, measuring the impact on project results and clearly calling out the impacts of applying change management in specific instances all contributed to successful deployments.

3. **Implementation approach that included collaboration**
   A number of participants identified having a clear implementation plan, which included coordinating and collaborating on the design approach with various parts of the organization. A passionate and effective deployment leader and team contributed to implementation success.

4. **Clear and open communications**
   Communications included information on change management and on the effort to deploy change management.

5. **Engagement of project teams**
   Integrating or embedding change management activities with the work of project teams contributed to success and gave project leaders and team members the ability to learn though application.

Obstacles to deployment

Participants who considered their deployment moderately successful, unsuccessful or very unsuccessful shared the greatest obstacles they faced. The top three obstacles were:

- **Lack of understanding of and buy-in for change management**
  Change management was not well understood or valued in the organization. Change management was perceived as: simply "good management," nice to have but unnecessary, irrelevant or extraneous work. Employees throughout the organization did not see the value of change management and were not committed to applying change management, particularly project managers.

- **Poorly resourced and executed deployment effort**
  The deployment effort either had no dedicated resources or had too few resources, and insufficient time was committed to the effort. A failure to treat the deployment as a project also contributed. The deployment work failed to arrive at an organizational standard or consistent approach.

- **No leadership commitment or consistent sponsorship**
  Leadership was not committed to the deployment effort, and sponsorship was inconsistent or completely absent.

Additional obstacles to deployment identified were:

- Lack of application of change management – including inconsistent application, lack of resources for application, insufficient time for change management and lack of integration with project management

- Lack of expertise – including not having sufficient change management competencies and turnover of change management resources

- Conflicting priorities – the organization was too busy with other change projects and those other efforts took priority

- Lack of focus or prioritization – the change management deployment effort was not made a priority or given adequate focus

- No participation by managers and supervisors – managers and supervisors did not have the capacity to take on change management responsibilities and were not effectively engaged

Mistakes to avoid when deploying change management

Study participants commented on the mistakes they would suggest others avoid in their efforts to build change management competencies. The top six mistakes identified by participants were:

1. **Failing to treat the effort as a project**
   Participants suggested it was important to treat the effort to deploy change management like a project and a change to be managed, which included creating a plan and approach, and assigning time and resources. Do not attempt the effort without clearly defined vision, outcomes, objectives and milestones. Avoid underestimating the necessary work, effort and resources required. Use change management to support the change management deployment effort.

2. **Moving forward without sponsorship**
   Participants warned against change management deployment without appropriate sponsorship. Sponsors needed to be at the right level and active and visible in their support. An attempt without adequate sponsorship resulted in numerous challenges.

3. **Failing to build the case for change management**
   Build an understanding of what change management is and why it is important. Secure buy-in for change management and create a business case. Participants emphasized the importance of building on successes and demonstrating the impact of change management.

4. **Approaching the effort with only one aspect of the solution**
   Change management deployment could not be limited to training that lacked real life application. Training had to be applicable and meaningful. Provision of tools without appropriate training and coaching was also identified as ineffective. Additionally, change management could not be viewed as solely a Human Resources competency.

5. **Failing to provide an effective methodology**
   The deployment effort must provide repeatable processes and tools that could be utilized by employees throughout the organization; the deployment effort needed a solid methodology as its foundation. Take steps to ensure consistency of application of the methodology. Avoid forcing a methodology that does not fit the organization and is not adaptable.

6. **Making change management a separate activity**
   Change management should not be viewed as a "separate" activity. It should be positioned as "everyone's job" and embedded as a competency necessary to be successful in the organization, regardless of the role in the organization. Competency models that clarified the responsibilities and roles in change management for each different audience in the organization enabled this embedding of change management as part of everyone's job.

Additional considerations included:

- Engage the right people. The deployment effort should include representation from throughout the organization and should have the support of key influencers. A skilled lead team should champion the effort. The effort should not take place too low in the organization.

- Take small steps. Avoid "biting off more than you can chew." Participants cautioned against being overly ambitious at the beginning of the effort, instead preferring small steps to move the effort forward.

- Understand the current climate, culture and competency level. Be sure to assess, understand and tailor the approach based on the current competency levels and the culture of the organization.

Definition of change management throughout organization

Figure 84 shows the study participants' level of agreement with the statement: *Throughout my organization, there is a single, common and shared definition of change management.*

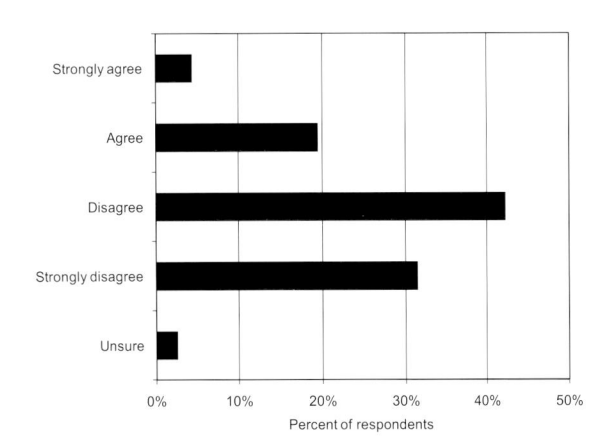

Figure 84 – Single, common, shared definition

Nearly three quarters (74%) indicated that they disagreed or strongly disagreed with the statement, indicating that most organizations are still faced with varied interpretations of change management.

Recognition of the value and need for change management

Study participants evaluated the level of recognition of the value and need for change management in their organizations on a scale of high, moderate, low and no recognition. Participants evaluated this recognition for five groups: project leaders and project managers; executives and senior leaders; middle managers, front-line managers and supervisors; and solution developers and designers. The graphs below depict study respondents' views of the level of recognition for these groups (Figures 85 – 89).

26% of participants rated project leaders and project managers as having a high recognition of the value and need for change management, the highest of the five groups. Over two thirds of participants ranked both project leaders and project managers (71%) and executives and senior leaders (67%) as having either a moderate or high recognition of the value and need for change management. Over half of participants ranked both front-line managers and supervisors (55%) and solution designers and developers (52%) as having low or no recognition.

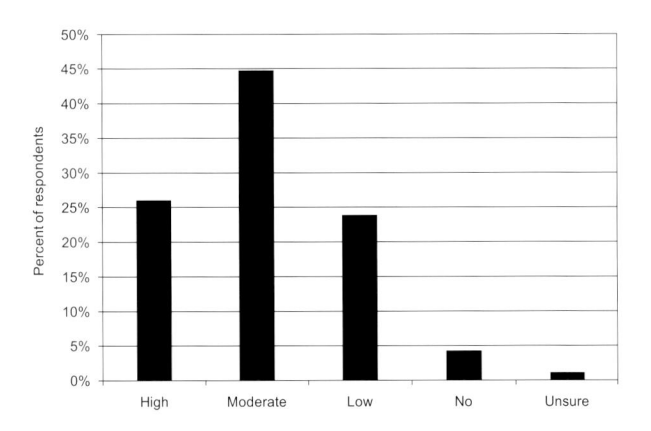

Figure 85 – Project leader and project manager recognition

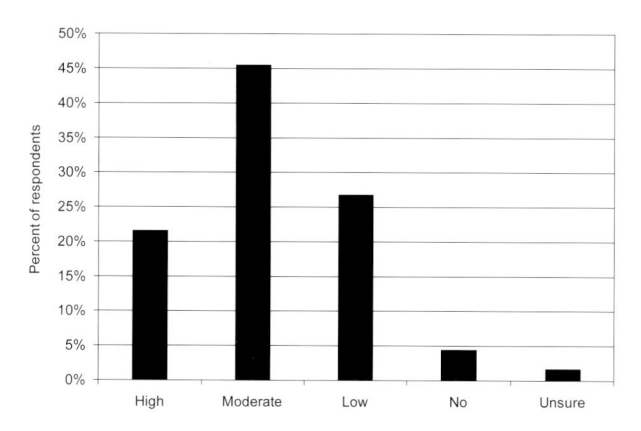

Figure 86 – Executive and senior leader recognition

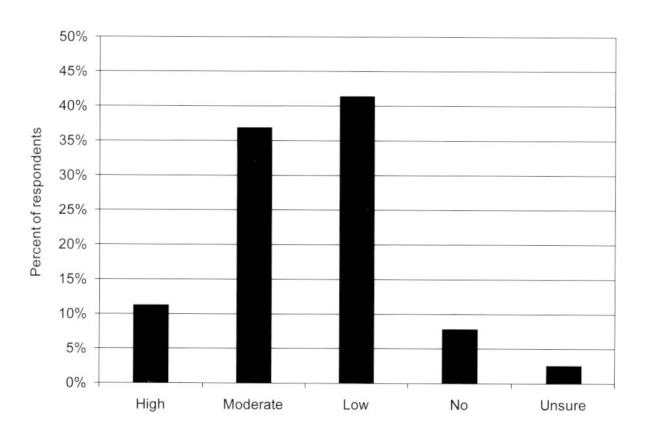

Figure 87 – Middle manager recognition

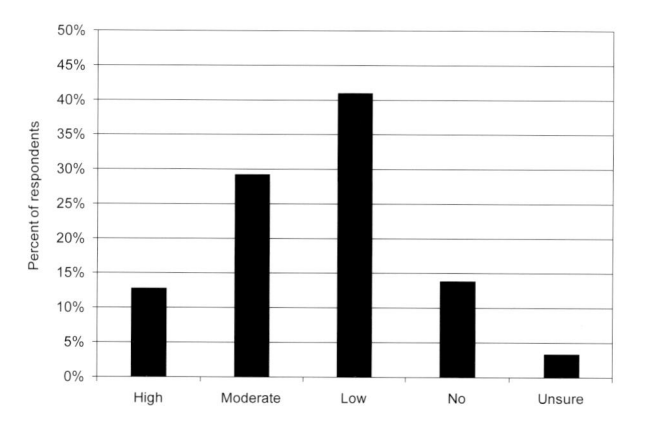

Figure 88 – Front-line manager and supervisor recognition

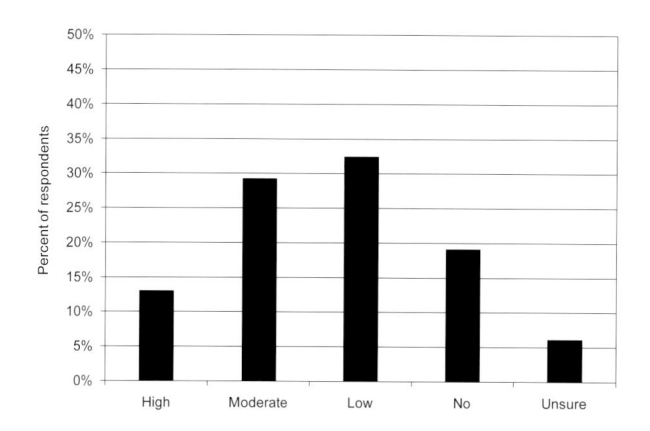

Figure 89 – Solution developer and designer recognition

Percent of projects applying change management

Participants in the 2011 benchmarking study reported on the percent of projects in their organization that were applying change management. Overall, participants reported an average of 35% of projects in their organization applied change management. The table below shows a more granular view of the percent of participants reporting 10% or fewer, 25% or fewer or 50% or fewer projects in the organization applying change management.

Percent of projects applying change management	Percent of study participants
50% or fewer	78%
25% or fewer	54%
10% or fewer	33%

Table 12 – Percent of projects applying change management

Figure 90 below shows the results for the percent of projects applying change management reported by participants.

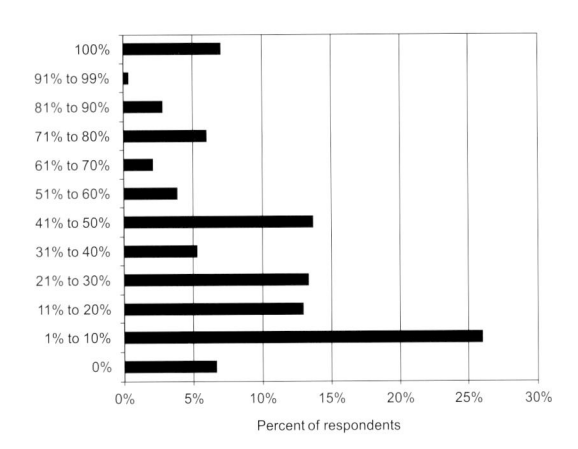

Figure 90 – Percent of projects applying change management

Change management effectiveness and measurement

Correlation between project success and change management effectiveness

Analysis was conducted correlating change management effectiveness with three dimensions of project success:

- Meeting objectives
- Staying on schedule
- Staying on budget

In evaluating change management effectiveness, participants were provided 12 factors that constituted effective change management (see Table 13) and then were asked to evaluate their overall change management effectiveness on a scale of poor, fair, good or excellent.

Actual number of responses vary in the three correlation charts because participants were able to indicate "too early to tell" for each of the project delivery categories. More participants indicated "too early to tell" for meeting project objectives than for schedule or budget adherence.

Figures 91, 92 and 93 show the percentage of projects performing at or above expectations correlated with change management effectiveness using data from the 2007, 2009 and 2011 benchmarking studies. For each change management effectiveness category (poor, fair, good, excellent), the chart shows the percentage of participants who were performing at or above expectations (i.e. those meeting or exceeding objectives, those on or ahead of schedule and those on or under budget).

Projects with excellent change management effectiveness were nearly six times more likely to achieve project objectives than teams with poor change management effectiveness, 95% to 17% respectively. Excellent change management also correlated directly with staying on schedule and staying on budget.

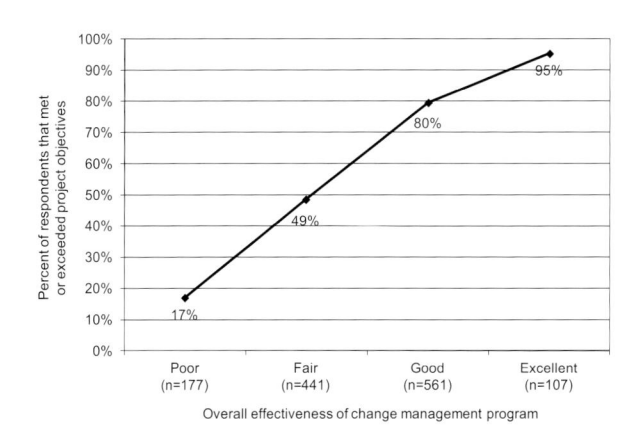

Figure 91 – Correlation with meeting objectives

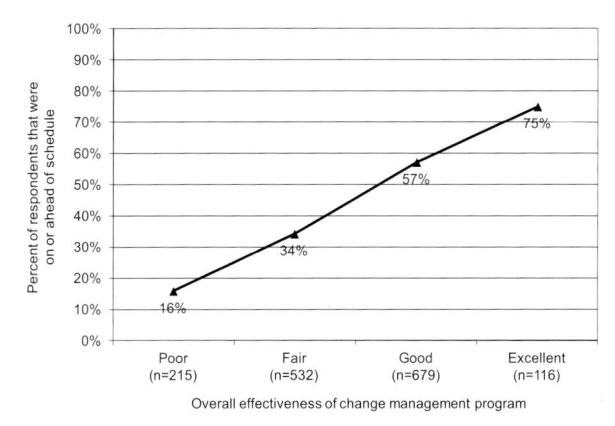

Figure 92 – Correlation with staying on or ahead of schedule

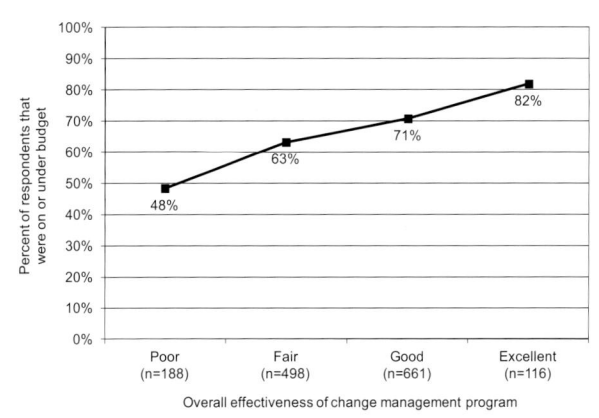

Figure 93 – Correlation with staying on or under budget

Change management effectiveness factors

The table below shows twelve change management effectiveness factors and the percentage of participants in the 2011 benchmarking study who indicated strongly disagree, disagree, agree or strongly agree for each factor. As in the 2009 study, the factors that received the most strongly disagree and disagree responses were factors 2, 6, 8, 10 and 12. Interestingly, these are the five factors that fall outside of the direct control of the change management practitioner. For the most part, the values in the 2011 study paralleled those in the 2009 study. The only meaningful change was a significant increase (9%) in those who indicated strongly agree with the first factor, the use of a structured change management process.

Factor	Strongly Disagree	Disagree	Agree	Strongly Agree
1. We applied a structured change management process.	5%	16%	50%	29%
2. We had sufficient resources on the team to implement change management.	10%	36%	42%	11%
3. Our change management activities were customized and scaled to fit the change and the organization being changed.	5%	16%	52%	27%
4. Our change management team had the necessary training and expertise in change management.	9%	29%	45%	17%
5. We integrated our change management activities into the project plan.	4%	17%	53%	26%
6. Our business leaders fulfilled their roles as effective change sponsors throughout the entire project.	12%	40%	37%	11%
7. We implemented an effective communications plan.	5%	22%	52%	21%
8. Managers and supervisors engaged in the change and effectively coached their employees through the change process.	10%	43%	42%	5%
9. We provided the necessary training to employees on new processes, systems and job roles.	4%	17%	60%	19%
10. Our senior leaders, mid-level managers and supervisors managed resistance to change effectively.	11%	44%	42%	4%
11. We measured compliance with the change and our overall performance in meeting project objectives.	8%	31%	54%	7%
12. We effectively reinforced the change with employees through recognition, performance measurement and celebrations.	10%	42%	43%	5%

Table 13 – Change management effectiveness factors

Overall effectiveness of change management program

Participants indicated the overall effectiveness of their change management program (Figure 94). Slightly fewer participants rated their change management program as excellent in 2011 than in 2009, while slightly more rated their program as good. Overall, the distribution remained fairly consistent over the last three studies.

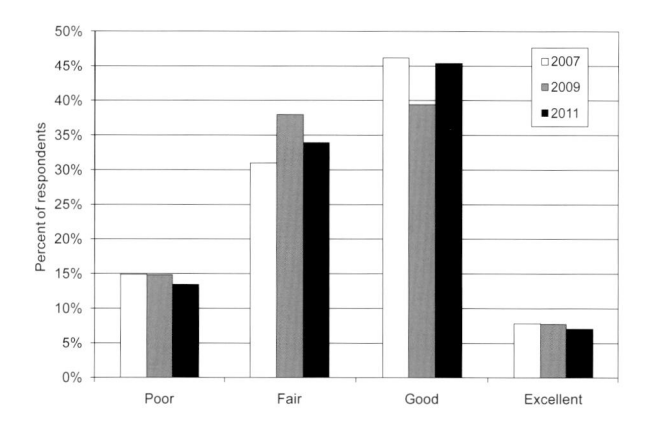

Figure 94 – Overall effectiveness of change management program

Change management effectiveness measurement

Half of the participants in the study reported measuring change management effectiveness (Figure 95).

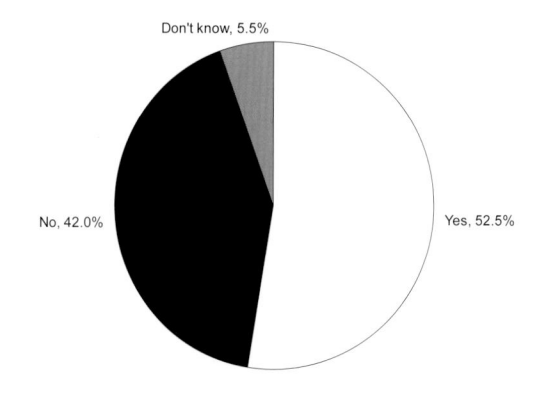

Figure 95 – Measured change management effectiveness

Those who measured change management effectiveness provided details about how they conducted the measurements. Analysis of results provided insights along four dimensions: methods, criteria, data sources and timing.

Methods
Participants commented on numerous methods or instruments used to evaluate change management effectiveness. The most common methods mentioned included:

- Surveys – directly collecting the feedback, perspectives and thoughts of employees within the organization who were impacted by the change

- Implementation reviews – including after action reviews and lessons learned sessions

- Interviews – face-to-face conversations with employees

- Focus groups – small group meetings and forums of employees involved in the project or impacted by the change effort

- Assessments – evaluations of individual competencies and adoption of the change through assessments

Criteria
In addition to the methods used, participants shared the criteria they utilized to determine change management effectiveness. The top responses included:

- Adoption, usage, acceptance, adherence – these evaluations focused on employee behaviors and processes, evaluating if employees were performing as required by the project or initiative

- Project performance – overall project success, benefits realization, data on project metrics and KPIs (key performance indicators), performance against deliverables, schedule adherence and timeliness

- Engagement and commitment – level of employee engagement and commitment to the change

- Awareness and understanding – level of employee awareness of the need for change and understanding of the details of the change

- Perception and attitude – measuring and evaluating the overall attitude about the change and perception issues

- Change management activities – completion and effectiveness of key change management activities including communications delivered and training delivered

- Indicators of change not occurring – including calls to help desk, resistance issues surfaced, unexpected obstacles, turnover, absenteeism and error rates

Data sources
While most of the measurement focused on end-users, participants collected data on change management effectiveness from others in the organization as well. The top sources of data included:

- End-users – those in the organization who had to change how they did their job and adopt the solution that was being deployed by the project or initiative

- Key stakeholders in the organization – managers and leaders within the affected parts of the organization

- Project team – the team leading the project and designing the change provided feedback on the effect of change management

- Change agents – including the primary change management resource or team and members of the extended change agent network within the organization

- Senior leaders – the primary sponsor and other sponsors spearheading the effort within their part of the organization

Timing
Finally, measurement of change management effectiveness occurred at various points during the project life cycle. The timeframe for measurement included:

- Post – measurements took place after implementation

- Pre and post – measurements took place before the project began to create a baseline and after implementation to gauge changes in performance

- At key milestones – measurements utilized at key points in time during the project life cycle tied to major developments or milestones

- Continuous – measurement occurred continuously throughout the project life cycle

Individual transition measures

Participants provided a number of tactics that were used to evaluate whether or not the change was taking place at the individual level. Overwhelmingly, the most common answer was direct feedback from impacted employees, followed by tracking of performance.

1. **Direct feedback**
   The top tactic used to evaluate whether individual changes were occurring was direct feedback from end-users. Surveys were by far the most common vehicle. Additional methods included interviews, direct conversations, focus groups and meetings. Feedback was collected regarding awareness, change readiness, engagement, commitment and understanding of the change.

2. **Tracking of performance**
   The second most common tactic was tracking the performance of individuals, including system usage, adoption of tools, adherence to processes, job performance and productivity measures. Evaluations following training and assessments of knowledge and skills were also used, as were general measures of participation.

3. **Feedback from managers and supervisors**
   Feedback was collected from the managers and supervisors who oversaw the employees impacted by the change to gauge the level of change adoption and acceptance.

4. **Feedback from change agents**
   The change agents, change champions and

change network supporting the change provided feedback on individual adoption of the change.

5. **Evidence of struggles**
Rather than tracking whether the individual change was occurring, some participants used tactics for evaluating that the change was not occurring. These tactics included tracking of questions posed by employees, error rates, resistance and help desk queries.

Half of all study participants reported that their organizations measured whether change was occurring at the individual level.

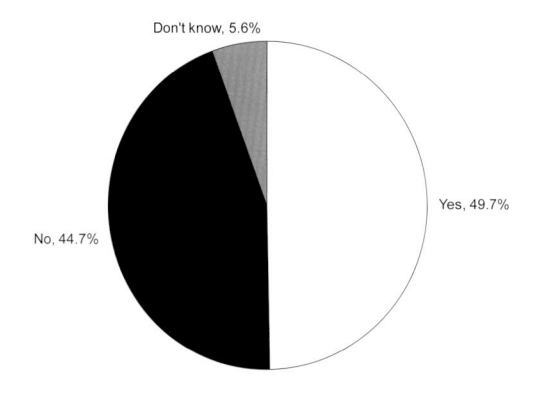

Figure 96 – Measured whether change was occurring at individual level

Definition of project objectives

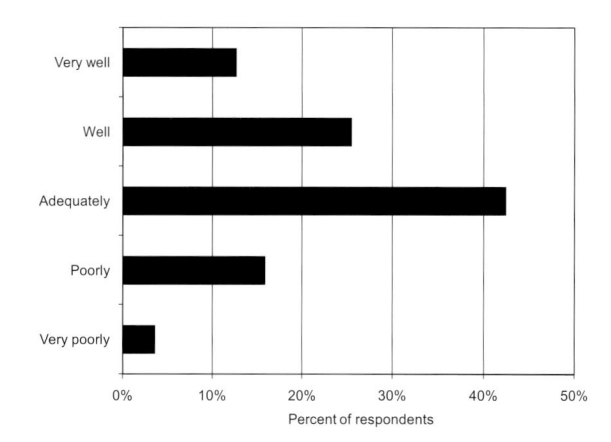

Figure 97 – How well were project goals and objectives defined?

For the first time, participants in the 2011 benchmarking study commented on how well the overall project goals and objectives were defined.

Only 38% of participants indicated that goals and objectives were defined very well or well. One fifth of participants said the project's goals and objectives were defined poorly or very poorly.

Project metrics and KPIs

Participants were asked to identify the key performance indicators (KPIs) that were tracked to evaluate project success. The two most frequently cited indicators were:

- The project adhered to the schedule and was completed on time

- The project was delivered on budget

In addition to delivering on time and on budget, the following indicators were mentioned by participants.

- **Achievement of intended outcomes**
Participants measured the degree to which the project met objectives, achieved the intended improvement in performance and realized expected benefits. Given the variety of changes reported on in the study, there were a number of different indicators tracked related to project outcomes. The most commonly cited indicators included customer satisfaction, cost savings, process time, sales or revenue, productivity, quality, efficiency gains, functionality, data integrity, service level targets and accuracy.

- **Usage by employees**
These indicators focused on the adoption of the change as demonstrated by employees. Indicators related to usage by employees included system usage, utilization, process adherence, adoption rates, usability, behavioral indicators, proficiency and acceptance.

- **User response**
Similar to usage, these indicators were aimed at evaluating end-users' satisfaction with and readiness to adopt the change. Indicators

included direct feedback satisfaction levels, training attendance, knowledge evaluation, communication effectiveness measures, participation at events, training feedback, and training effectiveness.

- **Achievement of interim milestones**
  Indicators related to monitoring project progress were tracked. These indicators included project milestone achievement, completion of deliverables and percent completion of project.

- **Error tracking**
  Instead of tracking positive adoption and metrics, some participants tracked metrics that would indicate the change was not taking place, similar to what was reported for assessing individual transitions. These negative indicators included support calls, calls to the help desk, error rates, problem and issue tracking, complaints and disruption measures.

- **Engagement measures**
  These metrics measured user perception and attitude toward the change. Indicators included engagement, awareness, morale, buy-in and understanding.

Speed of adoption, ultimate utilization and proficiency

For the first time, study participants indicated how the project was performing along the lines of speed of adoption, ultimate utilization and proficiency. Speed of adoption is how quickly employees adopt the change. Ultimate utilization is the terminal adoption rate (or the converse of the opt-out rate). Proficiency is how effectively employees performed as required by the change.

Generally, around 10% of participants indicated that performance was better than they expected and just over 50% indicated that performance was in line with what was expected (Figures 98, 99 and 100). More participants were able to evaluate speed of adoption performance than proficiency and ultimate utilization.

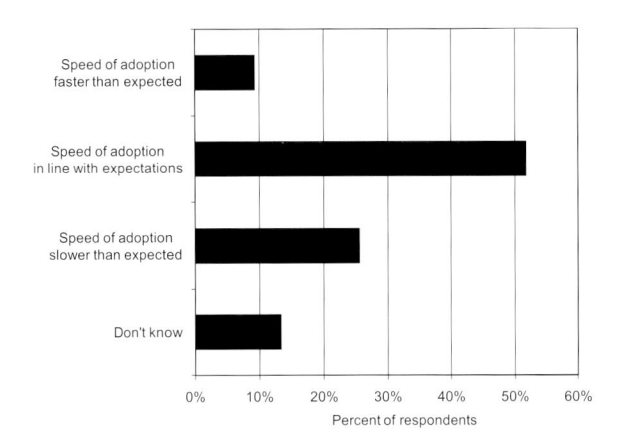

Figure 98 – Speed of adoption

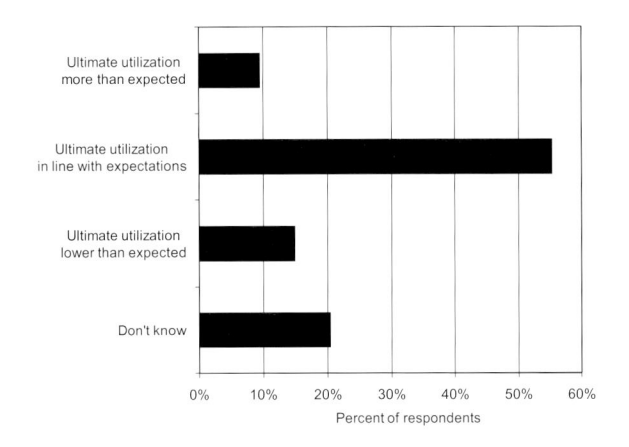

Figure 99 – Ultimate utilization

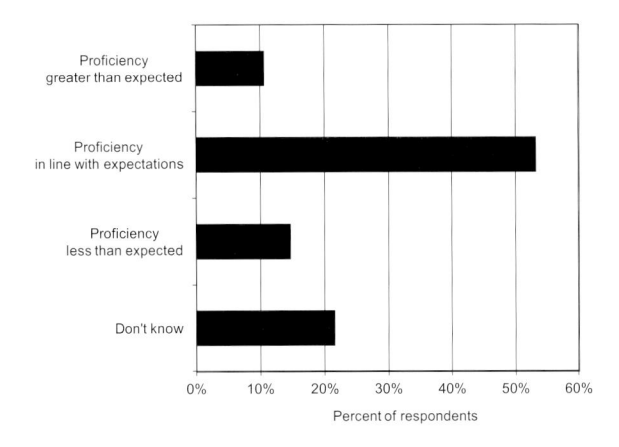

Figure 100 - Proficiency

Correlating people side ROI factors

The data for speed of adoption, ultimate utilization and proficiency were segmented by overall effectiveness of the change management program. The graphs below show the performance for these three variables (better or in line) for excellent, good, fair and poor change management programs (Figures 101, 102 and 103).

The data clearly show that respondents with more effective change management programs showed better performance in all three variables. Excellent change management programs resulted in faster speed of adoption, greater ultimate utilization and higher levels of proficiency. Poor change management resulted in slower speed of adoption, less utilization and lower proficiency.

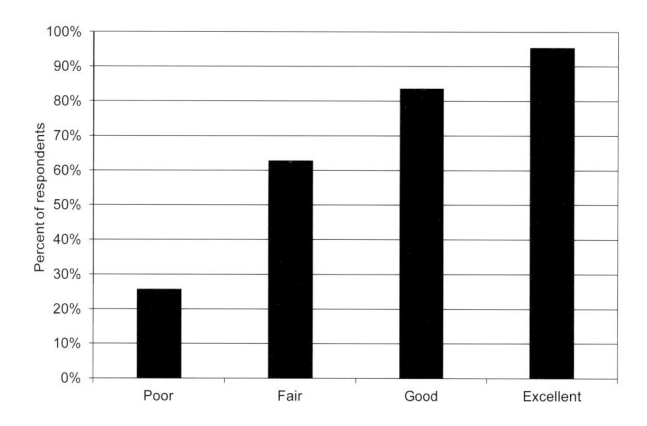

Figure 101 – In line or better than expected speed of adoption vs. change management effectiveness

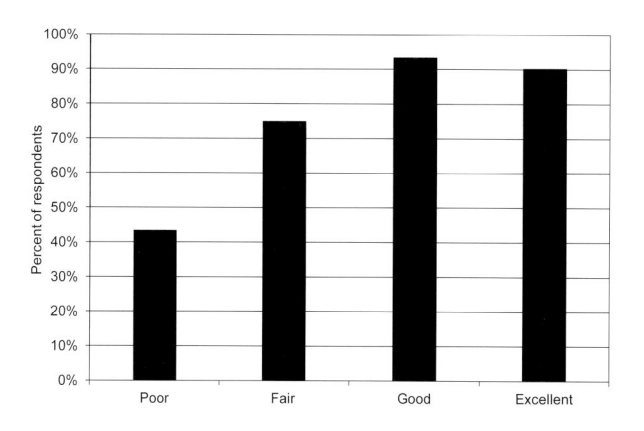

Figure 102 – In line or better than expected ultimate utilization vs. change management effectiveness

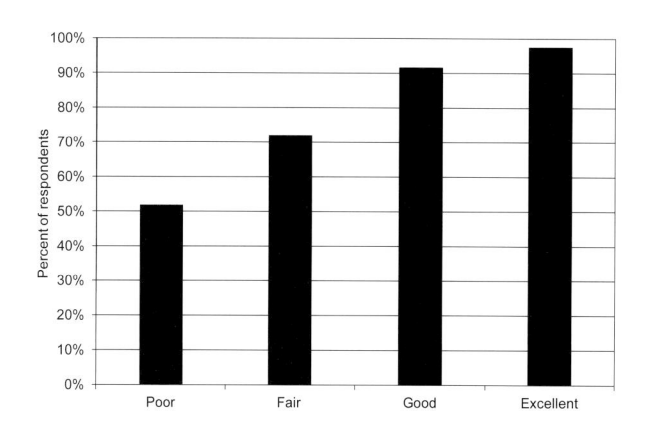

Figure 103 – In line or better than expected proficiency vs. change management effectiveness

If your project failed or only partially met objectives, what obstacles did you encounter?

Source date: 2009

Study participants in the 2009 benchmarking study whose projects failed or only partially met objectives reported obstacles in one or more of the following areas:

1. Leadership and sponsorship
2. Project management
3. Change management

1. **Leadership and sponsorship obstacles:**
   - Slow decision making by the sponsor
   - Lack of involvement of key business leaders; difficulty getting all key stakeholders on board to build the necessary sponsor coalition
   - Wavering support for the change; shifting or conflicting priorities of business leaders and managers
   - Competing initiatives (too many projects going on at the same time)
   - Insufficient resources or funding allocated to the project
   - Insufficient visibility and communication from the sponsor
   - Sponsor changed mid-project; lack of consistent leadership for this change

2. **Project management obstacles:**
   - Project changed or expanded in scope (scope creep)
   - Poor estimation of the project's magnitude; insufficient details to plan properly
   - Unrealistic schedule from the planning process
   - Poor project management throughout the project; failure to report progress honestly
   - Inadequate management of vendors; development was behind schedule or vendors did not meet commitments
   - Insufficient resources or lack of the correct resources for the project
   - Poor quality deliverables from vendors, specifically around the release of new technology
   - Poor assumptions about project's impact on the organization
   - Lack of a solid business case for change

3. **Change management obstacles:**
   - Employee resistance to the change; lacked buy-in and involvement
   - Middle managers resisted the change
   - Insufficient change management resources for the size of the change
   - Underestimated the impact this change would have on employees
   - Did not provide sufficient training to employees
   - Poor communication about the project
   - Lacked a formal change management process

Justifying change management

Working to justify change management
Source date: 2009

Over half of the participants in the 2009 study indicated that they had to justify change management to their leadership team (Figure 104).

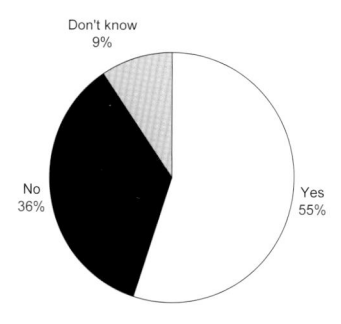

Figure 104 – Participants who had to justify change management to leadership team

Participants who needed to justify change management to their senior leaders used one or more of the following tactics.

1. **Learned from past failures**
   Study participants discussed recent project failures, especially those that people would remember and acknowledge did not go well, to demonstrate the risks and financial impacts of poorly managed change (used real-life, practical examples).

2. **Clearly showed the negative consequences of poorly managed change**
   Participants quantified the impact of "what can go wrong" and identified the potential risks to the organization if change management was not implemented effectively.

   "We created 'what if' scenarios to demonstrate the potential consequences of poorly managed change."

3. **Translated change management into tangible financial impacts**
   Participants linked change management to the ability to maximize project outcomes and focused all discussions on business results.

4. **Presented the outcomes of successful projects that used change management**
   Study participants contrasted successful projects with projects that did not use change management and were less successful.

5. **Used data to connect change management to the return on investment (ROI)**
   Participants provided senior managers with external research data that showed the correlation of financial success of a change project (or meeting project objectives) with the effectiveness of change management.

Some additional tactics participants shared were:

- Quantified potential impacts of employee turnover and productivity loss from poorly managed change

- Presented case studies and data from other companies that had used change management (benchmarking data was used to build credibility)

- Gained direct support of one senior leader who then became an advocate and spokesperson for change management with other business leaders

  "Found a few change champions."

- Connected change management activities to the specific outcomes that their business leaders were trying to achieve

- Gathered feedback from employees using surveys or interviews to show the negative impacts of poorly managed change; used organizational readiness assessments to demonstrate the impact of change management

- Used a current, real project as a testing ground or trial to show the effectiveness of change management
- Brought in a credible, outside speaker to provide an executive briefing to senior leaders on change management and why it is important for business success
- Integrated change management with project management and focused the discussion on the overall business objectives (not simply on the value of change management alone)

Participants who did *not* have to justify change management as part of their change project cited the presence of one or more of the following conditions.

- Past results with change management were very positive, preventing any further need to justify change management activities.
- Sponsors already believed in the need for change management or they specifically asked for change management to be implemented as part of the project.
- The project team or project leader was very experienced with change projects and made change management part of the project activities.
- Acknowledgement that past failures resulted from a lack of effective change management, and leaders did not want to see these mistakes repeated.
- Change management was already part of the requirements and process for implementing change.

Change saturation and portfolio management

Level of saturation

The percentage of participants nearing, at or past the point of saturation has continued to increase. 73% of participants in the 2011 study identified being past, at or near the point of saturation, up from 66% in 2009 and 59% in 2007 (Figure 105).

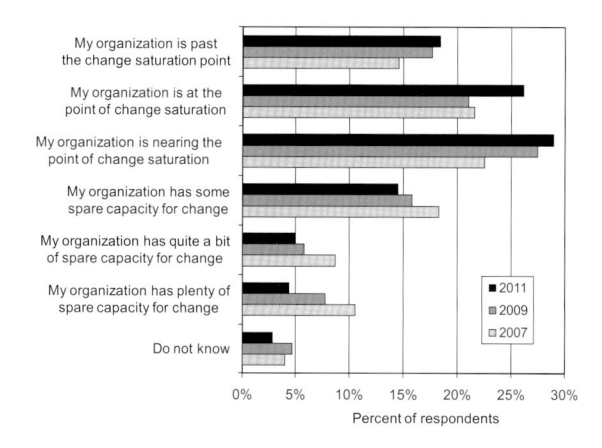

Figure 105 – Level of change saturation

Level of change saturation by region

The table below shows the percentages of participants who indicated being near, at or past the point of saturation by region represented in the study. The regions are ordered based on greatest occurrence of change saturation.

Region	Percentage of study participants past, at or nearing saturation
Canada	83%
United States	79%
Australia and New Zealand	75%
Europe	71%
Middle East	67%
Africa	65%
Asia and Pacific Islands	65%
Latin America	53%

Table 14 – Change saturation by region

Level of change saturation by industry

The table below shows the percentage of participants who indicated being past, at or near the point of saturation by industry. Data are provided for industries represented by more than 2% of study participants.

Industry	Percentage of study participants past, at or nearing saturation
Retail	92%
Telecommunications	86%
Health Care	84%
Finance/Banking	82%
Development/Manufacturing	81%
Oil and Gas	81%
Insurance	78%
Consumer Goods	77%
Food/Beverage	75%
Information Systems	75%
Mining	75%
Utilities	74%
Service Industry	71%
Education	70%
Government – State/Local	68%
Pharmaceutical	68%
Government – Defense	67%
Aerospace	67%
Government – Civilian	61%
Consulting	56%

Table 15 – Change saturation by industry

Change expected in the next two years

As in the 2009 study, participants indicated the amount of change expected in the next two years (Figure 106). 71% of the participants in the 2011 study expected an increase (either slightly or significantly), compared to 76% in the 2009 study. In both the 2011 study and the 2009 study, only 8% of participants expected the amount of change to decrease in the coming two years.

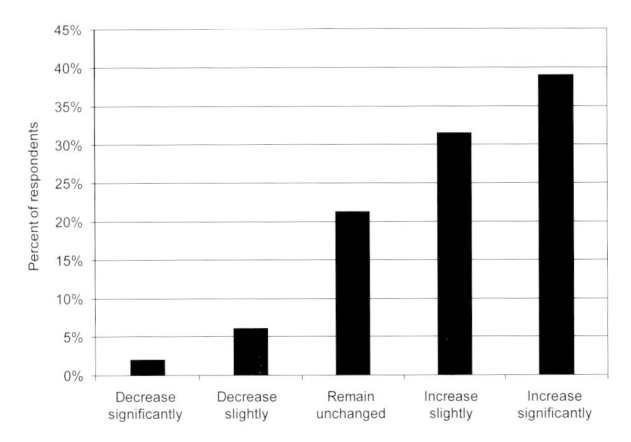

Figure 106 – Amount of change expected in the next two years

Identifying saturation

Source date: 2009

Participants in the 2009 study were asked how they identified when change saturation was occurring. Most participants shared the symptoms they could observe in a change saturated workplace. A small group of participants also shared proactive approaches they took to monitor saturation levels.

For those participants who took proactive steps to monitor change saturation, the following approaches were cited.

- Feedback gathered directly from employees and managers on their perception of the level and amount of change that was occurring
- Surveys and interviews that included questions on the amount of change, including small group sessions and satisfaction surveys
- Active management of project resource allocation and scheduling, including the use of mapping tools and Enterprise Project Management (EPM) tools
- Assessments of the changes and the impact they would have by group or stakeholder
- Evaluation of the number of change efforts underway
- Reporting by project teams and change management teams
- Assessment of the time available to handle change at the employee level
- Assessment of success rates of change efforts over time, taking into consideration the amount of change happening in the organization
- Comparative observation evaluating the amount of change happening and the level of discontent in different parts of the organization

In terms of the impacts of change saturation that participants observed in their organizations, the responses fell into three categories:

1. Individual symptoms
2. Organizational symptoms
3. Project symptoms

Individual symptoms:

- Disengagement, apathy and indifference – employees were not motivated to take part in the change or in their work and in some instances they began to shut down; a number of participants also cited a lack of questions and a lack of resistance as indicators of disengagement
- Burn out and fatigue – employees were visibly tired
- Anxiety, stress and weariness
- Confusion – about both the changes and the direction of the organization
- More complaints and "noise"
- Employees became desensitized, numb and lethargic
- Frustration
- Overloaded and feeling overwhelmed
- Cynicism and skepticism
- Anger – including more aggressive behaviors and quicker tempers
- Complacency

Organizational symptoms:

- Automatic resistance – employees reacted to any type of change with immediate resistance, no matter what the particulars of the change were

- Lack of focus on operations – participants cited productivity declines, "business as usual" tasks being ignored, issues not being addressed, a lack of flow, quality issues and difficulty in prioritizing work

- Attrition and turnover – valued employees left the organization

- Low morale throughout the organization

- Flavor of the month mentality – changes were constantly being introduced but not followed through to conclusion

- Absenteeism increased

- A lot of work being done but no progress or real change taking hold

- "Wait it out" mentality where employees simply ignored a change and hoped it would go away

- Changes viewed as distractions

Project symptoms

- Lack of necessary resources for projects, including budget and people

- Poor project delivery, including failure to produce expected results

- Delays and schedule implications, including slowed progress and missed deadlines

- Little direction and sponsorship from senior leaders

- Competition and conflict between projects

- Inability to finish out projects as the next change is started before the last one is solidified

- Non-compliance by employees, including lower adoption levels and requested changes being completely ignored

- Team members stretched too thin and working unmanageable amounts

- Project activities not occurring

Addressing saturation and collision

Study participants were asked to comment on what their organization has done to address change saturation and the collision of multiple initiatives in the organization. By a two-to-one margin, the top answer provided was "nothing," as many participants saw no actions being taken to address saturation and collision.

For those participants who did identify specific actions, the top responses were:

1. **Utilize a portfolio view and portfolio management tools**
   Organizations put in place portfolio and program management practices. These practices were aimed at developing a single, complete view of the portfolio of change and increasing visibility about the efforts underway. Portfolio management included steps to balance resources, make adjustments to governance, change release management efforts, identification and inventorying, coordinated planning, budget management and enterprise scheduling. Some participants indicated steps to evaluate saturation, change capacity and impact on people in the organization. Roadmaps, barometers and heat maps were used to present a view of the portfolio.

2. **Ensure prioritization**
   To address saturation and collision, organizations took on more rigorous prioritization. In some cases this meant establishing priorities, while in others it meant reevaluating priorities. Mechanisms were employed to ensure that changes were aligned with the direction of the organization and that the most important changes took precedence.

3. **Make adjustments to changes in the portfolio**
   Adjustments to the changes in the portfolio included reducing the number of changes, stopping some changes, intentionally sequencing or staggering changes, putting

some changes on hold, moving deadlines and timelines of projects, integrating or bundling similar initiatives, closing out changes that were nearing completion, and scaling back or adjusting the scope of some initiatives.

4. **Use structure**
The use of a group in the organization to manage saturation and collision was a commonly cited approach. Examples included a steering committee to oversee and evaluate the portfolio, a governance group that more actively managed approval, or councils or forums to coordinate efforts. This responsibility was most commonly assumed by the Project Management Office or Strategic Program Office.

5. **Increase communication efforts**
Communication efforts took place at two levels. First, communications to employees provided a view of the roadmap and status of the portfolio of change, including a clear articulation of how changes aligned with organizational direction. Communications to employees also aimed to build the expectation that change is natural and a certain level of saturation was to be expected. Second, communication was increased between project teams, leaders and representatives in the organization to build a more complete view of the magnitude of change underway.

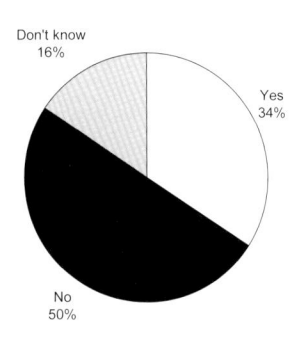

Figure 107 – Kept an inventory of all changes underway

Participants indicated who in the organization maintained the list or inventory of changes underway. The most common responses were:

- Project Management Office (PMO)
- Senior leadership – including a particular member of the "C-club" (CEO, COO, CFO, CIO), an executive team or staff members of senior leaders
- Change Management Office, group, team or council
- Distributed – department leaders kept their own inventory
- Strategy and Planning – including Office of Strategic Management, Strategic Planning Office or Business Planning Team

Inventory and portfolio management processes

Source date: 2009

Participants in the 2009 study indicated whether they kept an inventory of all of the changes underway and if they had a structured process for managing the portfolio of change in the organization. Over one third of participants kept an inventory or list of all of the changes underway (Figure 107), while just under one quarter of participants (24%) had a structured process for managing the portfolio of change (Figure 108).

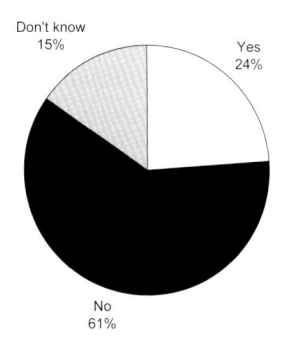

Figure 108 – Have a structured process for managing the portfolio of change

Tactics for managing the portfolio of change
Source date: 2009

Participants in the 2009 study were asked to identify the tactics they used to manage the portfolio of change – the collection of all change efforts underway. A small number of participants (approximately 6% of responses) indicated that they were taking steps toward portfolio management. The top approaches for managing the portfolio of change were:

1. **The use of tools to show the portfolio**
   These responses included a list or log of initiatives, a change dashboard, a central database of project plans, a vendor-provided tool, resource and time tracking tools, change impact maps and change calendars.

2. **Centralized planning by a project-focused body**
   Responses included a project office, a program office, a project committee or a steering group.

3. **Regular meetings**
   These were typically held monthly or quarterly to review status and progress.

4. **Senior leadership meetings and discussions**
   Executive meetings focused on the portfolio of change.

5. **Processes for managing project progress**
   These included prioritization tools and approval gates, demand management processes, planning and budgeting exercises that included multiple projects.

6. **Strategic planning oversaw the portfolio**
   Portfolio discussions included in the annual planning process and the use of a strategic project list or Office of Strategic Management.

7. **Dedicated group or resource**
   An employee or group of employees tasked with managing the portfolio of change.

Resolving project conflicts
Source date: 2009

Participants in the 2009 study were asked how their organization resolved conflicts between projects when there was competition for resources, budget or impact on people in the organization. By a fairly large margin, the two top responses were prioritization and senior leadership decisions and resolutions. The top approaches for resolving project conflicts were:

1. **Prioritization**
   The top response for resolving project conflicts was returning to some sort of prioritization process. Typically, prioritization took place ahead of the project launches and involved certain criteria for comparing projects to one another. The most frequently cited prioritization criteria included:

   - Highest value, benefit, impact or expected ROI for the organization
   - Strategic alignment and importance to the business
   - Business urgency
   - Regulatory or legislative mandates

2. **Senior leadership decisions and resolutions**
   The second most cited approach included the involvement of senior leaders. In some cases, decisions were simply made by the CEO, while in other cases this involved discussions with senior management teams. A number of participants indicated that when conflict did arise and could not be sorted out, the issue was escalated to senior management for resolution.

3. **Use of boards and oversight committees**
   A number of participants indicated that project conflicts were addressed by the collaborative work of an oversight group. Participants shared a number of names for this group including: steering group, steering committee, management review board, project control board, business exchange team, change control board and advisory board. Regardless of the name, this group

had visibility across multiple projects and made decisions to resolve conflict.

4. **Coordination by the PMO**
The fourth most cited response was oversight by the Project Management Office (PMO). In some instances, a project portfolio office existed within the PMO to coordinate the different projects and their requirements for time, human resources and budget.

5. **Negotiation**
Some participants said that conflict was resolved directly by the teams and sponsors of the projects through a negotiation process.

6. **Meetings and discussions**
A less formal tactic for resolving conflicts was the use of face-to-face meetings and discussions with project teams, leaders and representatives from the business.

A number of participants cited the role of individuals in influencing decisions when conflict occurred. Responses here related to politics, the use of influence and clout resulting in projects moving forward. Several participants also cited, with a negative connotation, that the loudest people were the ones who were heard – a "squeaky wheel" approach. Finally, several participants indicated that projects with the strongest sponsor were favored in times of conflict.

Unique change types

For the first time, the 2011 benchmarking study asked a series of questions about four types of specific changes with change management implications:

- Changes with impact across various cultures
- Changes that occurred over a long time frame (over two years)
- Changes that involved layoffs or significant staff reductions
- Mergers or acquisitions

Figure 109 shows the percentage of participants who reported on these four unique change types. Over 40% of participants indicated the change they were reporting on either had impact across various cultures or occurred over a long time frame. Just under one in five (17%) reported on a change involving significant staff reductions, while less than one in ten (8%) reported on a merger or acquisition.

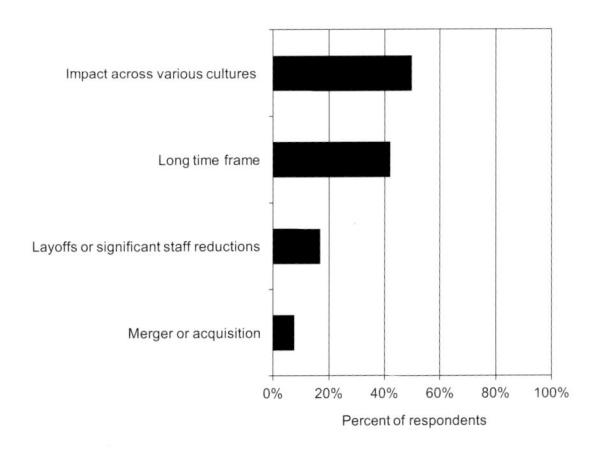

Figure 109 – Unique change types

For each of these unique change types, participants identified complexities or issues from a people side of change perspective and provided specific change management recommendations given the nature of the change.

Impact across various cultures

Issues

The participants who experienced a change which had impact across various cultures had four primary issues or complexities from a people side of change perspective. While research participants reported four challenges when introducing an intercultural change, the majority cited "overcoming cultural differences" as the number one challenge.

1. **Cultural differences**
   The majority of participants reporting on this type of change stated the overcoming of cultural differences as the biggest challenge. Cultural differences and challenges resulting from those cultural differences included: different ways of doing work, different perceptions of the change, different forms of resistance, different styles of communication, different backgrounds (e.g. IT, academia), cultural unawareness and different work ethics.

2. **Adapting to regional/cultural circumstances**
   Research participants reported understanding and adapting to the diverse needs of each impacted group as the second largest challenge.

3. **Changes to how work was done**
   Changes to how work was done included changes to business or organizational processes, integration of different cultures or different business units, changes to the reporting structure and roles, and changes to expectations and requirements.

4. **Language flexibility**
   Using simple language, translating into different languages and overcoming language barriers was the fourth challenge identified by research participants regarding an intercultural change.

Recommendations

Research participants who experienced a change across various cultures reported four recommendations.

1. **Build cultural awareness**
   Respondents stated the building of cultural awareness as the primary recommendation for others managing an intercultural change. Participants suggested acknowledging, honoring and understanding different languages, values and needs. Training to support this effort could include building cultural awareness through cultural workshops, cross-cultural interaction and change management training.

2. **Create a cross-regional change team**
   Research respondents recommended building a cross-regional change team that included local change leaders who were active and committed to the change. Cultural experts who specialized in intercultural changes could be used in the team as well.

3. **Customize plans for each group**
   A third recommendation included adopting and sticking to a method or change plan that could be adapted to meet the unique needs and preferences of each group. Participants also suggested representing all groups or cultures in teams and plans.

4. **Communicate clear and consistent messages for each group**
   Research participants recommended communicating transparently and consistently about the change and about the cultural differences and challenges faced by each group, including listening to employees experiencing these challenges.

Long time frame

Issues

The participants who experienced a change taking place over a long time frame (over two years) reported three main issues or complexities in regard to their changes.

1. **Retaining focus**
   The majority of respondents reported that retaining focus was the greatest issue during changes with a long time frame. Participants cited numerous reasons for losing focus, including: change saturation; change fatigue; other changes interfering; changing or interfering priorities; inconsistency of plan or approach; and frequent changes to vision, direction, timeline, content or scope.

2. **Maintaining momentum**
   Research participants stated that maintaining momentum or motivation was a major issue in changes occurring over a long time frame. They reported that lack of commitment, loss of interest or "burn out" occurred in the long period of moving toward the target.

3. **Retaining people**
   The third complexity regarding a change with a long time period was the retention of key people and knowledge-holders due to staffing changes, role changes, employee turnover or management replacements, including losing sponsors during the change.

Recommendations

The participants who reported having a change taking place over a long time frame (two years or more) provided four main recommendations for others applying change management over an extended project life cycle.

1. **Develop a structured approach**
   The number one recommendation by research participants was to develop a structured plan that would be realistic, flexible and sustainable. In addition, participants recommended communicating about the change and vision as soon as possible. Regular updates and reviews of the strategy were included in this structured approach.

2. **Break down the change into manageable phases**
   Research participants recommended building clearly defined milestones and manageable phases so that short-term successes and

progress can be not only noticed and sustained, but also celebrated.

3. **Communicate throughout**
The third recommendation by research participants encouraged planned, sustained communication regarding the change. These communications should be transparent and maintain key messages. Communications that were also fresh and informative were most effective.

4. **Identify and ensure support from sponsorship and leadership**
This recommendation also included assessing sponsor commitment and confirming both their engagement and continuity.

Layoffs or significant staff reductions

Issues

The 17% of participants who experienced a change that reduced staff had three primary issues or complexities from a people side of change perspective.

1. **Employee morale**
For changes effecting reductions to staff, research participants cited employee morale as the primary complexity experienced with impacts such as: decreased engagement in business processes, lack of buy-in, "quit and stay" behavior, loss of trust, negativity toward all changes, bitterness, guilt and sympathetic grief.

2. **Concern for the individual wellbeing of employees**
Research participants reported that during periods of staff reduction, a second issue involved giving the necessary attention to employees who were concerned about the personal impacts of the staff reduction.

3. **Logistical challenges of reducing staff**
The third complexity experienced was the logistical considerations surrounding the reduction of staff, such as: managing the layoffs, making arrangements for impacted staff, incorporating changes to business process, changing or creating new roles, engaging human resources and dealing with a lack of resources.

Recommendations

Research participants who reported having a change that involved a reduction in staff provided three specific change management recommendations.

1. **Provide support**
The primary recommendation provided by research participants was to provide support to impacted staff through means such as understanding and addressing unique needs, answering questions, offering career counseling and exit strategies, respecting the dignity of impacted employees and offering emotional support.

2. **Execute with a planned approach**
Research participants recommended a decisive, consistent and planned approach that accounted for resistance and challenges.

3. **Engage all levels and departments within the organization**
When experiencing a staff reduction, respondents also recommended engaging all levels of the organization, especially the impacted employees' direct managers.

Merger or acquisition

Issues

The 8% of participants who experienced a merger or acquisition listed three main issues or complexities in undergoing the change.

1. **Cultural differences**
Respondents reported that cultural differences were the greatest issue during a merger or acquisition. This issue often manifested in "us versus them" attitudes or internal "rivalries."

2. **Changes to structure**
The second most common issue reported by research participants regarded changes to the

internal or external structure of the business or organization, including different terminology, different expectations, different leadership, and different languages used for business transactions or in the work environment.

3. **Insecurity about future**
Research participants cited insecurity about the future as a third issue or complexity when experiencing a merger or acquisition. This type of change was often met with fear or skepticism.

Recommendations

Participants who experienced a change involving a merger or acquisition provided three primary change management recommendations.

1. **Communicate**
The research participants cited open and honest communication as the primary recommendation when undergoing a merger or acquisition. Recommendations included transparent communications focused on the individual, communications that included the rationale and benefits, and communications that brought the audience back to the vision of the change.

2. **Know the people and the cultures influenced by the change**
This recommendation included understanding strengths and constraints of employees, conducting cultural assessments and stakeholder analyses, and understanding the change from different perspectives.

3. **Invest in change management early**
Respondents recommended incorporating change management at the beginning or early in the merger or acquisition process in addition to elevating change management to the strategic business level.

Appendix A – Participant demographics

Geographic representation

Figure 110 shows the geographic distribution of study participants over the last five studies. The top three regions contributing to the 2011 study were the same as in the 2009 study.

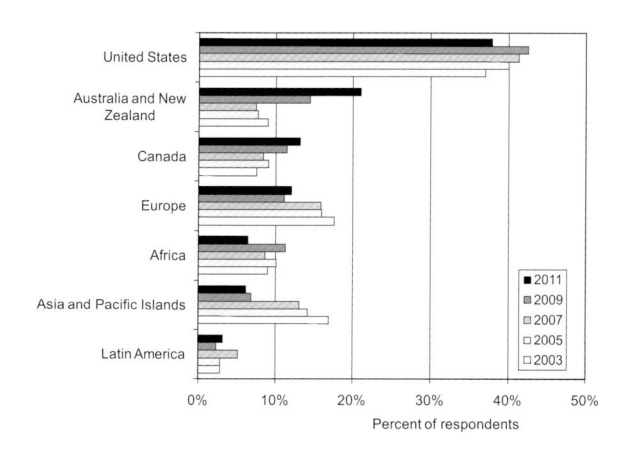

Figure 110 – Geographic representation of participants

Geographic presence

For the first time, participants in the 2011 study provided data on the geographic presence of their organization. Nearly half of participants had a presence in multiple countries (Figure 111).

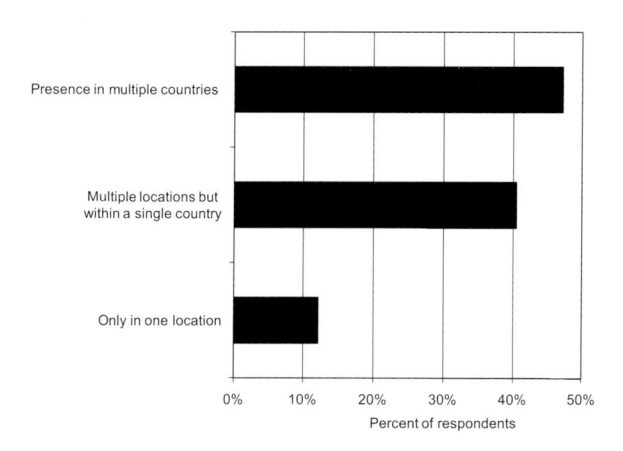

Figure 111 – Geographic presence

Industry representation

Finance/Banking, Government – State or Local, Health Care, Utilities and Insurance made up the top five industries in the 2011 study (Figure 112). Any industries representing less than 2% of study participants were included in the "Other" category.

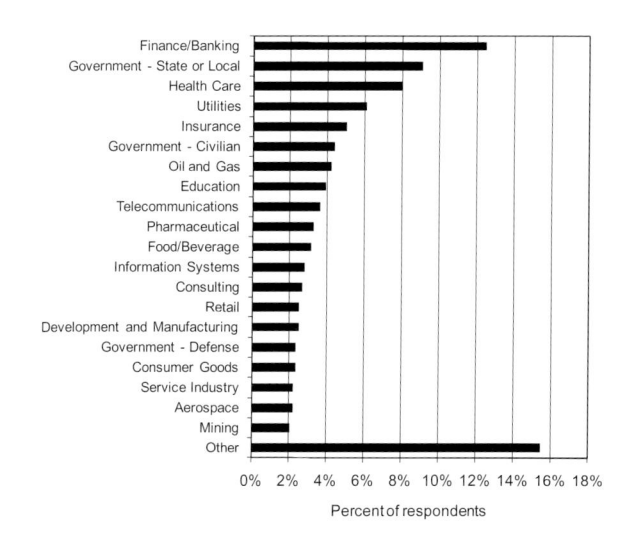

Figure 112 – Industry segment

Finance/Banking, Government – State or Local and Health Care remain highly represented industries as in previous studies. Representation from Utilities and Insurance increased, while representation from Development and Manufacturing decreased in this edition.

In this iteration of the benchmarking study, external consultants were specifically instructed to indicate the industry of the client they were representing, so the percentage of participants indicating "Consulting" decreased significantly from previous studies.

Size of organization

Participants in the 2011 study represented a wide range of organizations based on overall organization size (Figure 113). The largest participation came from organizations with more than $5 billion in annual revenue. Representation increased from organizations larger than $500M while representation from organizations smaller than $50M decreased.

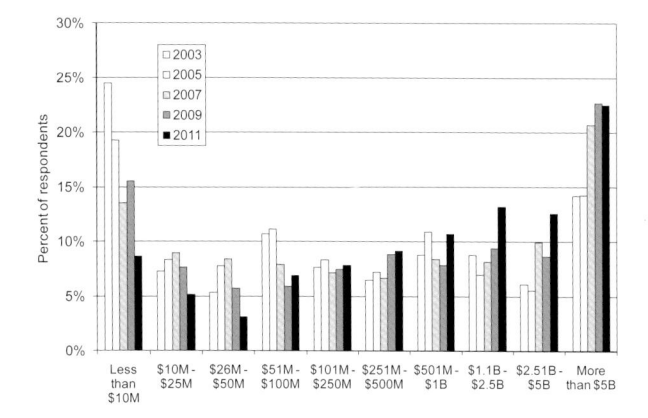

Figure 113 – Size of organization (annual revenue)

Appendix B – Project profiles

Project stage

In the 2011 study, as in the 2009 study, over 70% of participants reported on projects that were completed or in the implementation phase (Figure 114).

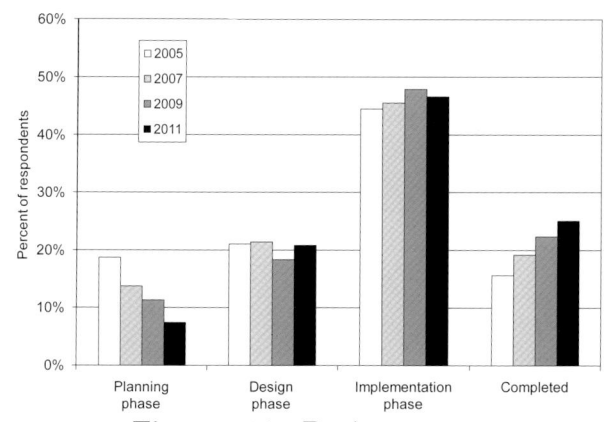

Figure 114 – Project stage

Project type

Participants indicated the type of change they were reporting on in the benchmarking study. As in previous studies, most participants were reporting on projects that involved changes to processes, systems, organizational structures and job roles (Figure 115).

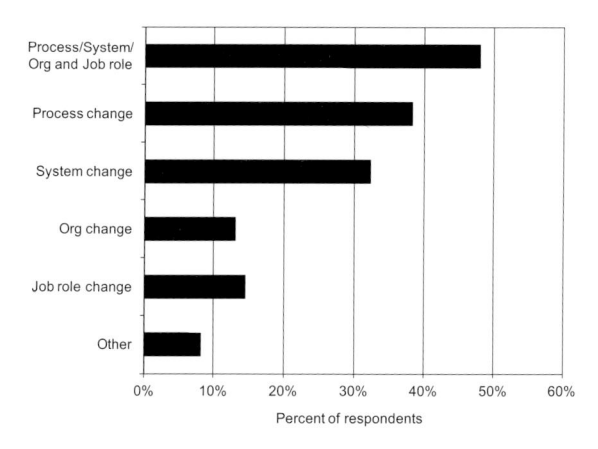

Figure 115 – Project type

Participants were able to select multiple responses, resulting in a total of more than 100%. The most common combinations of changes indicated by participants included:

Combination of change types reported	Percentage of participants
Process + System	15%
Process + System + Job role	7%
Process + Org + Job role	4%
Process + System + Org	2%
All types + Other	2%

Table 16 – Combinations of project types

Size of change

Participants provided several data points on the size of the project on which they reported. Participants indicated:

- Scope of the change
- Project investment
- Number of employees impacted

In terms of scope of the change, projects in the 2011 study matched those of previous studies, with the largest representation from projects impacting the entire enterprise (Figure 116).

From a project investment standpoint, the 2011 study had more large projects, those with budgets of over $5 million. The smallest projects, those with budgets of less than $100,000, were less represented in the 2011 study (Figure 117).

The 2011 study included reporting on more projects that impacted over 500 employees than previous benchmarking studies. The largest increase occurred in projects impacting more than 5000 employees (Figure 118).

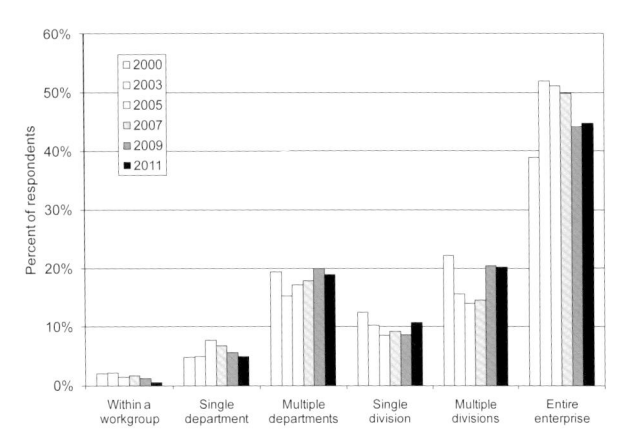

Figure 116 – Scope of the change

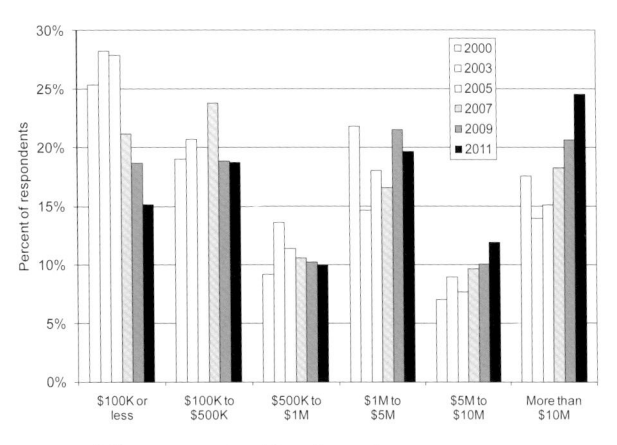

Figure 117 – Project investment

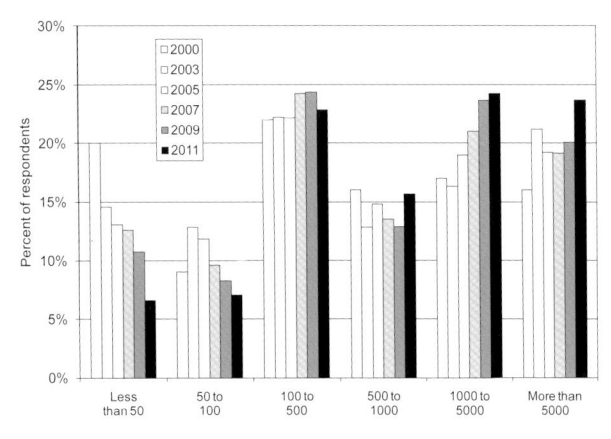

Figure 118 – Employees impacted

Duration of the change

For the first time, study participants shared data on the duration or length of the project on which they were reporting. Nearly 40% of participants reported on projects lasting over 24 months, and 70% reported on projects lasting over 12 months (Figure 119).

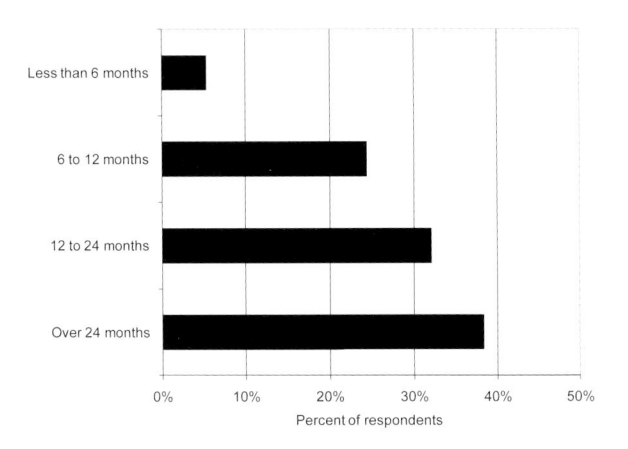

Figure 119 – Duration of the change effort

Measures of success: meeting project objectives, schedule and budget

As in the previous two studies, participants indicated the degree to which the project succeeded based on three criteria: meeting objectives, staying on schedule and staying on budget (Figures 120, 121 and 122).

Overall, 61% of participants reported that their project met, exceeded or greatly exceeded objectives, down from 64% in the 2009 study. 45% reported being on schedule, slightly ahead of schedule or drastically ahead of schedule, the same as in the 2009 study. Two thirds of participants reported being on or under budget, the same as in 2009.

The data on project success from the perspective of meeting objectives, finishing on schedule and staying on budget were used in a correlation to the overall change management effectiveness to see the impact of more effective change management on achievement of results and outcomes by the project.

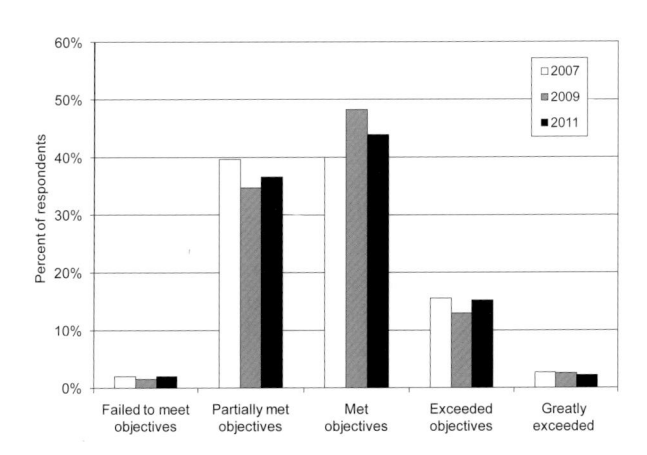

Figure 120 – Meeting objectives

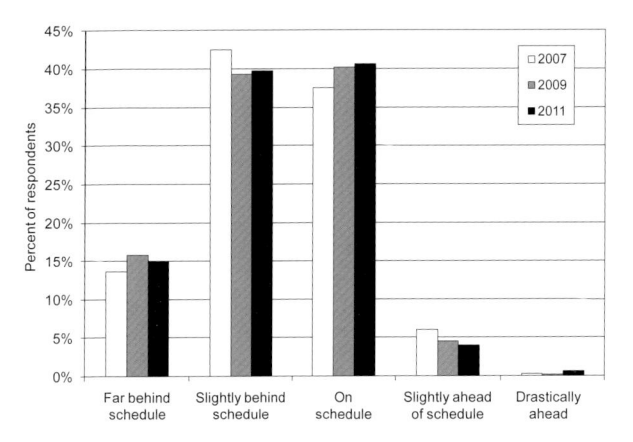

Figure 121 – Projects on schedule

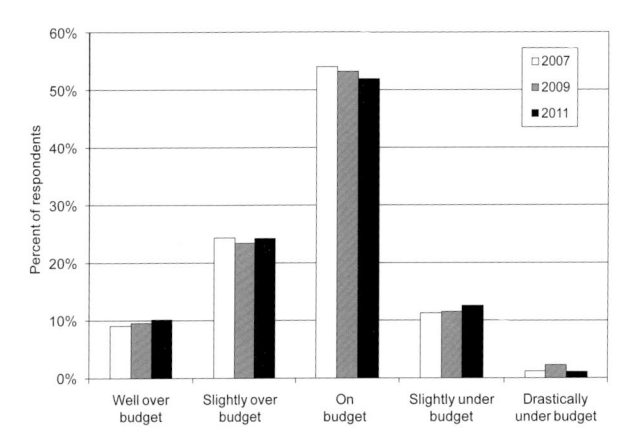

Figure 122 – Projects on budget

Appendix C – Prosci Change Management Maturity Model

Below are the complete descriptions of the five levels of the Prosci Change Management Maturity Model provided to study participants.

Level 1 – Ad hoc or absent

At Level 1 of the Maturity Model, project teams are not aware of and do not consider change management as a formal approach for managing the people side of change. Projects at this level can have one or more of the following characteristics.

- Project leadership is focused only on the "concrete" or tangible aspects of the project including funding, schedule, issue tracking and resource management.

- Communications from the project are on a "need to know" basis only and typically infrequent.

- Employees find out about the change first through rumors and gossip rather than structured presentations.

- Executive support is in the background as evidenced through funding authorization and resource allocation, but active and visible sponsorship is not present.

- Supervisors and managers have little or no information about the change, and have no change management skills to coach their employees through the change process.

- Employees react to change with surprise; resistance can be widespread.

- Productivity slows and turnover increases as the change nears full implementation.

When is change management used on a project at this level?

Change management is applied on a project at this level only as a last resort when employee resistance jeopardizes the success of the project.

Level of integration between project management and change management

At this level, change management is reactive and an add-on to the project. No integration with project management takes place at the beginning of the project.

Level 2 – Isolated projects

In Level 2, elements of change management begin to emerge in isolated parts of the organization. The effort to manage the people side of change is infrequent and is not centralized. Characteristics of this level are:

- A large variation of change management practices exists between projects with many different change management approaches applied sporadically throughout the organization; some projects may be effectively managing change while others are still in Level 1.

- Elements of communication planning are evident, but there is little sponsorship or coaching as part of change management.

- Managers and supervisors have no formal change management training to coach their employees through the change process.

- Change management is typically used in response to a negative event.

- Little interaction occurs between the isolated project teams using change management; each new project "re-learns" the basic change management skills.

When is change management used on a project at this level?

Change management is applied on a project when resistance emerges or when the project nears implementation with only isolated projects using change management at the beginning of their project. Some elements of communication planning occur early in the life cycle.

Level of integration between project management and change management

In Level 2, change management is not fully integrated into project management. On projects that use change management, the project team is aware and knowledgeable of change management. In certain instances, a change management advocate can encourage the integration of change management and project management.

Level 3 – Multiple projects

At Level 3, groups emerge that begin using a structured change management process. Change management is still localized to particular teams or areas in the organization. Organizations at this level can have one or more of the following characteristics.

- Structured change management processes are being used across multiple projects; multiple approaches and methodologies are being utilized.

- Some elements of knowledge sharing emerge between teams in the organization; experiences are shared between teams in some departments or divisions.

- While change management is applied more frequently, no organizational standards or requirements exist; pockets of excellence in change management co-exist with projects that use no change management.

- Senior leadership takes on a more active role in sponsoring change and considers this role part of their responsibilities, but no formal company-wide program exists to train project leaders, managers or coaches on change management.

- Training and tools become available to project leaders and team members; managers are provided with training and tools to coach front-line employees in future changes.

When is change management used on a project at this level?

Change management is initiated at the start of some projects, with a large fraction still applying change management as a reaction to employee resistance during implementation.

Level of integration between project management and change management

In Level 3, teams who are successful at change management integrate change management with their overall project management methodology at the inception of the project. Communication planning is integrated at the planning phase, and other plans are developed prior to implementation.

Level 4 – Organizational standards

In Level 4, the organization has selected a common approach and implemented standards for using change management on every new project or change. Note: a common methodology does not mean a "one-size-fits-all" recipe. Effective methodologies use repeatable steps but are built on understanding the situation and using the appropriate tools for the specific change. Organizations at this level can have one or more of the following characteristics.

- There is an enterprise-wide acknowledgement of what change management is and why it is important to project success.

- A common change management methodology has been selected and plans are developed for introducing the methodology into the organization.

- Training and tools are available for executives, project teams, change leaders, managers and supervisors. Managers and supervisors are provided formal training in change management.

- A functional group may be created to support change initiatives, with roles like Director of Change Management. Organizations may create a Center of Excellence with individuals, groups or administrative positions dedicated to supporting change management efforts and building change management skills.

- Executives assume the role of change sponsors on every new project and are active and visible sponsors of change.

- Resistance and non-compliance is expected in isolated instances. Some project teams still do not understand why they are using change management. Adoption is not yet at 100% and the organization is in the process of building change management skills throughout the organization.

When is change management used on a project at this level?

At Level 4, teams regularly use a change management approach from the beginning of their projects. Change management work begins at the planning phase of the project.

Level of integration between project management and change management

Project management and change management are integrated from the beginning, to the point where they are not separable. Project teams follow both project and change management milestones.

Level 5 – Organizational competency

Level 5 is having change management competency as part of the skill set of the organization. Organizations at this level can have one or more of the following characteristics.

- Effectively managing change is an explicitly stated strategic goal and executives have made this a priority.

- Employees across the enterprise understand change management, why it is important to project success and how they play a role in making change successful.

- Change management is second nature – it is so commonplace that it is nearly inseparable from the initiatives.

- Managers and supervisors routinely use change management techniques to help support a broad range of initiatives from strategy changes to individual employee improvement.

- The organization gathers data to enable continuous improvements to the common change management methodology, tools and training.

- Extensive training exists at all levels of the organization.

- Higher ROI, lower productivity loss and less employee resistance are evident across the organization.

When and how is change management used on a project at this level?

Change management begins before projects begin.

Level of integration between project management and change management

When organizations have developed a high level of change management competency, change management steps are completely integrated into project management. Planning and design phases have both project and change management elements and are viewed as standard practice.

Appendix D – 2011 study participant list

- A Plus Transition
- A.C.T. Advanced Consulting & Training
- AB Volvo
- Absa Bank Ltd *
- Acaché Pty Ltd
- Accomplish Business Solutions Pty Ltd
- Acquiro
- ADP, Inc.
- Agility Factor Inc.
- Airservices Australia
- Ajilon Consulting
- AKKADIS Change Practice
- Alaska Airlines
- Alberta Government
- ALC Ltd (UK)
- Almarai Company
- APA Group
- aplus transion
- Aqua America
- ARGOS Consulting Group
- ASB Bank Ltd
- Asgard / BT Financial Group
- Assochange
- AST Corporation
- Atomic Energy of Canada
- Australia Department of Defense *
- Australian Capital Territory Department of Human Services *
- Australian Unity
- Avbob
- Avto Union
- AXA GROUP SOLUTION *
- Baker Hughes, Inc.
- Bank of Canada
- Bank of Ireland
- Bartecko Consulting Ltd.
- Bayer AG
- Bayer Healthcare
- Bayer MaterialScience
- BC Hydro
- BD
- BDM Directions
- Being Human
- bendigo Bank
- Bio-Rad Laboratories
- Birmingham City Council
- BJC Healthcare
- B-Line, LLC
- Blue Heron Consulting
- BMA Grupo Alianza
- Bombardier Aerospace
- Bon Secour Health System
- Bonneville Power Administration
- Boomerang Management Inc.
- Booz Allen Hamilton *
- Botswana Collge of Agriculture
- Brighton Leadership Group
- Brightstar Corp
- Brisbane City Council *
- British Telecom - Openreach
- Bruyere Continuing Care
- Business Solutions - The Positive Way
- Canadian National Railway
- Canadian Tire Ltd.
- Canadian Wheat Board
- Canon Business Solutions, Business Services Division
- Capacity Development Africa
- Capgemini India Business Ltd
- Capgemini Italia
- carbon group
- CareFusion
- Cargotec *
- Carla Carter & Associates, Inc. *
- Carrier
- Carus Consulting Group
- Caterpillar Inc.
- Caterpillar Logistics Services Inc
- Catholic Healthcare West
- CCG/DVI
- CDS
- CedarCrestone Inc.
- Cegos
- Central Bank of Nigeria
- Central Health
- Central Statistical Agency of Ethiopia
- CEVA Logistics
- CGI
- Change Connections
- Change Factory
- Change Guides LLC
- Change Logic
- Change Matters Australia
- ChangeLeaderU.com
- Changeworks Consulting *
- Chaucer Consulting
- Chebais Consulting
- Christchurch City Council
- Cirque du Soleil
- Cisco Systems Inc. *
- CITEC
- Citrix Systems
- City of Calgary *
- City of Regina *
- CMPC Celulosa S.A., Planta Santa Fe
- Coca-Cola Amatil *
- Coca-Cola Amatil New Zealand Ltd
- Coldwater Creek
- Commonwealth Bank of Australia
- Commonwealth Centers for High Performance Oragnizations (CCHPO) Network
- Community Youth Services
- Compassion International
- Comunicación y Cambio S.A.S. (Medellín - Colombia)
- Consumers Energy *
- Co-operators Life Insurance Co.
- CPS Energy
- Crowe Change Specialist Services
- Crystalmount Solutions Inc.
- Cue 7 Consortium

- David Marklew Ltd
- De Adviespraktijk B.V.
- Delegata
- Deutsche Bank
- Development Strategies Plus
- Dibena Enterprise Sdn Bhd
- Diversified Consulting
- DNV-ITGS
- DOXA Cambios Inteligentes
- DSD Laboratories, Inc.
- Duke Energy
- Eastern Health
- Emerson Human Capital Consulting
- Enterprise Transformation Group Ltd.
- eProcesses Consulting
- Ergon Energy
- Ernst & Young LLP *
- Essential Energy
- Ethier Associates
- Ethiopian Management Institute
- evolve! People and Process Management
- Exervio Management Consultant
- Express Scripts
- Federal Aviation Administration
- Federal Government/Treasury
- FIG Consultants Ltd
- Finest Business Consulting
- Fireman's Fund Insurance Company
- First National Bank (South Africa)
- Focus First Consulting
- Fontys University of Applied Science
- French Chemical Company
- Fujitsu Consulting India
- GARMCO
- Gas Natural Fenosa
- Georgette Rouncefield
- GEP Business Solutions
- GFIA (Gobodo Forensic and Investigative Accounting)
- GlaxoSmithKline
- GrameenPhone Ltd.
- GRUPO JUMBOPACK
- GSK
- Halkjær Human Univerz
- Halliburton
- Harris Bank
- Harriss Wagner Management Consultants
- HCL-AXON
- Health Care Services Corporation
- Health Insurance Department of Bermuda
- Health Quality Council
- HEC Paris
- Hennepin County
- Herman Miller Inc.
- High Grade Professional Education Centre
- Hitachi Consulting *
- Hoffmann La Roche
- Honduras AKC
- Hong Kong Productivity Council
- Housing Industry Association
- Housing New South Wales - Department of Human Services
- HRSB Concepts Inc.
- Hyundai Capital America
- IKEA
- Impact@work inc.
- Implementation dynamics
- Industry and Investment, NSW, orange
- InfoChoice
- Infosys Consulting, Inc. *
- Inland Power and Light Company
- Innovative Health Solutions, OptumHealth
- International Crops Institute for the Semi Arid Tropics
- Investor IQ
- Investors Group
- IP Australia *
- IUTUM
- J Wagner Consulting Inc.
- Jemena
- John Holland
- Jon R. Wallace
- Joy Mining Machinery
- Kaiser Permanente
- Kaleido Consulting NV
- KPMG *
- Krauthammer International
- Kusha Madan Consulting Engineers
- Kuziva Huni Consultants
- La Société conseil Lambda
- Lambda
- Landpower
- LECG
- Lifeline Education Resource Development Centre
- Lloyds Banking Group
- Logica
- Mack Center for Technological Innovation - Wharton School
- Maersk Line
- MAFC
- Make Change Positive
- Malawi Institute of Management
- Malayan Banking Berhad
- Manitoba Public Insurance
- Marriott International
- MBTelehealth
- McKesson Corporation
- Mediabloc Consulting Limited
- Mensard
- Micron Technology
- Microsoft
- MillerCoors
- MindPeace Consulting
- MLP Consultants, LLC
- MNP
- Moen Inc
- Molson Coors Canada
- Moon Holt Solutions
- Mouchel
- MRC Group Spzoo
- MTN Group
- Mutual of Omaha *
- Nab/JBWere
- NASA Enterprise Applications Competency Center
- NASA's Marshall Space Flight Center
- Nathan Consulting Group
- National Australia Bank *
- NATIONAL BANK OF COMMERCE LTD

- National Bank of Egypt
- National E-Health Transition Authority *
- National Institute for Smart Government - NISG
- National Institute of Allergy & Infectious Disesases, Office of Research Operations
- Natura Cosmetics
- Natural Resources Canada
- Navigator Management Partners
- Navistar International Corporation *
- NCS Pte Ltd *
- Necron Benchmarking Consutants
- NEHTA
- Nelson Consulting Group
- Nelson Marlborough District Health Board (NMDHB), NZ
- Neoris
- Netahenx Corporation
- New Rubicon Limited
- Newton-Wellesley Hospital
- Nextlevel Consulting
- NIE
- NiSource, Inc.
- northern exposure
- Northern Trust Co.
- NouvEON *
- Nycomed
- Oakton *
- OCBC Bank
- OLG
- Onirik
- Online Business Systems Inc
- Ophelo Ltd.
- OppenheimerFunds
- Optus Pty Ltd *
- OVAL Tech & Training Services
- Pacific Blue Cross
- Panduit
- Park Nicollet Health Services
- PCGI Consulting Services
- People & Performance A/S
- People and Organisation Development
- PEOPLE ISSUES LIMITED
- PeopleFirm, LLC
- PeopleSense
- Pepco Holdings Inc.
- Petroleum Development Oman
- Pfizer, Inc *
- philips
- Picourseware CC
- Pitt County Memorial Hospital
- PNC Financial Services
- PNC Mortgage *
- Pole emploi
- Police & Nurses Credit Society Ltd
- Primavera BSS
- Private Contractor
- proacteur *
- Progressive Insurance
- Projector Communication GmbH - Communication for Change
- Providence Health Care
- PS Consulting
- Public Trust *

- Purple Apple
- Ramse Consulting Oy
- Region of Peel
- Reinsurance Group of America
- Repars Inc.
- Resources Global Professionals *
- RFadera & Associates
- Rhythm Consulting Inc.
- Rich Products
- Right Management
- Robert Ayling Incorporated
- Rogers *
- Roosevelt University / Next Level Consulting
- RSL Care
- RWD Technologies
- RWE npower
- SABMiller Plc
- SAIC
- SAJE Consulting
- Sallie Mae
- Salt River Project
- Sandia National Laboratories
- Santos
- SAP
- Saskatoon Health Region
- SaskEnergy
- Sasol
- Schneider National
- School of Industrial Management, HCMC University of Technology
- SCI International
- SELEX Communications (UK)
- Serco Consulting
- Shape Consulting
- Singapore Government
- SIS División Information Management
- Slalom Consulting
- SMS Management & Technology
- SN Consulting Ltd
- SOJE Consulting Services
- Sole trader
- Soltius Indonesia
- Solvera Solutions
- Sonar6
- Sovereign
- St John of Health Care
- Standard Bank of South Africa
- Standard Bank, Personal and Business Banking
- Starfish Consulting Inc.
- State of California
- State of Delaware, Department of Technology & Information *
- Sui Southern Gas Company Limited
- Sun International
- Suncorp
- SunGard Global Services
- Suntiva
- SunTrust
- Superpartners
- Surrey County Council
- Sutter Health Sacramento Sierra Region
- Symantec
- Tacoma Public Utilities *

- Talent Partners
- Talisman Energy
- TASC Management Consulting, LL
- Tasmania Department of Health and Human Services
- TD Bank Financial Group
- Teachers' Retirement System for the City of New York
- Teched Consulting Services Ltd
- Tenaris
- The Coca-Cola Company
- The Critical National Infrastructure Authority of Abu Dhabi
- The Dominion of Canada General Insurance Company
- The Hartford
- The Home Depot
- The Housing Authority of the City of Atlanta, Georgia
- The J.M. Smucker Company
- The Litmus Group
- The Mersky Group
- The Parliamentary Service
- The Synthetic Family
- The Taligens Group, LLC
- The University of Auckland
- The Wespac Group (Westpac Institutional Bank Division)
- Thiago Lelis ME
- Tim Hortons
- TLC
- TOTVS
- Townsville City Council
- Transfolign Consulting LLP
- Trasys
- Treasury Wine Estates
- Trexia
- Tribunal Superior do Trabalho
- tw telecom
- Tyler Technologies
- U. S. Government Accountability Office
- UGL Limited
- Umtha Management Services Pty Ltd
- UNISYS
- Universiti of Utara malaysia
- University Hospitals of Cleveland
- University of Melbourne
- University of Southern Queensland
- University of Vermont
- Urbanizadora del Bajío, SA de CV
- Valassis Communications Inc. - IT
- Valassis, Inc. *
- VALSOUSA
- VeriScope, Inc.
- Vertex, Inc.
- Victoria Department of Human Services
- Victoria Department of Treasury and Finance
- Volkswagen Financial Services UK
- West Monroe Partners
- Western Management Consultants
- Western Power
- Westpac Banking Corporation *
- Westpac NZ Ltd
- WesTrac Pty Ltd *
- Wipro Consulting
- Your Purpose Consulting Limited
- Zurich
- Zurich Insurance

Appendix E – 2009 study participant list

- 3rd i Consulting
- A.C.T. Advanced Consulting and Training
- Abbott Labs
- ABC (Australian Broadcasting Corporation)
- Absa Bank Ltd
- ABSA, division of Barclays
- Accretive Solutions
- Adams-Gabbert & Assoc., LLC
- ADP Inc
- Adult Multicultural Education Services (AMES)
- AEROFLOT Russian Airlines
- AFMC/A2
- Africa Crisis Management Team
- AHM
- Alberta Justice and Attorney General
- Alex Apouchtine
- ALTEC Training Centers
- Ambuja Realty Group
- Amertron Global
- Anderson Alliance Pty Ltd
- Applied Data Trends, Inc.
- Archstone Consulting
- ARGOS Consulting Group
- Artis Rei
- ASB, Auckland, New Zealand
- Ashland Inc.
- Astral Consulting Services
- AT&T
- Atos Origin
- Auckland City Council
- Australian Government Solicitor *
- Australian Human Service Organisation
- Avnet
- Bank of Canada
- Barnsley MBC
- Bartholomew Corporate Solutions p/l
- Bayer AG (The Bayer Group)
- BDM Directions
- BearingPoint
- Being Human
- Bell Canada
- BHP Billiton *
- Blue Oceans Information Solutions
- Blueshield of CA
- BMW Manufacturing
- Bombardier *
- Bonneville Power Administration *
- Booz Allen Hamilton *
- Bristol Myers Squibb
- British Telecommunications, Openreach division
- Brown-Forman Corporation
- BTS
- Bulyanhulu Gold Mine
- CA (Australia) *
- Comptroller and Auditor General of India
- California Manufacturing Technology Consulting
- CalPERS
- Canadian National
- Canadian Tire Financial Services
- CapGemini *
- Capita (National Strategies)
- Capital City Fruit
- Capital One
- Carbon Group *
- Cardinal Solutions Group *
- Caterpillar Inc. *
- CBA
- Central Bank of Nigeria
- Centre For Excellence, LLC
- Centre for Strategic Development
- Cetna Consulting Limited
- Chameleon Adventure Academy
- Change Consultoria
- Change Guides
- Change Management Consultants of Maryland, LLC
- ChangeWright Consulting
- Chevron *
- CIBC *
- Ciber Inc *
- Cirque du Soleil
- Cisco
- Citibank
- City and County of San Francisco
- City of Calgary
- City of Minneapolis
- City of Regina *
- City of Tacoma
- Clorox
- CMA Holdings Incorporated
- CMTC *
- Coaching Counts
- Coldwater Creek *
- Cole Consulting, LLC
- Commonwealth Bank
- Comptroller of the Currency (USA)
- County of Santa Clara
- Courtyard Group
- CPS Human Resource Services
- Croken Enterprises Inc
- Crystalmount Solutions Inc.
- CSIRO
- Cue 7 Consortium, Inc.
- Daar
- Dan Murphy's
- Danske Bank
- DBHG
- De Adviespraktijk
- Delaware Department of Insurance
- Delegata *
- Dell, Inc
- Deloitte Consulting
- Department of Correctional Service (South Africa)
- Department of Health and Human Services, Housing Tasmania *
- Department of Land Affairs (South Africa)
- Department of Planning and Economy (Abu Dhabi)
- Department of Treasury and Finance, Victoria, Australia
- Desjardins general insurance group
- Development Bank of Ethiopia
- Development of Malawian Enterprises Trust (DEMAT)

- Distinct Consulting
- District of Columbia Department of Small, Local Business Development
- Dreamhouse Consulting
- DSD Laboratories, Inc.
- Duke Energy
- EADS CASA
- Eastern Health
- EDS, an HP Company *
- EduServe/Amarillo College
- Egerton University
- Emerson Human Capital
- Enaxis Consulting, LP
- EnteGreat, Inc.
- Enteprise Community Partners, Inc.
- EQE Bulgaria AD
- Ergon Energy
- Erne Enterprise Ltd
- Esterline Defense Group
- Ethiopian Civil Service College [ECSC]
- Ethiopian Management Institute
- European Central Bank
- evolve! People and Process Management SA de CV
- Experian
- Farm Credit Canada
- Fireman's Fund Insurance Company
- Firestone International Associates, Inc.
- Focusphera Consulting
- Fonterra Brands Australia (P&B) Pty Ltd
- Fontys University
- Frank McGrath Change Management Ltd
- Freeman
- Friedkin Companies, Inc.
- Gambia Revenue Authority, Directorate Of Technical Services
- George Weston Foods Limited
- Georgia Technology Authority
- GHD
- GK Associates
- GlaxoSmithKline
- Goodwill Great Lakes
- Government Department (United Kingdom)
- Government of Canada
- Grupo Ultra
- GSI Group
- Guiness Ghana Breweries Ltd
- Gulf Water Company
- Harriss Wagner Management Consultants
- Hawassa University
- HBOS
- HCL Axon
- HD Supply
- HEC Paris
- High Plains Library District
- Hitachi Consulting *
- Housing Tasmania, Department of Health and Human Services
- HP Global eBusiness
- Humadyn-Center for Human Relations, Growth & Achievement
- Hungarian Foreign Trade Bank
- Hyosung Corporation
- IAT Program Management Office
- iB4e, Inc.
- IDC of South Africa Ltd
- Imagineering Solutions Inc.
- Impact Management Consultancy
- Incahoots Consultancy
- Infotek Systems
- Ink Business Development Services Ltd.
- Insurance Australia Group
- Intel Corporation
- Internal Revenue Service (USA)
- Inventure Solutions
- IPLAN
- J.R. Simplot Company
- Johnson & Johnson
- JP Morgan Chase
- Kansas Department of Revenue
- Keane Inc.
- Kenya Revenue Authority
- Kirsten Davies Consulting
- KPMG LLP
- Kusha Maadan Consulting Engineers (KMCE)
- La Société conseil Lambda inc
- Lakelanand HealthCare
- Leprino Foods
- Level 5
- LGFC
- LIBERTAS Zagreb - Business School of Economics
- Limited Brands
- Limpop Health Consortium
- Lions Clubs International, Multiple District 308
- LM Dulye & Co.
- Logisource
- Louisiana Machinery Co., LLC
- Lower Colorado River Authority (LCRA)
- MAC Carpet
- Maersk, Inc
- Dept. of Transport and Main Roads, Queensland
- Malawi Institute of Management
- Manship Associates
- MAP
- Marshall Manufacturing Co.
- Maryland Food Bank
- McKesson Canada
- McMaster University
- mdb Consulting
- Medavie Blue Cross
- Microsoft Corporation
- Milbank Manufacturing Company *
- Ministry of Education (Trinidad)
- MJ Medical
- MKR Consulting
- MMHE Sdn. Bhd.
- MOHSS
- Montana-Dakota Utilities
- Moshood Abiola Polytechnic
- Motorola
- Mutual of Omaha
- MWH Global *
- Namibia Institute of Pathology (NIP) Ltd
- NASA
- National City Corporation *
- Navistar, Inc.
- NCS Pte Ltd *

- Nedbank
- Nelson Consulting Group
- Network Rail Ltd
- New Brunswick Power Holding Corporation *
- New York State
- Nexen Inc.
- Nextant
- North Highland *
- NORTHPARK ZIM
- Oakton *
- OCBC
- Oklahoma Department of Human Services
- Online Business Systems
- Pacific Blue Cross
- Panduit Corp.
- Parramatta City Council
- PCGI Consulting Inc
- PeopleFirm, LLC
- PeopleNRG, Inc.
- Performance Path TM
- performanceglobal
- Philip Morris International
- Picourseware
- Plante & Moran, PLLC
- PMI Service Center Europe Sp. z o.o.
- POLITEC
- POQ
- Prime Therapeutics LLC *
- proacteur *
- PROJECT A LA CARTE, Inc.
- Projectology Pty Ltd
- Prominence Pty Ltd
- PT SOLTIUS Indonesia
- Qedis Consulting
- Quartzdyne Inc.
- Queensland Health
- RAAF
- Raiffeisen banka ad
- RAMSE Consulting
- Raytheon Company *
- RBC
- Reach Select
- Region of Peel
- Repars Inc
- Resources Global Professionals
- Rio Tinto - People and Organisational Support
- Robert Ayling Incorporated
- Roche *
- Rockwell Collins
- Roshcon / Highveld PFS
- RWD Technologies
- SAIC
- Saje Consulting
- Salalah College of Technology
- SAP Business Objects
- Saratoga Professional Services
- Sasol Technology *
- SATRENO AFRICA
- Satreno Change Management
- Satyam Computer Services
- Saudi Arabian Mining Company (Ma'aden)
- SBSA - Corporate and Investment banking
- SC COCA-COLA HELLENIC ROMANIA

- Scheltema & Co (Pty) Ltd
- Schneider National
- Schuyler County Community Services
- See Results, Inc.
- Sentry Insurance *
- Service Corporation International
- Severn Trent Water
- Shell *
- Shengquan Group
- Siemens Healthcare Diagnostics
- Sirius Solutions LLLP
- Solution Dynamics
- South Somerset District Council
- SouthWest Water Company
- Sovereign
- Spatial Information Services Pty Ltd
- Standard Bank of South Africa *
- State of Delaware *
- State of Nevada
- State Street Corp
- Stegmeier Consulting Group
- Sui Southern Gas Company
- SunTrust
- Symphini Change Management Inc.
- TASC Management Consulting, LLC
- TCWTUIF (Ethiopia)
- Teacher Training and Development (Botswana)
- Teched d.o.o.
- TechTeam Government Solutions *
- TEKsystems
- Tenaris
- Texas Childrens Hospital
- Textron, Change Management
- The Bremer Institute of TAFE
- The Dominion of Canada General Insurance Company
- The Hackett Group
- The Minto Group
- The New River Group
- The Student Loans Company Ltd
- Thomas Cook
- Thomson
- TMS Consulting
- Toyota Financial Services
- TradeDoubler AB
- Transnet
- Transocean
- Tri-Opus Technologies LLC
- tw telecom
- UCS
- Uganda Revenue Authority *
- UNISYS
- United Airlines, Information Technology Division
- United States Coast Guard
- University Hospital Maastricht
- University of Auckland *
- University of Ballarat
- University of Melbourne
- University of Southern Queensland
- University of Technology
- University of Tennessee Center for Industrial Services
- University of the West of Scotland
- University of Vermont
- Urbanizadora del Bajío, SA de CV

- UT Southwestern Medical Center
- Valsousa
- VeriSign
- Vertex Inc.
- VIP/Training
- Virginia Retirement System
- Wachovia Corporation
- WAPDA (Pakistan)
- Water Corporation of Western Australia
- Wawa, Inc.
- West Sussex County Council
- Whirlpool Corporation *
- World Omni Financial
- Wyeth
- Wyeth Pharmaceuticals
- Yarona Management Consulting
- Z. KefaLlinou & Co
- Zurich *

Names followed by an asterisk (*) had more than one individual participate in the study. Some organizations are not listed, per the specific request of a participant from that organization.

Appendix F – 2007 study participant list

- 2020 Management Ltd.
- ABSA Bank Limited
- Accenture
- Acxiom Corporation
- Ada County Highway District
- Adaptis
- ADP
- Aegility.com
- Aflac, Inc.
- African Development Bank
- AFRICHANGE
- Albemarle Corporation
- Alcan
- Alchemists International*
- American Express Company
- ANZ Banking Group Limited
- Apis Consulting Group
- Appleton
- Applied Telemanagement Inc.
- Area Agency on Aging District 7, Inc.
- ARGOS Consulting Group
- Ascodi Services
- Associated Press
- Atos Origin
- Attorney General's Department of New South Wales
- Attorneys' Title Insurance Fund, Inc.
- Aurora Loan Services
- Australian Commonwealth Scientific and Industrial Research Organization (CSIRO)
- Australian Government Department of Finance and Administration
- Ayurvet Limited
- Bay Consulting Group
- Bell Aliant*
- BHPBilliton Iron Ore*
- Blue Cross Blue Shield of Michigan
- BlueOrange Consulting
- Blue Shield of California
- BMO Financial Group
- Boise Cascade
- Bombardier
- Booz Allen Hamilton*
- BP America Inc.
- Brisbane City Council*
- BT Group
- Bureau Veritas Group
- Buro Happold
- California Public Employees' Retirement System
- Caltex Australia Limited
- Canada Post Corporation*
- CapGemini
- CapGemini Italia
- Carbon Group Change Consultants
- Catalise*
- Caterpillar Inc.*
- Chait and Associates, Inc.
- ChangeWright Consulting
- Chery Automobile Co., Ltd.
- China Oxford Scholarship Fund
- Christensen/Roberts Solutions
- CIBC
- CIBER
- City of Boise, Idaho
- City of Edmonton
- City of Toronto
- City of Tshwane
- CK Consulting
- Clever Output Strategic Consulting
- Collin County Government
- Comenius University
- ConseQuent
- Consultus
- Co-operators General Insurance Company
- Corporate Systemics, Inc.
- Crawley Borough Council
- Crystal Lake Central High School
- CTG Health Care Solutions
- Datico
- DCP Midstream Partners, LP
- Defense Logistics Agency
- DeLaval Services LLC
- Derby Homes
- DeVry University
- DSD Laboratories
- EDS*
- Electric Insurance Company
- Engen Petroleum
- Entergy
- eProcesses Consulting
- Ergon Energy
- Ernst & Young
- ESNAAD
- Ethicon Endo-Surgery, Inc.
- Ethiopian Management Institute
- Etisalat
- Expressworks International
- Fairlead BVBA
- Farm Credit Canada*
- Fiberweb
- Financial Services Authority
- Firestone International Associates, Inc.
- First Data Corporation*
- Fontys University of Applied Sciences
- Ford Motor Company
- Forma Change Inc.
- Fujitsu Consulting*
- Fundacao Getulio Vargas
- GBM Corporación
- Getronics
- GKNM Hospital
- GlaxoSmithKline
- Government of Nova Scotia*
- Grupo Pão de Açúcar
- Hanover
- Harman/Becker Automotive Systems
- Harriss Wagner Management Consultants
- HCMC University of Technology
- HDR Inc.
- Hellmuth, Obata + Kassabaum
- Heron Advisory Group

- Hewlett-Packard
- Hi-Performance Learning
- Hitachi Consulting*
- HOK Visual Communications*
- Homeserve
- Honeoye Falls-Lima Central School District
- ICTS Global
- Impact Management Consultancy
- InfoChoice
- Infosys Consulting
- Inova Health System
- InSightec Ltd.
- Instituto de Logistica, S.C.
- Insurance Corporation of British Columbia
- Intel
- InterActive Financial Services Inc.
- Internal Revenue Service
- International Truck and Engine Corporation
- Isagen S.A.
- ITP New Zealand
- IUTUM
- JD Lowry Computer Service
- Jet Propulsion Laboratory
- JLT Mobile Computers
- Key Performance Consulting
- Kimberly-Clark
- KLA-Tencor
- L-3 Communications
- Laboratories Esteve
- Lascelles de Mercado & Co. Ltd.
- Leaders Training & Consultancy
- Leadership Intelligence Inc.*
- Lejara Enterprise Solutions
- Liberty Systems
- Limited Brands, Inc.
- Lion Nathan
- Liverpool John Moores University
- London Borough of Croydon
- MAC Carpet
- Make Change Positive, LLC
- Malaysia Marine and Heavy Engineering
- Massachusetts Convention Center Authority
- Medtronic, Inc.*
- Memorial Sloan-Kettering Cancer Center
- Middle East Contact Center Management Association
- Mississippi Valley Surgery Center
- MLP Consultants, LLC
- Molson Coors Brewing Company*
- Motorola, Inc.
- MUSE Consulting Inc.
- NASA
- National City Corporation*
- National Defense and Canadian Forces*
- Nelson Consulting Group
- Neoris Consulting Services
- Nestle
- Nevada Division of Child & Family Services
- North Highland
- NorthKey Community Care
- North-West University
- OCBC Bank
- Old Mutual plc
- Option One Mortgage Company
- Oregon Department of Transportation
- Pacific Gas & Electric Company
- PartyLite
- People and Process Management S.A. de C.V.
- Peoplematters
- PETROTRIN*
- Philippine Airlines
- Pier 1 Imports
- Plus Human Resources
- Pomeroy IT Solutions
- PricewaterhouseCoopers
- proacteur
- Prominence Pty Ltd
- Qedis Consulting
- Queensland Homicide Victims' Support Group
- RAMSE Consulting
- RBC Financial Group
- Results Kurumsal Verimlilik
- Reuters
- Rich Products Corporation*
- RWD Technologies
- SAIC
- SAJE Consulting
- Saline Water Conversion Corporation
- Sanofi-aventis
- SaskTel
- Sasol Infrachem
- Satyam Computer Services Ltd.
- Schneider Electric
- Sentry Insurance
- Serco Consulting
- SERVICOM
- Severn Trent Water
- Shakti Masti Overseas Pvt. Ltd.
- Shell Canada
- Shell*
- Silterra Malaysia Sdn Bhd
- Simeka BSG
- Sinclair-Cockburn Financial Group
- Skanska Brasil
- Soltius Indonesia
- South Carolina Department of Parks, Recreation & Tourism
- Southern California Edison
- Spirit Aerosystems, Europe
- Sprint Nextel
- Standard Bank of South Africa*
- State of Delaware
- Stegmeier Consulting Group
- Stored Energy Systems
- Student Loans Company Limited
- Sui Southern Gas Company Limited (SSGC)
- SunTrust Banks, Inc.
- SUPERA
- Swedish Social Insurance Agency
- Symantec
- TAM Iran Khodro
- TASC Management Consulting, LLC
- Tata Consultancy Services*
- Tata Sky
- Teched Consulting Services
- Technological University of Panama
- Tekla Corporation

- Tenaris
- Tennessee Valley Authority
- The Gillette Company
- The Hartford Financial Services Group, Inc.
- The Insolvency Service
- The Revere Group
- Theo Consulting Ltd.
- Transat A.T. Inc.
- Transformaciones Estrategicas
- Tri-Global Solutions Group Inc.
- Unisys
- United Nations
- United Nearshore Operations
- United States Army Reserve
- University of Bolton
- University of California - Davis
- University of Melbourne
- University of Paisley
- University of Texas Southwestern Medical Center
- University of Vermont
- Urbanizadora del Bajio
- Valsousa
- Vulcan Flight Management
- Wachovia Corporation*
- Warri Refining and Petrochemical Company
- Wayne County, Michigan
- Western Cape Education Department
- Western International Bank
- Whirlpool Corporation
- Wipro Technologies
- World Vision Inc.
- xwave
- Yucel Boru
- Zurich American Insurance Company

Names followed by an asterisk (*) had more than one individual participate in the study. Some organizations are not shown, per the specific request of the participant from that organization.

About Prosci

Formed in 1994, Prosci is the leading provider of research and tools that enable organizations to manage the people side of change. As a research company, Prosci has conducted seven studies since 1998 to create the most complete body of knowledge available in the change management field. Research participants include more than 2,600 organizations from 65 countries, including many of the largest companies and government organizations worldwide.

Prosci sponsors the Change Management Learning Center at **www.change-management.com**. This online resource provides access to Prosci's change management tools and a collection of books, articles, case studies and other change management resources. The nearly 60,000 registered members receive regular tutorials featuring the latest research and models in change management.

Resources for the entire organization

Prosci has developed holistic models, processes and tools for effective change management. The Prosci ADKAR® Model and the Prosci 3-Phase Change Management Process have become two of the most widely used approaches for managing the people side of change in corporations and government agencies. Prosci's change management approach provides a common language, customized tools and training for multiple levels in your organization:

For change practitioners:
Change Management Certification Program
Change Management Toolkit
Change Management Pilot Professional

For managers and supervisors:
Change Management Coaching Program
Change Management Guide for Managers
ADKAR® Worksheets

For senior leaders and sponsors:
Change Management Sponsor Program
Change Management: the people side of change
Executive Guide to Change Management

For employees:
Change Management Orientation for Employees
Employee's Survival Guide to Change

Prosci has also developed a licensing framework to enable organizations to deploy change management to all employees and to customize or tailor the materials to meet their specific needs. Contact Prosci for more information on licensing options and costs.

Training

Prosci has been directly engaged in knowledge transfer and coaching of executives and project teams for very diverse groups, including many Fortune 500 companies and large government organizations. Prosci's popular Change Management Certification Program includes training credits from Colorado State University, the Project Management Institute® (PMI) and the Society for Human Resources Management (SHRM). Training programs are offered in open enrollment, public programs around the world or onsite at client locations. These programs are delivered by Prosci directly and by accredited members of the Prosci Global Affiliate Network. Prosci also offers a robust Train-the-Trainer Program that enables internal resources to deliver Prosci change management training programs.

Contact us

Web: www.change-management.com
Email: changemanagement@prosci.com
Phone: +1 970-203-9332
Prosci Inc.
1367 South Garfield Avenue
Loveland, CO 80537 USA